Chief Justice

John Marshall
and the Growth of the Republic

OTHER BOOKS BY DAVID LOTH

The Brownings, a Victorian Idyll
Lorenzo the Magnificent
Charles II, Ruler and Rake
Philip II, Master of the Armada
Public Plunder, a History of Graft in America
Alexander Hamilton, Portrait of a Prodigy
Woodrow Wilson, the Fifteenth Point

J Marshall

Chief Justice

John Marshall

AND THE

Growth of the Republic

BY DAVID LOTH

W · W · NORTON & COMPANY · INC · New York

PRINTED IN THE UNITED STATES OF AMERICA
FOR THE PUBLISHERS BY THE VAIL-BALLOU PRESS, INC.

RG

To Helen, who has been the court of last resort for this book—and for the author, too.

☆ ☆ ☆

Contents

I.	The Quality of Justice	11
II.	Education of a Judge	15
III.	Education of a Nationalist	28
IV.	A Warrior's Courtship	49
V.	Leader of the Bar	65
VI.	A Nation Is Born	81
VII.	The Making of a Federalist	106
VIII.	A Mission to Paris	125
IX.	From Congress to Cabinet	142
X.	The Highest Court	162
XI.	Last Stronghold of a Party	172
XII.	The First Offensive	189
XIII.	A Judge on Trial	203
XIV.	Building the Barricade	215

XV.	The Meaning of Treason	221
XVI.	Measures Short of War	251
XVII.	Obligation of a Contract	263
XVIII.	Death of a Party	278
XIX.	A Day in Court	290
XX.	Era of Good Feeling	307
XXI.	Lottery and Monopoly	313
XXII.	Last of the Federalists	332
XXIII.	Justice and the Indians	356
XXIV.	The Final Decision	370
	Bibliography	383
	Index	389

Chief Justice

John Marshall
and the Growth of the Republic

I

☆ ☆ ☆

The Quality of Justice

THERE IS MORE truth in law than in lawyers, more poetry in justice than in judges. But once in a while a man mounts the bench with the salt of life, the spice of wisdom, and the sweetness of humor blended in him so subtly yet so successfully that those who are quite unlearned in the law glimpse some of its beauties. An Oliver Wendell Holmes or a Learned Hand shows them to us. So does John Marshall.

Of all the judges who ever lived, Marshall contributed the most to the way in which his country is governed—and the way in which it governs itself. For he established, maintained, and left to us as a cherished heritage the principle that, in the blunt words of one of his successors, Charles Evans Hughes, "the Constitution is what the judges say it is."

Fortunately for themselves, most of the people all of the time have liked it that way. Grumbling is confined largely to those against whose beliefs or interests of the moment the Supreme Court of the United States has ruled. That Court's power is unique in the world. There are enthusiasts who argue that this is the main reason why the government of our country, by and large, has been uniquely successful in operating the machinery of republican institutions. Of course there are other enthusiasts who argue that the power of the Court has been a brake on progress. But there is no dispute as to the reality of the power.

It exists today, shaping to some extent the lives of all Americans, because John Marshall was the kind of man he was. Littler lawyers sometimes say that his influence has long since disappeared because the rules he made in some of his notable opinions have been reversed by his successors. Yet this very fact testifies to his survival. His successors would not be exercising the power of final decision in these matters at all, but would be taking the last word meekly from another branch of government, if Marshall had not been there before them.

Such power is nowhere stated in the Constitution. Marshall found it there by implication. So had others. But Marshall was the man who made the principle live. Would it have happened without him? Probably. The thirteen colonies would have won their independence, no doubt, if there had been no George Washington, but not in the same way, nor would they have consolidated that independence quite so fruitfully. The Union would have been saved perhaps if Lincoln had never emerged from the backwoods, but it would not have been quite the same Union. So with the Supreme Court if there had never been a Marshall.

Speculation along these lines is often entertaining, but scarcely ever profitable. Without inquiring into might-have-beens, there is enough food for thought in the hard fact that this man sat at the head of our judiciary for thirty-five years. It was an unpleasantly hard fact to Thomas Jefferson, to Andrew Jackson, and to many a statesman in between. Out of it grew the legend of a judge somewhat larger than life-size, so large that most Americans who know the name think of him as the first Chief Justice, a Virginia aristocrat, a dry and excessively learned jurist. He was none of these.

The things he really was added up to a great deal more than this cold, stuffy portrait because what he was had a very important

share in making this country what it is for us. The republic, it is
said by the historians, was moulded in its formative years by the
titanic struggle between Jefferson and Hamilton. Yet it was Marshall who did more than any other man (except perhaps Jefferson
himself) to fix the Hamiltonian principles of government so firmly
in our political structure that they have never been dislodged.

In doing it, Marshall displayed qualities which his two great
contemporaries lacked. His work lives partly because he brought
to it a broad humanity which was based on both experience and
intelligence. Jefferson, who loved the people, never knew them
and was uneasy in their company. A political philosopher of the
widest possible sympathies, he was at his best in the study. Hamilton, who knew the people and could be charming to them when it
suited his purpose, never loved them. To Jefferson, the agricul-
tural masses of his day were "the chosen people of God." To
Hamilton "your people are a great beast, sir." But in their lives,
both were as far removed from the bulk of their fellows as intellectual superiority and fastidious tastes could make them.

Marshall on the other hand was born of the people. He did not
have to think about it or philosophize about it. He accepted it and
was happy. Like Franklin, he believed a man was human, neither
a specially noble creature nor yet a mere animal. Marshall liked
people, all kinds of them, a fact which gave him a far better understanding of them and a far greater pleasure in their society,
even after he became one of the landed gentry, than could be
achieved by the passionate but abstract devotion of a Jefferson.

So when he came to the bench, he brought with him a humanity
which Hamilton and his closer disciples despised. It gave Marshall the strength to withstand the onslaughts of the Jeffersonians
in their years of triumph. It gave him a certain humility in his own
power. It gave to his decisions a flavor which, quite as much as
their substance, enabled them to project their influence through
generations and into the settlement of questions never dreamed of
in his own time.

His court has become peculiarly American. Foreigners, therefore, often are puzzled in their studies of our institutions to find that the Supreme Court can be hailed as the most cherished bulwark of property rights and at the same time as the protector of personal liberties. They are bewildered by a tribunal which has brushed aside the edicts of overwhelming Congressional majorities in one breath, and in the next professed itself (or anyone else) powerless to coerce a citizen on a matter of conscience.

Foreigners also are puzzled—as are some natives—to find the political descendants of Hamilton seeking to maintain their dominant position by appealing in the name of Jeffersonian principles to the successors of Marshall. The radicals of a later day than his canonized the author of the Declaration of Independence as the patron saint of political progress. But they have achieved their most recent and most substantial successes by following Marshall's reasoning. They have found that the Federal authority which Marshall divined and Jefferson viewed with alarm can be a boon as well as a burden. The first beneficiaries, the holders of property in bulk, bewail the fact that the principles on which they thrived for so long can cut both ways.

The story of how that Federal authority was established is not the biography of a single man. It is the story of an idea adventuring in a world where the old ideas of government had been tested by war and revolution, and had been found wanting. Those old ideas of government were exposed during Marshall's youth in all their pitiful inadequacy by the novelty and complexity of current problems. New machinery and new uses for the old machinery were establishing what later generations would view as the traditional bases of American democracy, American capitalism, American privileges, and American freedom. John Marshall's life spanned the change, and he was no mere spectator; he was an increasingly important actor in the drama.

II

☆ ☆ ☆

Education of a Judge

S EEN FROM A Virginia farm in the 1760's, the world had
a deceptively placid appearance. Turmoil and change, misery and tyranny existed, of course. But all that was far
away, among unhappy people whose fate surely could not influence the lives of independent and self-reliant husbandmen content to mind their own business.

Even the devastating wars of the century had touched Virginia
—and all America—lightly. Threats of new conflicts growing
partly out of European rivalries and pressures, partly out of American trade and ambitions, were more menacing. Another war
might come closer home. But most Virginians were content to
shrug aside their fears—if they had any, after a peace which had
removed Frenchmen from their borders—and concentrate on
problems they could understand. That meant the personal and
local rather than the political and international.

Yet the men of the 1760's, without being aware of the fact, had
outgrown the social and economic machinery by which they
managed their affairs. The world had grown too big to be man-

aged by a few cloistered gentlemen in ancient capitals. Property
was changing hands so rapidly under the whip of expanding commerce that whole new classes, let alone new individuals, were asserting that they had a stake in their countries.

A few of the men of the time were groping for new principles.
More of them were seeking new procedures within the frame-
work of accepted philosophy. But all of them, thanks to the increasing complexities of civilization, were being forced out of old,
comfortable grooves. While philosophers explored the roots of
the social system, all sorts of enterprising, practical fellows knew
only that they were being chafed in tender places of their economy by the current methods of dealing between nations and between various segments of society within nations.

A boy growing to manhood in this time might not understand
the change—few of his elders did either—but his character and
his future were inevitably moulded by it. If he was a Virginia boy,
the moulding forces were English. He would have to go to other
colonies to find the influence of other nationalities.

Life in Virginia was the result of transposing English habits and
traditions, beliefs and doubts, hopes and dissatisfactions to a new
land. The native populations had supplied a few place names, some
hunting techniques, a new style of fighting, and the new crops of
tobacco and corn. A far more important contribution was that of
nature—the vastness of the country, the great forests and rivers,
the apparently inexhaustible fertile soil.

The people who had built the Virginia way of life came from
all classes of the home country except the two extremes. There
were very few of the British aristocracy of blood, place, or money.
There were almost as few of the most underprivileged of British
subjects, the slum-dwellers of London. The bulk of the immigrants were gentlemen, merchants, traders, artisans, and displaced
workers from town and country.

John Marshall had in his veins the blood of nearly all of these
classes. On his mother's side, he was descended from the Ishams
and Randolphs, who could trace their ancestry back two and

three hundred years to gentlefolk in England. It was this line which made him third cousin once removed to Thomas Jefferson, a young man of means and fashion from Shadwell, then preparing to master the law. The Marshalls were humbler, small farmers and workers.

The first fairly well-identified member of the Marshall family was a carpenter who settled in Westmoreland County and died in 1704. One of his sons was a John Marshall, usually called "of the forest" because his farm was carved out of the woods some distance from the river. This John Marshall married a girl whose parents had come to America from Wales. Among their ten children was a son, Thomas, born in 1730, whose childhood was chiefly interesting to posterity because he was a boyhood friend of George Washington, two years his junior. Both learned surveying as well as farming; both were tall and athletic; both were by nature dignified and rather reserved in manner. They were such close friends that when young Washington got a job surveying the principality of the "Northern Neck" which belonged to Lord Fairfax, he took Thomas as his assistant. Together the young men rode through the Virginia forests, sleeping on the floors of settlers' cabins as near the fire as they could get, reviling the fierceness of the vermin in their bedding when they were lucky enough to get bedding, but acquiring a new concept of the vastness of their country.

When he was twenty-four, Thomas Marshall married. The girl was a sprightly seventeen-year-old, Mary Keith, the daughter of an elderly clergyman and of Mary Isham Randolph, whose personality must have impressed itself upon her contemporaries because they invented a number of romantic but unlikely stories about her early loves and adventures. James Keith, a Scotsman of Tory leanings, had been a soldier before he took holy orders, and became noted among the hard-drinking, hunting, careless parsons of his day as one singularly devoted to the duties of his calling. Well along in middle age when he married, he was almost an old man by the time his children were grown.

His daughter received a rather better education than fell to the lot of most Virginia maidens. Reading and writing were accomplishments generally regarded as unnecessary for women. Even among the girls of Mary's mother's class, the wealthier planters, there were many who never achieved literacy. Miss Keith, moreover, had other accomplishments. She was trained in household duties. She was robust—an enviable quality on the frontier—and attractive. She had a high forehead, a clear gaze from handsome eyes under arched brows, a mouth which even in repose seemed ready at any moment to curl into a smile. Everyone thought that Thomas Marshall was a lucky fellow, and during their long life together he never had any reason to disagree with them.

The young surveyor had abandoned the paternal acres—literally, it appears, since there is no record that he sold the unproductive farm in Westmoreland County. This was no indication of improvidence. Land was plentiful, and unless it was either fertile or well-placed it might not command a purchaser. Mary Keith Marshall, therefore, went as a bride into the backwoods, some thirty miles further up the Potomac. There, in Prince William County, her husband had built the usual log cabin with an even ruder shelter near by for the two slaves he had inherited from his father.

It was a pleasant spot if not a very good farm. The cabin looked down over a roughly cleared field to a stream flowing gently toward the river, and beyond was the green of unbroken forest marching over the hills as far as the eye could see. Here on September 24, 1755, Mary gave birth to her first child, John, named for his recently dead grandfather.

[2]

The boy was born into a frontier that was filled with fear. Just eleven weeks before, General Edward Braddock had marched his brightly uniformed army, to the accompaniment of fine military music, into a death trap on the Monongahela. In hundreds of frontier cabins like that of the Marshalls, settlers knew that only their own resources stood between them and the French and Indian conquerors. There was some consolation in the way Marshall's young friend Washington and his Virginia rangers had covered the disaster and preserved the lives of a few Britishers. (The Colonel was getting his first but by no means last taste of the bitter glory to be won by managing defeat well.)

Of course the fears and recriminations formed no part of little John Marshall's consciousness. In the cabin above the stream he grew from babyhood to boyhood with a profound sense of security. At least that was how he remembered it many years later. His parents were almost entirely responsible for this. In his first six or eight years, he hardly ever saw anyone outside of the immediate family. The nearest neighbors were miles away. Visitors were scarce, and so for companionship the boy had his mother, father, and sisters, the latter only one and two years younger than himself, followed by a baby brother six years younger.

John was eight or nine years old when his father decided to move to better land, and also to keep nearer the frontier. Thomas Marshall had improved his worldly position. His surveying had brought in a bit of income; the neighbors had recognized his quality of leadership in 1761 by electing him to the House of Burgesses. There he sat with his friend Washington and mingled cautiously in the cultivated society of Williamsburg, the colonial capital.

The spot he selected was only about thirty miles on a straight line from his old home and twenty-odd miles west of Warrenton. It was situated in a singularly beautiful valley of the Blue Ridge, on Goose Creek. The Marshalls apparently went there as squatters, for it was not until a year or two later that Thomas, newly appointed to the modestly lucrative post of Sheriff, leased from the Lees a tract of 330 acres "whereon the said Thomas Marshall now lives." The rent was five pounds a year plus taxes.

Although the distance was only thirty miles from their old home, the family required several days for the journey, and John began his lifelong acquaintance with the hazards of the road. The

Marshall possessions—a matter of bedding, a few tools and household implements, some modest clothing, dishes, a couple of books,
the master's guns, and a few sticks of furniture—did not unduly
crowd the wagon, but the faint track through the woods was in
such a state of mud and stumps and holes that they crawled at a
snail's pace.

However, once arrived at Goose Creek, they found waiting for
them a house of more ample proportions and more ambitious construction than most frontier farmers attempted. Thomas Marshall
treated his family to a one-and-a-half-story house made of sawed
timbers with a tremendous fieldstone fireplace and chimney. The
dwelling boasted two rooms below and two above. Near by was a
stone structure for keeping meat and other food, a log cabin for
the slaves and a log stable for the livestock.

Perhaps association with Washington and contact with Lord
Fairfax, coupled with the easier mode of life he saw during the
sessions in Williamsburg, led Marshall to indulge in such lavish
building. Young Colonel Washington was fairly elegant and was
accustomed to the well-furnished homes of the Tidewater gentry,
of whom his brother Lawrence was a modest example. Lord Fairfax, one of the rare British noblemen who made their homes in
America, had built certain upper-class comforts into his home in
the wilderness, although Tidewater Virginians of far lesser rank
would have regarded Greenway Court, in the Shenandoah Valley
near Winchester, as a stone cottage of mean proportions hardly
worthy of its rather grand title.

The Fairfax tradition, the Fairfax name, and, in the end, the
Fairfax land itself had a lifelong influence on John Marshall. The
land had come into the Fairfax family through the Baron's mother,
a Culpepper, whose father had been a Stuart favorite and had
gained, among the substantial rewards of his careful work at
Court, a grant to five million acres between the Potomac and Rap-
pahannock Rivers. About the size of the present State of Massachusetts, this grant had come to Lord Fairfax in return for allowing the entail of his paternal English estate to be broken in order

to help his mother's family out of a financial crisis. In spite of his generosity—or perhaps because of it—he did not get along very well with his relatives. After his fiancée threw him over for a Duke, he found English life, English manners, and English society distasteful. The prospect of an ocean to separate him from ungrateful relatives, fickle girls, and perhaps contemptuous friends was balm to his spirit.

In the mood engendered by his private misfortunes, the young man preferred the loneliness of the Northern Neck to the society of Williamsburg and the hospitality of the planters. He was no hermit, however. He took an interest in settling his vast estate. He was a generous and helpful landlord to those tenants who maintained a properly respectful gratitude for noble benevolence. He was a discerning employer—witness his selection of Washington and Thomas Marshall. He brought to the wilderness a few refinements of urban life, especially some books which were the chief reading of more households than his own—the Marshalls and Washington were among the borrowers.

[3]

In the frame house on Goose Creek, children were more frequent arrivals than books. (Between 1755 and 1781, Mary Marshall bore Thomas seven sons and eight daughters. Contrary to the common fate of such broods, all of them survived to maturity—a formidable clan.) As the eldest, John early became accustomed to responsibility, but it was not sufficiently onerous to dampen his spirits. He was remembered as a happy, cheerful child, but the memories about any one individual in such a large family are usually unreliable in detail. He was as a matter of course a woodsman and a hunter, taking his gun into the forest for game at an age when children of later generations were cautioned if they played with popguns.

On Goose Creek, the older children learned to read from their parents, probably their mother. The Bible and Pope's Essays were the chief items of literature which at the end of his life Marshall remembered from this time. These were supplemented by Shake-speare and an occasional volume from the Fairfax library. Of equal educational value were the accounts of debates and issues which Thomas Marshall brought back from the House of Burgesses. He had been present to hear the great arguments over the Stamp Act when Patrick Henry introduced resolutions which had a highly revolutionary ring. Marshall, like all the back-country burgesses, was an ardent supporter of the resolutions and a great admirer of what young Jefferson, a spectator, called "the sublime eloquence of Henry." The revolutionary ring of the oratory and the resolu-tions was not diminished by the contrast between the somewhat uncouth spellbinder and his elegant, be-laced opponents. It was these gentlemen of careful dress and big estates who interrupted Henry's "Caesar . . . had his Brutus, Charles the First his Crom-well and George the Third—" with cries of "Treason! Trea-son!" It was to these gentlemen that he addressed the first of his great phrases which were to be published in schoolbooks, ". . . may profit by their example. If this be treason, make the most of it!" It was the backwoodsmen, reinforced by a few Tidewater gentlemen of vision and courage, like Washington, who backed the eloquence with votes.

The story lost nothing in Thomas Marshall's telling of it. The big man, no very facile speaker in public, had a concise simplicity in conversation which helped his ten-year-old son to see and hear the incidents described. Listening to his father, whom he admired for physical prowess as much as for legislative position, the boy came to take it for granted that the representatives of the people should be the governors of the people.

Shortly before John was fourteen, more formal teaching than his mother's instruction and his father's conversation entered his life. A new parish was formed, taking in the whole county, and the vestrymen (Thomas Marshall was their chief) selected a Scot-tish deacon of thirty, James Thompson, to act as minister. En-gaged for a year on trial, Thompson lived in the Marshall home which, although crowded by the nine sons and daughters who had so far blessed the family, was more commodious than most of the near-by cabins. In return for his board and lodging, Thompson held school for the children old enough to profit by his instruction. His class was not as large as might be supposed, for four of the little Marshalls—Judith, Lucy, and the twins, William and Charles—were less than three years old.

The schoolmaster-deacon made good, and at the end of the year went to England to be ordained. On his return he married, set up his own home, and was far enough away that if John Marshall was among his pupils at all it was only on rare occasions. For a few months, however, John was sent East to school. His father was becoming a man of substance, and wanted his oldest boy to be a lawyer. As partial preparation, the lad was dispatched to the Reverend Archibald Campbell's academy in Westmoreland County. This was one of the better schools in Virginia although its proprietor was the only teacher. The reverend gentleman had versatile talents, considerable learning and some gift for pedagogy. Marshall gained added acquaintance with the classics during his brief stay, but more notable was his acquaintance with a gangling boy nearly three years his junior, James Monroe. Perhaps of more significance than either, was the backwoods boy's introduction to a softer life than that of the frontier.

[4]

He came home to find that his father had become subscriber to a book just published (1772) in America. The *Commentaries* of Blackstone were destined to be the backbone of many a lawyer's professional education, and there is enormous temptation to attribute to the possession of a first edition some of the remarkable legal attainments of a much older John Marshall. Actually there is little evidence that he absorbed any considerable amount of legal lore from Blackstone. He was too much engrossed in what to a lad of seventeen were more important affairs.

First of all was a new home. Thomas Marshall had risen to the ranks of the landed gentry. He had not achieved any such estate as his friend Washington acquired through marriage, but his hold-ings totaled 2,000 acres. Most of them were purchased in January, 1773. The plantation was a little nearer to Warrenton and was large enough to remove the Marshalls from the class of backwoods farmers.

The new house, which the older boys helped to build, was in keeping with the family's new status. It had seven rooms, four below and three above, and was said to have the first glass windows in that part of Virginia. It looked somewhat small after Thomas Marshall's grandson and namesake added a "wing" which was larger and taller than the original, but the dwelling was impressive to visitors in 1773. From the vantage point of this home, Oak Hill —which later generations would easily confuse with James Monroe's estate of the same name only a few miles away—the Marshalls observed the sweep of politics and economics. These also were more interesting to young John than law. They were rush-ing this family and 300,000 other Virginians tumultuously into a war.

The machinery for colonial government, never of the soundest construction, had fallen apart. The first experiment in replace-ment was proving a dismal failure.

The old machinery had been a careless disregard of the colonies because they were not worth attention. The serious misgovern-ment up to the end of the French and Indian Wars was perpetrated by officials on the spot rather than by absentees in London. With that sort of misgovernment, colonials had learned to deal.

At the end of the wars in 1763, England had acquired a vast American Empire, all of Canada and undisputed claim to the land as far west as the Mississippi. She also had acquired a debt of 140,-000,000 pounds, almost double the pre-war figure, and Chancellor of the Exchequer George Grenville was not alone in believing that this was nearly an intolerable burden. In every age in every land there have been politicians who set national debt apart from all other economic factors and tremble before it. Taken by itself, the debt seems to fill the fiscal firmament, scaring the daylights out of self-styled political economists in much the same way that an eclipse of the sun terrified savages.

With one eye on the ledger in which that 140,000,000-pound debt was entered and the other on British taxpayers, the Chancellor inquired why America, which had benefited from the war, should not help pay for it. Why not? echoed an enthusiastic House of Commons, and promptly voted duties for Americans to pay on molasses, sugar, wines, and a considerable list of luxuries. This had happened in 1764 and was followed the next year by a stamp tax.

There were more reasons than the affront to colonial autonomy behind the storm which blew up suddenly and promptly to amaze the London politicians. The duty on molasses, for example, had actually been cut in half under the new law, but the rum distillers of New England were as angry as if it had been doubled. They had been accustomed to ignore the higher duties altogether—except for the modest bribes they tossed to underpaid customs officials—but England was preparing actually to collect the new rate. This was not to be borne by free men.

"Rum," as John Adams remarked later, "was an essential ingredient in the American Revolution."

There were even more heady elements. Importers and merchants chiefly were annoyed with the duties, but all men of business or property were outraged by the stamp tax, partly on principle, partly because it would take all their very scarce "hard money." In those days of limited specie, men of real wealth often found it difficult to rake actual cash together. Dealers in land, therefore, joined lawyers, bankers, and merchants in protesting the tax. They in turn were joined by settlers, plantation owners, men with grandiose development projects. Their rage seemed out of all proportion to the new legislation, politicians in London thought, and they were right. What the politicians did not understand was that the colonists saw their whole future threatened by the archaic system of which the Stamp Act was a symbol, the smoke which merely showed that there was a fire underneath.

[5]

Not the least of the deficiencies of the governing machinery was
the inability of Englishmen in office to obtain adequate information about America. The calm assumption that all the colonies had
benefited immediately and substantially from the war was based
on almost complete ignorance of the facts. Hundreds of millions
of acres had been added to the Empire. But the new land was not
legally available to colonists; indeed, they had seen the area actually open to them shrink. In order to avoid the expensive Indian wars, London had ruled that settlement should stop at the
Alleghenies. Men like Washington, who had explored beyond the
mountains, who had fought for their country's rights there, who
had promoted land development industriously, were not likely to
submit tamely. Men like Franklin, who had formed a truly imperial plan for a colony about the size of New York State over the
mountains, were not likely to agree that their years of planning,
lobbying, and investment should be sacrificed to fit a new English
policy, and a timid one at that. Men like the Lees and the Carrolls,
who had organized ambitious land companies, were not likely to
give it all up just to save a few English Ministers trouble.

Thus the territorial gain from the war could be realized in
America only by changing the colonial system as then operated.
Furthermore, most of the colonies had done some spending of
their own, both blood and money. Their public debts were not so
big, but their hidden contributions to English revenues were substantial. Because they were hidden, they were magnified in the
eyes of the contributors. British merchants and shipowners
skimmed the cream from colonial trade, valued at 2,000,000
pounds a year. Colonials sold their produce cheaply in England—
unless they went in for smuggling—and bought dearly. The war
had increased their actual commerce, but the profit was reaped in
England.

The colonial response to the creaks in governmental machinery
was an increasingly rebellious spirit. Thomas Marshall, returning

from the turbulent sessions of the Burgesses, was convinced that American rights could be maintained only through a show of force, and the use of force if necessary. After the Boston Tea Party in the winter of 1773, as one of Washington's Virginia rangers and an experienced Indian fighter, he began a preparedness campaign in eminently practical fashion. He drilled his older boys in military arts during their spare time, and as spring came to the Virginia hills in 1775, they were fairly accomplished militiamen.

Spring brought news both exhiliarating and tragic along with the dogwood and the laurel. The shots fired on the road to Concord echoed in due course through the forests of Virginia, and Thomas was home again from legislative duties—this time a convention at Richmond—with perhaps an even greater eloquence echoing in his calm voice. For during the debate on the Virginia "Resolutions for Arming and Defense," he had sat not far from young Jefferson to hear those stirring phrases from the most memorable of all Henry's orations:

"Is life so dear or peace so sweet as to be purchased at the price of chains and slavery? Forbid it, Almighty God." And, "I know not what course others may take, but as for me, give me liberty or give me death."

Thomas Marshall remembered those phrases. He repeated them to his sons. They talked, they discussed the rumors from Massachusetts, they agreed that the boys should become members of a new company of militia forming in the neighborhood. So on a day in May—the Second Continental Congress with Jefferson elected as a member convened that month in Philadelphia—John Marshall dressed himself carefully in a blue hunting shirt, trousers with a fringe of white down the seam, and a hat with a bucktail for cockade. He took down his gun from the rack, slipped a hunting knife in his belt, and set off through the forest for the mustering place. There was no Blackstone in his pocket, no thought of law in his head. John Marshall was off to the wars in the light-hearted spirit which nineteen has always brought to these grim affairs.

III

☆ ☆ ☆

Education of a Nationalist

THERE WAS NOTHING in his first experience of sol-
diering to dim John Marshall's high spirits. The first
Virginia regiment of Minute Men was being discussed—
those troops of whom John Randolph later spoke as "raised in a
minute, armed in a minute, marched in a minute, fought in a minute and vanished in a minute." Thomas Marshall was to be Major
of one battalion, and prospective recruits to form a company were
being mustered in a field some ten miles from Oak Hill when the
Major's son arrived. The nominated captain did not show up, so
young Marshall as Lieutenant proceeded to take charge.

One who was present remembered sixty years later that he
opened his military career with a speech. It seems to have been
indistinguishable from a thousand orations then delivered by ardent lads all over the country. If the speakers later became eminent
enough, their youthful eloquence was recalled, perhaps exaggerated, in the minds of old men who confused the youthful promise with the mature achievement. The speeches themselves were
inevitable. Among human beings, fighting is always preceded by
talking.

On this particular day, standing tall and slim and straight in the late spring sunlight, Marshall spoke to his comrades of liberty and of their share in maintaining it. He repeated as fact the rumors of British defeat at Lexington—the authentic news of these April events around Boston did not arrive until days later. He cried out that more fighting was inevitable and it was time for good men "to brighten up their fire-arms."

The spectator remembered how his round dark face was flushed with excitement and perhaps a little with a feeling of triumph as he saw his words visibly affecting an audience. But at last he stopped talking and ordered the men to fall into line so he could show them the manual of arms. This he demonstrated as his father had taught it to him, and then led them through the drill. When their enthusiasm began to wane, Marshall made another speech. This one lasted for an hour, and in the main was an exhortation for his hearers to join the new regiment of Minute Men.

Even at nineteen, however, Marshall shied away from bombast and exaggerated dignity. He finished his oration on a more homely note than might have been expected, his conclusion being no more than a challenge to a friend to pitch a game of quoits. With shouts and laughter, the military formation broke up for games and foot races. Marshall, who already had won neighborhood fame as a runner, took part in all of them. It was sheer sport, not designed to harden recruits for the field. For these recruits were already in a physical condition which veterans seldom achieve. Their lieutenant, an average specimen except for his height, his speed of foot, and his gift of gab, concluded the day's strenuous exercise by walking the ten miles home through the May dusk.

In Virginia the summer wore on slowly, with news of tremendous events trickling into the hills months late. Ethan Allen's capture of Ticonderoga and Crown Point, the Battle of Bunker Hill, Washington's arrival to take command of a Continental Army besieging Boston made New England almost popular in Virginia. The stirring tidings and reports of ringing debates from Philadelphia, where the Continental Congress was giving its most impressive demonstration of colonial unity, seemed to promise an easy triumph. Virginia, however, clung to peace until, just after John Marshall's twentieth birthday, a rider galloped by express, which meant by relays of fast saddle horses, westward along the trails to plantation, farm, and village. He was carrying Patrick Henry's message of warning and command. The warning was that Lord Dunmore, the Governor, had proclaimed martial law, was freeing slaves who would work for the Crown, arming additional men, accumulating munitions. The command was for the Minute Men to march upon him before he grew too strong.

Marshall's regiment hastily responded. Gathering near the village of Culpeper, they formed untidy columns and set out with the woodsman's easy ground-consuming stride for Williamsburg. The regiment, known as the Culpeper Minute Men, had a fine determined appearance. In effect they were in uniform, for all of them wore fringed deerskin trousers, colored hunting shirts with "Liberty or Death" embroidered across the chest, a leather belt for tomahawk and knife, a buck's tail in the hat. The popular rattlesnake flag with the legend "Don't Tread on Me" floated over the marching column.

In Williamsburg, the eager militia learned that Dunmore was consolidating his position in Norfolk, Virginia's chief port and largest city. Their leaders, pleasantly surprised by the number of men who had answered Henry's call, sent half of them home. The Marshalls, father and son, went on with the other half toward Norfolk.

They were stopped twenty miles short of the city by a fort which the Governor had erected beside a causeway crossing a swamp. The Minute Men threw up a breastwork of their own and made camp. Here, even before any fighting started, Marshall learned the truism that war is mostly mud. It was turning cold, but not freezing, and the two little armies, damp and dirty, watched each other across the swamp. All the men were eager and uncomfortable, but their leaders hesitated to prod them out of the mire for an attack because of the obvious advantages which defenders would have on that ground. Lord Dunmore's patience was the first to break. John Marshall thought he was "participating probably in that contempt for the Americans which had been so freely expressed in the house of commons." Of what followed on that December morning, Marshall wrote:

"Lord Dunmore . . . ordered Captain Fordyce, the commanding officer at the Great Bridge, to storm the works of the provincials. Between daybreak and sunrise, on the morning of the ninth of December, this officer, at the head of about sixty grenadiers of the 14th regiment, who led the column, advanced on the causeway with fixed bayonets, against the breastwork. The alarm was immediately given; and, as is the practice with raw troops, the bravest of the Americans rushed to the works, where, unmindful of order, they kept up a tremendous fire on the front of the British column. Captain Fordyce, though received so warmly in front, and taken in flank by a small body of men who were collected by Colonel Stevens of the minute battalion, and posted on an eminence something more than one hundred yards to the left, marched up under this terrible fire with great intrepidity until he fell dead within a few steps of the breastwork. The column immediately broke, but the British troops, being covered in their retreat by the artillery of the fort, were not pursued.

"In this ill judged attack, every grenadier is said to have been killed or wounded, while the Americans did not lose a single man."

The Minute Men pushed on to Norfolk after their victory while the Governor and his aides retired to the British warships in the harbor. From time to time the frontiersmen amused themselves by taking pot shots at the ships, the principal effect of their marksmanship being to provoke Dunmore to retaliation. The guns of the men-o'-war were heavier than anything the rebels could muster, and most of Norfolk had been burned by the time the Minute Men had disbanded in March. A regiment of North Carolina regulars who had come to Virginia's aid completed the destruction of the town to prevent Dunmore from establishing a naval

base there. A few days later Lieutenant Marshall was home in Oak
Hill to tell admiring younger brothers and sisters about war and
victory.

[2]

Complacency could not last long. Resting from his share in the
little triumph, Marshall could hardly fail to be disturbed by news
from the north. The brave little army with which Benedict Arnold and Richard Montgomery had set out to capture Canada was
reeling back. Sir William Howe had evacuated Boston but was fitting out at Halifax for a decisive blow, probably against Washington, who had moved down to hold New York for the Conti-
nentals and was calling for more men.

Shortly after news of the Declaration of Independence penetrated to Oak Hill, John Marshall accepted (on July 30, 1776) a
lieutenant's commission in the Third Virginia Regiment. He thus
became a Continental officer, splendid in blue and buff with a
sword, a three-cornered hat and boots, rather than picturesque in
hunting shirt and fringed trousers with a tomahawk, a musket,
and buck's tail. He was inspired less by Jefferson's momentous
phrases, although he admired and approved them, than by the
more prosaic fact that his father had been for months the Major
of the Third Virginia, and was eager to lead fighting men to the
help of his old friend Washington.

The Third Virginia, marching north through the late summer
heat and early autumn rains, was met by consistently discouraging
news. Washington's army, beaten on Long Island, routed by panic
on Manhattan, driven from Westchester, was retreating across
New Jersey. When the Third Virginia joined the Commander,
his forces had shrunk by desertion and expired enlistments to a
few thousand footsore but dogged men.

Participation in their barely orderly flight was a far different
experience from the brief glorious encounter with a charging foe
outside Norfolk. This was a battle against despair, against hunger
and discomfort and vermin, against mud. But some remarkable

characters were being formed, at least in part, by those terrible days of retreat and despondency.

There was the Commander in Chief himself, presenting a wonderful front of dignified calm to his men while he seethed with rage against those who held up supplies, against militia who refused to re-enlist in the face of the enemy, against incompetent officers, against a Congress which would not or could not establish its own authority. There was the ungainly Englishman, Thomas Paine, lugging his long musket through the mud and writing the army's chief inspiration on a drumhead beside the fire at night. Although they joked about it, his gaunt comrades were immensely cheered by such phrases as "summer soldier and sunshine patriot" and "the times that try men's souls."

There was Nathaniel Greene, the Rhode Island Quaker who had abandoned the pacifism of his preacher father to become the best military tactician in New England, Benedict Arnold perhaps excepted. There was Harry Knox, the huge young Boston bookseller turned artillerist who had worn himself down to a mere 280 pounds in the arduous march across the Jerseys but retained the loudest voice and one of the clearest minds in the army. There was Captain Alexander Hamilton, a year younger than Marshall, commanding a New York field artillery battery and writing long philosophical treatises on political economy and government finance in his spare time. There was Marshall's schoolfellow at Campbell's academy, James Monroe, also a lieutenant in a Virginia regiment.

Among the blaspheming, dirty, tired men who followed these more conspicuous figures, young Marshall gained a reputation. He won it for good humor, a quality even more rare and certainly more highly valued just then than courage or genius. Fortunate in the robustness of his body and the excellence of his health, the Lieutenant was able to jest at misfortune and make others laugh, too. He probably had a few of the more professional qualities of a soldier as well, for on the first of December he was promoted to the rank of Captain-Lieutenant.

Transfer to the Fifteenth Virginia went with the promotion; so Marshall missed or was spared (depending upon the point of view) the terrible but heroic raid on Trenton. The bitter march through the snow and over the ice-rutted roads on Christmas Eve, the attack upon the Hessians on Christmas morning, the bone-wearying struggle back across the Delaware on Christmas Day were performed by others, his father among them. Another was Monroe, one of the four Americans wounded in the brief, wonderfully successful fight. The whole army was encouraged by the victory, but not so much so that there was a man among them who would not have said a fervent "amen" to Robert Morris's New Year greeting to Washington:

"The year 1776 is over. I am heartily glad of it, and hope you nor America will ever be plagued with such another."

Later generations of Americans have held a more exalted view of 1776 than could the men who lived through it.

[3]

Captain-Lieutenant Marshall, moving with the rest of the army back across the Delaware to take up post at Trenton on the last days of the year, was developing in common with the majority of his fellows who were interested in public affairs some mildly heretical views about the organization of society. He was beginning to think that a passion for liberty was not enough. There ought to be some provision for supplying free men with the means to guard their freedom. Order and discipline began to have attractions for men who were suffering because of the lack of these ingredients in the body politic.

The system, or lack of system, by which the Continental Congress theoretically governed seemed to resemble chaos more closely than liberty. Congress exhorted the states, wheedled and cajoled and wrote out requisitions which the states ignored. Marshall himself observed that the militia "abandoned" the army at their own free will. What was worse, they took their muskets and blankets with them, leaving better men to fight without arms and sleep without covering. While he had not lost his faith in the cause of independence, he was coming to the conclusion that there must be another way of winning and maintaining it than through the spasmodic efforts of an unreliable militia and the well-meant but ineffective resolutions of an impotent Congress.

He had little time for these reflections. The army, raised to 5,000 men by the sudden glamour which it attained after the capture of Colonel Rall's Hessians, was subjected to strenuous work —mostly leg work—in the next few days. Waiting at Trenton for a British attack, Washington knew he had nothing but the stamina of his troops and a rather desperate stratagem of his own to oppose to the superior numbers, superior discipline, and superior equipment of the British. Furthermore, he was facing a very annoyed General. Lord Cornwallis at Christmas time had been preparing to go home to report that the rebellion, in a military sense, had been crushed. The fragment he had chased across the Delaware was no longer an army, he thought. The Earl's baggage actually had been put aboard ship in New York when he heard of the raid on Trenton. Furious, he cancelled his passage, brought his possessions ashore, and rode south through the cold to give the presumptuous Virginia squire another lesson in the art of war. Collecting his troops from winter quarters, he led 8,000 of them toward Trenton. They arrived late in the afternoon of January 2, in time to exchange a few artillery shots with Captain Hamilton's battery, but not in time to attack in force.

Cornwallis, however, was a patient man. He was quite willing to wait a day for his revenge, and he was in no doubt as to just when and how he would have it. Washington had a river at his back and an army he had never beaten in front of him. His Lordship went to bed after uttering the only one of his phrases which posterity remembers. He said with satisfaction that now he was sure he had "the old fox in a trap."

At one o'clock in the morning, Captain-Lieutenant Marshall struggled out of sleep with the other 5,000 trapped Americans and started walking through a freezing mud. Their task was to beat the British in a foot race. John Marshall was an uncommon man on his feet, and he found that day's march a little less exhausting than most of his fellows. They started easily enough by slipping around Cornwallis's flank in the darkness. Then they really began to work, the leaders setting a killing pace.

At dawn they were two miles from Princeton, but there were only 4,000 left. During the night, 1,000 of the militia who had joined up in the brave days after the Trenton raid thought they saw a Hessian. They were in Burlington before they stopped running.

A small British force on its way to join Cornwallis held the main army briefly at Princeton; then the ranks re-formed for the most gruelling part of the march. Cornwallis, in a tremendous rage at his quarry's escape, was driving his men relentlessly in pursuit. Fortunately the Earl was worried about a lightly guarded supply of munitions and 70,000 pounds in cash at New Brunswick. He turned that way to be sure the treasure was safe, but Washington kept his men moving until eleven at night. They dropped in their tracks at Somerset Court House, some of them too exhausted to get out their blankets so that they froze to death where they fell. They had been on the go for twenty-four hours, and the survivors had walked out of a trap. Three days more of marching, not quite so strenuous, brought them to the hills of Morris County while Cornwallis drew off in exceedingly bad humor to join Howe in New York.

Young officers like Marshall had little opportunity to relax that winter, although there were a few dances at the old Freeman Tavern and a good deal of card-playing and sports. The troops were drilled intensively in a routine which bore most heavily on the junior officers. Marshall seems to have been unsuccessfully inoculated for the smallpox at this time, too—it did not "take" in his case—for Washington forced this precaution upon the whole army.

Not the least of the evidence pointing to the force of character which was in this man, who was referred to with immense respect as "His Excellency," is revealed by the fact that the order for inoculation was carried out. The sheer power of his personality overwhelmed the "religious" objections that he was interfering with the laws of God. Brushed aside with equal success were the fears of the ignorant and the natural perverseness of soldiers. Inoculation was a serious business in those days. It involved getting a so-called "mild" form of the disease, and most of the army spent some time in uncomfortable, makeshift hospitals that winter. But by the time spring arrived, Marshall and the rest were fit and hearty and about half-trained in infantry drill. They were in excellent shape for a walk to Philadelphia.

Howe had loaded his troops aboard ship, obviously with the headquarters of Congress as his objective. Washington got there first, but his army was as badly supplied as in 1776. Summer soldiers had joined up in droves—Washington was able to parade 11,000 through the streets of Philadelphia. However, he was far short of 11,000 muskets; few of the parading troops were adequately clothed although they had been ordered to make themselves as neat as possible to impress the Tory citizenry of the capital, and nearly all of them were dirty. Soap was one of the supplies for which Washington appealed in vain. Curiously enough, relatively few of the new recruits were Pennsylvanians.

"Those nearest danger were, as usual, most slow in assembling," Marshall commented bitterly.

The young officer himself was one of a picked band of 117 men and officers assigned to harass the British advance. Since the battle near Norfolk, Marshall's military experience had been confined to out-walking the enemy. Now he met a column of them in a sharp fight, short but so fierce that the Americans suffered 40 casualties among their 117 men before they fell back to join the rest of the army along Brandywine Creek.

Here Washington made his first effort to keep Howe from Philadelphia. For most of one September day detachments from the two armies skirmished, with Marshall taking part in some warm fighting at the left of the American line. His father, recently promoted to full Colonel, led the Third Virginia on the right. Then the British attacked with fury. Marshall noted that the men who had seen service in '76 held their own, but new recruits broke and ran. He blamed them the less because, he learned, they had muskets of several different calibers and it was only a happy coincidence if the ammunition issued to them fitted their pieces.

The army's left crumpled rather easily, the right only after such a fierce struggle that the Third Virginia, young Marshall heard with admiration, lost half its officers and a third of its men before being driven from the field. Their Colonel himself was safe, so the son's pride in the exploit was not dimmed by personal mourning.

Nearly four weeks of marching, skirmishing, and manoeuvring followed, made miserable for the troops by increasing cold and wet. Then Washington tried a very complicated, daring attack on the British position at Germantown. Success depended upon careful, not to say exact, timing and upon the good judgment of subordinate commanders in meeting unpredictable emergencies. The troops were not sufficiently well trained to keep to a rigid timetable, and the commanders were not notable for judgment. The General under whom Marshall served that day allowed himself to be held up with his whole force by a few Englishmen in a stone house instead of passing them by to follow up a successful charge which had driven the main British column back in some disorder. Even then, he did not take the stone house; a fog rolled up to confuse the fighters, and behind the fog came a reorganized British column. The battle was over, turned into a defeat of the Americans who ended the day's fighting by a retreat of seven or eight miles.

It began to seem that the year 1777 would close as gloomily as had the year 1776, and without the spiritual lift provided by a Trenton raid. But then, as the army looked down from the hills at the British establishing themselves comfortably in Philadelphia, they got news of a greater victory, won within two weeks after the Battle of Germantown. In the forests of New York State near Saratoga a magnificent army led by that darling of London, Gentleman Johnny Burgoyne, had surrendered to a combination of daring militia, brilliant wilderness tactics, and grim wilderness hardships. This was even better than the capture of Colonel Rall's Hessians. Those in the know said that Saratoga would bring France into the war on the side of the colonies.

Enthusiasm in the army was tempered by caution, discomfort, and bitter experience. Camped after Germantown on high ground above the Schuylkill, the soldiers anticipated one more battle before winter. But Howe did not like the looks of those Pennsylvania hills, and besides he had sent his resignation in just before authentic news of Burgoyne's surrender reached him. He was content to wait for the appointment of his successor unless Washington should be foolish enough to heed the advice of hotheads in Congress. These gentlemen, ignoring the demands of their Commander in Chief for supplies and troops and munitions, exhorted him to take Philadelphia by storm. What he was to use for this purpose, they did not say.

Washington by now was too experienced a General to venture his army out of those protecting hills. He was by no means sure he could hold his own even within their advantageous slopes. He was worried when Sir William brought his men out for exercise, because the British might be planning an attack for all the Americans knew. Captain-Lieutenant Marshall remembered how General Washington rode through the ranks that day, the big calm man so easy in the saddle and so skillful at concealing his doubts behind a mask of serene confidence. Marshall heard him warning the troops that they should rely upon their bayonets—in view of the uncertain quality of their ammunition, this was probably a counsel of necessity—in case the British charged. But the British drew off again to the comforts of Philadelphia, and the Americans trailed away to Valley Forge.

[4]

John Marshall entered that camp of horror as a Deputy Judge Advocate. His appointment was announced in the same order which named Lieutenant James Monroe as aide-de-camp to the hard-drinking General Alexander whom the Americans called Earl of Stirling. Marshall's assignment was a tribute to his common sense, his popularity, and his durability rather than to any recognition of budding judicial genius. A Deputy Judge Advocate had to rely upon his own judgment rather than on legal learning. It was helpful to him if his fellow officers thought highly enough of him to carry out his decisions. And in that army, where fever, cold, hunger, and despair kept two men out of three from their posts, Marshall's robust health was a decided asset.

He had still another advantage. He managed to keep enough clothes on his back that winter for decency if not for comfort, although he had to wrap himself in his single blanket on the days when his only shirt was being washed. Plenty of his comrades had neither shirt nor blanket. As for the men, 3,000 of them were incapacitated solely by nakedness before the new year, and by February this number had swelled to more than 4,000. Nearly twice as many at one time were unfit for duty because of disease, unhealed wounds, sores, and sheer feebleness from malnutrition. One-third or less of the men in camp could be called upon for some sort of chores, whether standing sentry with their feet in their hats to keep from freezing, or burying dead horses or cutting wood for fuel.

Men and officers lived in log huts about the size of an ordinary modern bedroom. The soldiers were packed together so closely that on the average each man had the same space in which he would one day be buried—six feet by three. This crowding helped them keep warm perhaps, but it spread disease. In the absence of anything which would now be considered as sanitary facilities, dysentery and fever ran riot through the camp. Men sickened from the very stench of the huts in which the sick lay virtually untended. Those who were strong enough to gather rags or tar or anything else that would burn with a strong odor, flung it on their fires for relief.

The well-wooded hills did not have enough trees for all the huts and all the fuel. Living in what had been groves of handsome oaks, the army could not find enough wood by the time winter was over. As for food, even Washington's staff was reduced to frozen potatoes, coarse bread, a few scraps of meat, hickory nuts for dessert, and plebeian rum and water for drink. The common soldiers subsisted chiefly on a foul watery soup and a horrible concoction of meal, water, leaves, and ashes called fire cake. Junior officers generally enjoyed a fare somewhat less luxurious than that of the staff, a little better than that of the common herd.

Years later, Marshall was privileged to see the correspondence which Washington was carrying on at this time with Congress. His Excellency's letters blazed with fury and contempt, apparently hot enough to melt the hide of a brass monkey, but they brought no warmth to the huts at Valley Forge. Although surrounded by some of the richest farm land in America, the army got precious little food from its neighbors. Most of the Pennsylvania farmers were displaying a good deal of ingenuity to get their produce smuggled into Philadelphia where a well-heeled British staff paid hard money for beef, butter, chickens, vegetables, and grain. Even when farmers sold to the American army, the produce seldom reached camp. Enough shoes and blankets for even more men than packed the dismal huts of Valley Forge had been paid for. But the gentlemen in charge embezzled the money, used army teams and wagons for private business, sold army food and clothing to civilians or even to the enemy.

"The naked and distressed soldiers," as Washington described them in his milder outbursts, were punished more severely for infractions of discipline than the dishonest plunderers who had forced this misery upon them. The commissariat was manned by civilians then, and Deputy Judge Advocate Marshall's authority over such people was virtually nil. A private soldier might be sen-

tenced to 100 lashes for attempting to desert. A civilian in the
commissary department, caught selling army food for his own account, was drummed out of the camp. His worst punishment consisted in being mounted backwards on his horse with his coat
turned inside out and his hands tied behind him. Few were of such
delicate sensibilities that this deterred them from theft.

In spite of hardships which have made the name of Valley
Forge synonymous with misery, there was a fair amount of bitter
jesting, and even some genuine good humor among the minority
healthy enough to crack a joke. Marshall remained one of the
favored few throughout the ghastly winter. At twenty-two he
was so rugged not even the perils of that contaminated camp
could weaken him in body or spirit. Lieutenant Philip Slaughter,
who shared Marshall's mess with three others, thought him "the
best tempered man I ever knew." Young Slaughter found Marshall's good-natured drollery one of the redeeming features of the
Valley Forge nightmare. Marshall told stories well. He had a gift
for witty remarks which inspired laughter but not bitterness. He
had the strength for mimicry and absurd stunts. Slaughter remembered for years the nonsense which Marshall managed to extract
from possession of a tattered pair of silk stockings, the grotesque
costumes he contrived for the amusement of his comrades, the
mock fuss he made over damages done to his treasures.

"He was an excellent companion, and idolized by the soldiers
and his brother officers," Slaughter wrote.

He was not, for all this, indifferent to the plight of the army.
He saw that there were other reasons for the suffering around him
than the sheer perversity of human nature or bad luck. He was
acquiring, as were a great many military men in those days, a contempt for their government. It was hard not to have such sentiments about the body of impatient, impractical, bewildered, and
quarrelsome gentlemen who called themselves the Continental
Congress. Only a few of the members remained at York, and even
when their resolutions made sense, there was no authority behind
them, so that the army benefited not at all.

Congress could plead, recommend, demand. The States quietly or noisily did as they pleased. The lesson was not lost upon men who served at Valley Forge. The great majority of them, including Marshall, had a good deal of their future politics determined by their experiences that winter. The great majority of them became convinced believers in the necessity for authority as well as liberty, order as well as freedom. Some of them put the authority and the order first in their philosophy. They had suffered more from chaos than they ever would from tyranny, and the fact deprived them of a measure of philosophic calm, which was more easily attainable by men who had never seen Valley Forge.

[5]

The food problem at camp was solved finally in the spring when the shad began to run in the Schuylkill. Men hauled the fish ashore with gusto and ate their fill for once, while sun and fresh air replaced smoke and smells. Under this course of treatment, the survivors of dysentery and fever and hunger slowly regained their strength. Each day saw more and more of them exposed to the attentions of Baron Friedrich Wilhelm von Steuben, the huge Prussian who had become the drillmaster of the Revolution. Clothing had ceased to have its midwinter importance; a man could be comfortable in shirt and socks.

Baron von Steuben could not exhaust the men's reviving energies on the drill ground. Valley Forge became a sports center, with races organized at the drop of a hat, and even the grave Washington joined selected officers in a sort of predecessor of baseball. A young Deputy Judge Advocate who had not been sick once all winter was in the forefront of all the games. His mother had sent him some new socks, the heels made of white yarn, and he won so many races that his fellows gave him the nickname of "Silver Heels." Fortunately it did not last.

In these sports, the caste system of the army was rigidly observed. It was as much as an officer's commission was worth to be seen associating on terms of anything like equality with enlisted men. There was never any question of matching young Marshall against some other speedy fellow who might happen to be a sergeant. The Deputy Judge Advocate never dreamed of pitching quoits against anyone under the rank of ensign.

Even on the great day in May when news of the French alliance reached camp, the celebration was conducted along lines of strict segregation. There should have been an equally enthusiastic celebration among the Americans over a change in the British Army, too. On the day the French treaty was laid before Congress, Sir Henry Clinton replaced Sir William Howe in command. Howe's whole conduct of the war had been based on a theory that he could chastise the rebels with one hand while the other held out inducements which would lead them to re-enter the imperial fold. Clinton had no such statesmanlike visions.

Sir William knew his business, his military business that is. He had outmanoeuvred Washington easily every time they met. Sir Henry's talents would not extend to this. When he took over the command, he decided to return to New York by land, and he set his troops in motion on June 18. Ten days later the Americans caught up with him near Monmouth, New Jersey.

It was one of the hottest days which men who took part in the battle were ever able to recall. Some of them even thought with perverse longing of the nice cool snow at Valley Forge only a few months before. Washington's generals were not very eager for the fray. At a Council of War they voted against risking battle at this time. Their arguments—"which," young Colonel Alexander Hamilton sneered, "would have done honor to the most honorable society of midwives, and to them only"—were overruled by the Commander in Chief. He thought he had a good chance to teach Clinton a lesson and seize most of the 1,500 wagons of supplies with which the British commander had encumbered his march. Orders were given. General Charles Lee was to attack the British columns as soon as they broke camp.

Captain-Lieutenant Marshall was a member of Lee's division that day, serving under "Mad Anthony" Wayne. Lee, an English professional soldier whose talents were greatly overrated by the American amateurs among whom he served, was not then known to be a traitor. He had spent part of a recent captivity (the result of being trapped in dressing gown and slippers through his own carelessness) in drawing up an itinerary and a program for Howe's invasion of Pennsylvania and ending the war. Exchanged, he was on the ground at Monmouth to disorganize one of Washington's best conceived plans of battle. Lee's unsavory reputation has led to some dispute as to his motives this hot June day. Cowardice, jealousy of Washington, stupidity, and active treason have all been offered.

The fact is that, whatever influenced Lee, Marshall and his comrades were led to the rear instead of forward. Washington himself rallied them on the brink of defeat and turned them back against the red-coated British columns. Through mud and sand they struggled, tortured by heat and thirst, attacked at every step by clouds of the famous Jersey mosquitoes, which did more damage than British bullets that day. It was a very confusing battle for all concerned, but since the British drew off, taking all their wagons with them, the Americans could claim a victory. Marshall was not so much worried with the verdict just then. He and all the others wanted nothing but water and rest. He had been marching and fighting for twelve hours. His clothes were wet through with sweat as he flung himself down on a level bit of ground. There was no cover for anyone that night. Washington, Lafayette, Hamilton, Colonel Aaron Burr, Wayne were all sleeping where they fell, like common soldiers, trying to protect their faces from the merciless mosquitoes.

[6]

They had expected to renew the fighting at dawn, but when they awakened, the British were gone. The weary ranks followed, and on July 1, while they were marching toward New York, Marshall was gratified to receive news of his promotion to Captain. It was all the more welcome because his next brother, Thomas Jr., al-

though six years his junior had held this rank for some months
past.

Captain Marshall shared with hundreds of other young officers
a sense of frustration after the Battle of Monmouth. Distributed
on both sides of the Hudson where they could watch Clinton,
they fought almost exclusively for subsistence. There was little
military glory in the continual scraping for supplies.

Washington was also worried by the fact that the British held
the most advantageous spot for crossing the Hudson and thus
hampered communication between the two wings of his army.
This spot was a naturally strong defensive position just before
the river spreads out into the wide reaches of the Tappan Zee.
Here two forts, Stony Point and Verplanck's Point, commanded
a crossing known as King's Ferry.

The desperate enterprise of capturing Stony Point was entrusted to Wayne. He was allowed to pick his men from all the
light infantry regiments, and Marshall was one of the chosen, but
only with the greatest of difficulty could three days' rations, de-
cent uniforms, and serviceable weapons be gathered for the picked
men.

Wayne made extremely careful preparations. Stony Point
could be reached only from one side, across a low swampy neck of
land. The fort was defended by strong batteries, and any attackers could be fired upon from British warships in the river. The
plan, therefore, was a night attack. First a select band would creep
forward in the darkness, silence the sentries, and knock down some
of the stakes which formed the outer British defenses. Then the
first wave of the actual storming party would pour through the
gaps in the barrier. A second wave would wait on the edge of the
swamp to support the attack where needed. The whole business
was to be done silently, with cold steel. Wayne's orders called for
the men to advance without shot in their muskets, "placing their
whole Dependence on the Bay^t." If a soldier dared fire his piece
in the face of these orders, the nearest officer was to kill him on
the spot.

Marshall waited with the second wave, a bit of white paper in his hat to serve for identification, at the swamp. It was very dark on this night of July 15, 1779, and the men had been warned to expect heavy losses. They were all the more triumphant, therefore, when the first wave of attackers carried the fort in a few minutes and almost without casualties, the British throwing down their arms with cries of "Mercy, mercy, dear, dear Americans"— or so Marshall later reported. His own detachment was never called into action at all.

Wayne held Stony Point for only a few days. Verplanck's across the river proved a harder nut to crack. In fact it could not be cracked at all, and without command of both sides of the ferry, Washington's position was untenable. Reluctantly he drew the men out of the captured fort and retreated with his whole force to the Hudson Highlands. Captain Marshall did not immediately go with him. Detached to join a scouting party under his fellow Virginian, Major Henry Lee, the Captain spent several weeks patrolling on the very edge of the British lines.

Risky and arduous as this was, the scouting was a little tame for Major Lee. He decided on one of those raids which were the chief American triumphs of the war—and which filled the British with rage because they were so unorthodox. One August night the Major led his men some fifteen miles over hills and through ravines to a place called Paulus Hook, which was supposed to be impregnable. Not only was it deep inside the British lines, but the garrison had dug a ditch which cut them off from the mainland. Captain Marshall and his companions reached the ditch about an hour before dawn, jumped over it, seized 159 sleepy Britishers and made off with their prisoners before daylight.

There was no special military advantage to the incident unless annoying the British was an advantage. But the raid was hailed for its sheer audacity. It was a considerable morale builder. It was one of the little victories which kept the American army's spirits proof against the grim disappointments of major inactivity and inadequate supplies.

These disappointments grew more frequent and intense as 1779 wore on. Clinton sat stolidly in New York, giving a perfect example of how to lose a war if only the Americans could manage to exist during the leisurely demonstration. Washington perched unhappily in the hills, watching the ranks of his army thinning faster through desertions and expired enlistments than would have been likely even in the most deadly battle or epidemic. The Virginians had kept their regiments better filled than most, but now even these were reduced to such slim proportions that there were more officers than men to be commanded. John Marshall fell into the category of surplus. On December 9, 1779, while the remnants of Washington's command began settling into quarters at Morristown for a winter of hardships which were to rival those of Valley Forge in everything except the publicity, the twenty-four-year-old Captain ended his active service and turned toward the home which he had not seen for more than three years.

IV

☆ ☆ ☆

A Warrior's Courtship

THE VIRGINIA to which Captain Marshall returned on a winter's day had changed in a good many subtle ways. Outwardly this was not very noticeable, for the scars of war were few. Life in the big houses of the plantations and the mansions of the towns continued its easy, rather wasteful way. The Tidewater gentry sported less finery from London, but men still ate and drank extravagantly, gambled and hunted, talked politics and crops. Ladies maintained as much state as separation from the centers of world fashion would permit.

Behind that familiar façade, however, was a new spirit—two new spirits, in fact. One had been introduced largely by Jefferson and his colleagues in the state government, the other mainly by Continental officers who had served in the North. One was the spirit of liberty and the other the spirit of order and nationalism. Virtually everyone was in favor of both—Tories had been pretty well eliminated or cowed in Virginia—but there was a definite difference of emphasis.

Jefferson had been Governor for nearly a year in succession to

Patrick Henry, and was probably the most popular man in the State. Resigning from Congress within two months of the Declaration of Independence, he had led the State legislature in a series of revolutionary reforms which frightened the representatives of the big planters, as any interference with property rights always alarms the owners of property. It was a great victory for good sense, and in the end for property rights, too, when Jefferson forced through the abolition of entail—that feudal system by which property was handed down through a previously fixed line of heirs no one of whom could alienate a bit of it, whether to pay his debts or for any other reason. He introduced and saw passed without opposition a law forbidding the future importation of slaves. He led the fight to abolish the law of primogeniture—that other feudal hangover by which a man's real estate went to his eldest son, no matter what reasons there might be for leaving it elsewhere. The State adopted the wild radical notion that a father might, with safety to society, divide his land among his children as he could his personal property. The dire consequences freely predicted at the time failed to materialize.

Jefferson's administration made a start on public education, opened a great fight for religious freedom, began a salutary revision of the laws. But perhaps an achievement greater than all of these was the interest which his measures aroused among the people and the part which that interest led them to take in public affairs.

At the same time, there were men who were disturbed by this preoccupation with Virginia and reform. Not all of them were animated by a desire to preserve the old aristocratic order. Their point of view was that of Washington, who, in one of his letters deploring the weakness and folly of Congress, deserted by the best men who had composed it in '75, demanded:

"Where is Mason—Wythe—Jefferson?"

His Excellency thought that, great as these men's reforms might be in Virginia, the pressing need was for a civilian administration which would help him win a war. Unless he won, the reforms would be worth less than the ropes by which their authors would be hung. The General, and the army, were more preoccupied just then in winning the right to set up a new form of government than in what that form would be.

It is the fashion in an army, too, to attribute failures of supply to the civilians. Marshall and his comrades were more than usually right in 1779, but Marshall was one who realized that the system was as much at fault as the men. He thought it was the fault of "enthusiasm uninstructed by experience."

The difference between the two schools of thought was that one supposed Americans were making a revolution while the other thought the colonies were merely seeking independence. Jefferson was the true revolutionary. Marshall was attaching himself to those who were well enough satisfied with the old institutions, the old distribution of power, and wanted to change nothing much except the galling British sovereignty.

This was the ancient struggle between those who have and those who have not. The returning soldiers—some of them at least —contributed the second of Virginia's two new spirits, the spirit of nationalism, which had not yet acquired unsavory connotations. They were not content with the old ways, but they did not accept Jefferson's revolution as adequate either. The abolition of entail and primogeniture provided no muskets or powder for the army. The imbecility of Congress (as the soldiers saw it) was too dangerous for them to wait until the full effects of the new educational system would bring more intelligent men to office. They were impatient, of course, and army life had given them an exaggerated regard for discipline, especially if the discipline was applied to others. But they supplied a new element in politics, an element which wanted results, and wanted them without delay.

[2]

The new order in Virginia did not burst upon Marshall all at once. He came to Yorktown on what he hoped would be military business, the raising of new troops to take back to Washington. However, there were no new troops, and in the process of falling in love, Marshall had no time for regrets.

Yorktown had been his destination because his father commanded the artillery regiment there. But Colonel Marshall was also a Virginia State Councillor, and in both capacities was in close friendly and political relations with the leading men of the place. Apparently the Colonel was also a fond parent, and he seems to have entertained his friends with anecdotes about his children, or at least about his eldest son, for a young lady of Yorktown who lived next door wrote of those days to her sister:

"Perhaps no officers that had been introduced to us excited so much interest. We had been accustomed to hear him spoken of by all as a very *paragon;* we had often seen letters from him fraught with filial and paternal affection. The eldest of fifteen children devoted from his earliest years to his younger brothers and sisters, he was almost idolized by them and every line received from him was read with rapture."

A less dutiful generation might think this was not the best possible build-up for a young man, at least among susceptible young women. But Captain Marshall's domestic virtues were enhanced by the glamour (for those who had never seen a camp) of four years of war, Wayne's exploit at Stony Point, the raid on Paulus Hook. So, said the gossipy letter writer, "our expectations were raised to highest pitch and the little circle of York was on tiptoe on his arrival."

Captain Marshall met the ladies of Yorktown at a ball which was graced by all the girls in the village who mattered, and all, we are told, "were emulous who should be first introduced." The *"paragon"* bowed to all, but he succumbed to the charms of the youngest of them, and apparently at first sight. The gallant Captain was twenty-four, little Mary Ambler just fourteen. But they were immediately and obviously smitten with each other, and continued in that condition so completely that forty-five years later the distinguished Chief Justice of the United States could find no greater relief from the pain and tedium of the bed to which a nasty fall had confined him than to remember his courtship and to write to the object of it:

"I have plenty of time on my hands in the night as well as the day. How do you think I beguile it? I am almost tempted to leave you to guess till I write again. But, as I suppose, you will have rather more curiosity in my absence than you usually show to hear my stories when I am present, I will tell you without waiting to be asked. You must know then that I begin with the ball at York, and with the dinner on the fish at your house the next day; I then retrace my visit to York, our splendid assembly at the Palace in Williamsburg, my visit to Richmond where I acted Pa for a fortnight, my return the ensuing fall and the very welcome reception you gave me on your arrival from Dover, our little tiffs & makings up, my feelings while Major Dick was courting you, my trip to the cottage, the lock of hair, my visit again to Richmond the ensuing fall, and all the thousand indescribable but deeply affecting instances of your affection or coldness which constituted for a time the happiness or misery of my life and will always be recollected with a degree of interest which can never be lost while recollection remains.

"Thus is it that I find amusement for those hours which I pass without company or books."

Marshall was ardent, but he never was in the position of having to debate with his wife which of them had been the pursuer and which the pursued. Mary Ambler, the "dearest Polly" of his correspondence for more than fifty years, knew what she wanted and how to get it even at fourteen. Before she ever met the young Captain, and apparently on the strength of his father's stories about him, she calmly told her sisters, one of them wrote, "that we were giving ourselves useless trouble, for that she, for the first time, had made up her mind to go to the ball, though she had not even been at dancing school, and was resolved to set her cap at him and eclipse us all."

John Marshall had not been at dancing school either, which was about the only obvious and immediate bond between them. But they were able to find other common interests and experiences without much interruption. Miss Ambler had unexpectedly little competition in snaring her Captain because at first sight of him the ardor of the other girls cooled precipitately. The army had not taught him to carry himself gracefully. He was unkempt, even for a veteran of Valley Forge. His swarthy face and rather small features were not especially prepossessing at first glance. He did not seem at all worth the feminine consideration which had been bestowed upon him in advance.

"Awkward figure, unpolished manners, and total negligence of person" was the verdict of Polly's sister, expressing her disappointment at that first meeting when she had expected to see "an Adonis."

The Ambler girls—even the one who had not been at dancing school yet—did not need to waste their time on awkward young men unless they very much wanted to. They were the acknowledged belles of Yorktown. They had inherited good looks and absorbed charm in the cradle. Their father, Jacquelin Ambler, was the most attractive of the delightful Ambler brothers, each of whom had married a beauty. Jacquelin's wife was the Rebecca Burwell who had inspired a great deal of extravagant rapture in a very young Thomas Jefferson. The Ambler fortune had disappeared in the war. The Ambler mansion had been given up for quite modest quarters in the village. But the Ambler girls, Eliza, Nancy, and Mary, attracted youths in swarms, and Jacquelin Ambler was still a charming host.

Somewhat to the surprise of Eliza Ambler, it turned out that Marshall could be a charming guest. The fair Polly's even fairer sister found that he had become "truly a brother to me," and she confided to another sister that she had been able to overcome her aversion to his dress and manner.

"Under the slouched hat there beamed an eye that penetrated at one glance the inmost recesses of the human character," she wrote with somewhat conscious literary care, "and beneath the slovenly garb there dwelt a heart complete with every virtue."

Eliza had plenty of opportunity to observe both the garb and the virtue as winter gave way to spring, for Marshall spent an inordinate amount of time in the Ambler home. The *"paragon"* endeared himself to the whole family, partly by his good nature and partly by long readings "from the best authors, particularly the Poets." Eliza, who was not in love with him, thought he did it "with so much taste and feeling, and pathos, too, as to give me an idea of their sublimity which I should never have had an idea of." Polly, who was in love, was even more enchanted. But reading from the poets was not the only way Marshall had of expressing his sentiments. He and Polly had little walks and long talks in which he told her of his adventures and ambitions. In the spring he was saying that he intended to follow the law, and as it was obvious by now that there would be no immediate military duties for him, it was time to begin preparation for the pursuit of a civilian career.

The nearest law school happened to be the best, but Marshall probably would have chosen it anyway. Twelve miles was as far as he cared to go from Polly Ambler. There was the state of his own affections to be considered, but also there was the dangerous rivalry of "Major Dick." This dashing individual had the surname of Anderson, and just eighty years later that name was to be much in the news as his son, a "Major Robert," defied the might of the sovereign State of South Carolina at Fort Sumter. The father was a stubborn fellow, too, and Marshall set off for William and Mary College with some misgivings. He need not have worried. His beloved's fourteen-year-old mind was made up as firmly as it had been before she met him.

[3]

Williamsburg was sadly shrunken from the glory which had enfolded it in the days, seemingly a lifetime before, when Jefferson had studied there and Thomas Marshall had listened entranced to the eloquence of Henry. The capital had just been moved to the new raw village of Richmond, and the college was fighting a battle to remain open. But in May, 1780, there were at least forty law students enrolled, and they were fortunate in having a most distinguished faculty.

The faculty was George Wythe, a little man with a big head and an erect carriage who was teacher to two generations of exceptionally accomplished Virginia lawyers. With his hair brushed back from a magnificently domed brow and collected in a little roll at the back of his neck above his collar, he beamed in kindly fashion upon his students as he talked. He had this year adopted the newfangled practice of lecturing to them. He also presided as judge in a mock court where they tried pretended cases and as speaker in a make-believe legislature where they framed and debated laws with much freedom and spirit.

Marshall took his place easily in these activities, but he could not keep his mind on them. That was frequently twelve miles away at Yorktown, as his notebook testifies. In this little volume, Marshall had started in scholarly fashion, neatly writing at the top of blank pages the titles of the various subjects on which Wythe was to lecture. But many of these pages remained blank and others are adorned with scribbled variations on the name of Mary Ambler, sometimes alone, sometimes blended in happy intimacy with his own.

Academic life for a war veteran of twenty-four was a very different thing than Jefferson, for example, had found it when he entered upon his college career here at sixteen. Marshall was in a hurry. From the standpoint of civilian success, his four years in the army had been four years lost. He wanted to make up for them because he wanted to be in a position to support a wife as soon as Polly was old enough to become one. That, in the eighteenth century, would not be long.

Therefore, it was perhaps just as well that there were no more of the receptions, the promenades, the dramatic performances, the gaming, and the elaborate balls which had made young Jefferson's years at William and Mary delightfully gay. Not that life was especially grim, either. There were possible excursions to Yorktown and animated debating meets in the Phi Beta Kappa Society —Marshall was elected as "a gentleman who would make a worthy member" on May 18—and on a particularly fine June day there was as magnificent a dance as Williamsburg could stage in honor of the Misses Ambler. The coaches with their splendid horses and bright trappings were gone or put up "for the duration." The liveried servants were in the army or working on the plantations or attending their masters at the new capital. The elaborate feasts of Jefferson's time were beyond the means of the gentlemen of Williamsburg in 1780.

The young ladies suffered from no regrets. If the food was almost ostentatiously simple, the company was brilliant—"more Beauty and Elegance than I had ever witnessed before," wrote the impressionable Miss Eliza. She was "transported with delight," but had time to notice and report to a friend how devotedly Marshall danced attendance upon her sister.

The ball put an end to the enamored young man's formal legal studies. Wythe's lectures, the charm of Williamsburg, the debates of the Phi Beta Kappa Society lost their allure, for Polly Ambler was moving to Richmond where her father was to take up the duties of Treasurer of Virginia. Marshall promptly abandoned his college career and set out for the capital in pursuit of the Amblers. It was undoubtedly at this time that he so much enjoyed a fortnight of acting "Pa."

He tore himself away for a short visit to his own family at Oak Hill, and because he was seeking a license to practice law. His academic qualifications were slim, even for that day in which inclination, good family, and a ready tongue were of considerably more influence in gaining admission to the bar than familiarity with Blackstone or precedents or the ponderous phraseology of the courts. Examinations were of the most cursory nature, and in his home county a Marshall would not be unduly bothered by them. On August 28, Thomas Jefferson, therefore, exercised his prerogative as Governor and signed the document by which John Marshall, Gent., was licensed to practice law.

Then he was back in Richmond, which was pretty well crowded with lawyers already, but which possessed the ultimate attraction of the Amblers who, although living in a house so small that "our whole family can scarcely stand up altogether in it," were dispensing their famous hospitality.

[4]

Richmond made a sad excuse for a capital after the comforts, even luxuries of Williamsburg. Jefferson's government had been there for a year, hardly time to build a capital. As a village, the place had been in the past a mere convenience for Scottish factors who used the James River as their highway for trade. Shockoe Hill, which had virtually all the houses the town could boast, looked as if the Scots had brought their houses with them, so small they were, Colonel Marshall commented on one of his visits. He thought they had carried the shacks up on their backs, measuring their strength by the height they climbed.

There was no business for a young lawyer, very little for established members of the profession, since the courts were closed most of the time. Nevertheless, the first autumn of his professional career remained in Marshall's memory as a pleasant time of tiffs and makings up, of excursions to a little place in the country where Polly's aunt lived, and occasional visits back to Oak Hill.

He was probably on one of these last when he heard that Benedict Arnold had landed at Westover on January 3, 1781. Next day Arnold led 800 British troops into Richmond, thirty miles away as the crow flies but a good deal further as the soldier walked. An arsenal, warehouses filled with tobacco, and such ships as were in the river were burned.

Captain Marshall was among the men who rushed to the defense of the Commonwealth. He was in a group which hurried to catch up with Arnold, and on the march Captain Marshall was impressed all over again with the all-pervading role of mud in war.

It was raining. It was cold. The roads were brown streaks of sticky mire. For once the British were walking as fast as if they had been Americans—Arnold knew well the value of speed—and no serious opposition could be gathered against him before he was back in Westover.

Here there was an inconsequential skirmish, a rather shameful affair in which the militiamen who had boasted the loudest of what they would do to the Traitor—Arnold always rated the capital letter—ran the fastest. To a man who had taken part in real battles and at least two heroic raids himself, the terror of his comrades was a little disgusting. Captain Marshall spent a few days in the futile marching and running which found the Traitor safely dug in at Portsmouth for the winter. Captain Marshall returned home and on February 12, 1781, he resigned his commission.

He missed a possible chance at some more fighting, although inactive officers with equal claims to command were left idle in the closing campaign of the war. Certainly it did not seem likely in February that this year would see victory for America. Troops were mutinous and no better fed or armed than they ever had been. Cornwallis was marching north from the Carolinas to have one more try at ending the war by capturing Virginia. He ended the war, but not as he had planned.

At first Cornwallis swept everything before him. The legislature, called by Jefferson to meet at Richmond on March 1, hastily abandoned the capital in the face of a new British advance and adjourned to Charlottesville. Cornwallis's cavalry was not far behind them, and the legislature moved on to Staunton, while Jefferson had just time to escape from Monticello.

Oak Hill was well out of the way of this excitement. Only rumors, travelling fast, and news, travelling slowly, reached the Marshalls. They heard of Cornwallis's futile efforts to bring young Lafayette and Wayne to a decisive battle. They heard of the British withdrawal to the coast to await reinforcements and orders. They heard that he had selected Yorktown, and then they heard that Washington and his army were on the way. With all Americans, they rejoiced unreservedly when on October 19 Cornwallis surrendered.

John had enlivened the tedium of that summer by walking to Philadelphia. Whether it was because inoculation had not "taken" during his army service or because he had managed to avoid it, he felt himself still susceptible to smallpox. Virginia, despite the enthusiasm of Washington, made it almost impossible for a citizen to be inoculated within her borders. He had to obtain the consent of every person living within two miles of him in any direction as well as the written permission of all the justices of his county. Philadelphia was more liberal. However, Oak Hill could not spare a horse for such a journey. Between the requisitions of the British and American armies, horses had become exceedingly scarce, but a stout young fellow like Marshall moved almost as fast afoot. He averaged thirty-five miles a day, and such a pace over such country was hard on the clothing. Marshall looked so disreputable that the first tavern he approached refused to admit him, but there were less discriminating lodgings to be had. In a few days Marshall was recovered from his inoculation and marched home again.

He found himself faced with an important domestic decision. His father had decided to settle over the mountains in that part of Virginia called Kentucky, and had an appointment as surveyor of one section of the territory. He had already sold about half his land in Fauquier County, and the price he got was a pitiful commentary on the state of the currency. He had bought the land eight years before for approximately ten shillings an acre. He sold it for thirty pounds an acre, but he did not feel sixty times as rich by any means. For he had to take paper money, and in actual value he was probably a loser.

Kentucky, however, had no lure for the Colonel's eldest son. He was as far from Richmond and Polly Ambler as he cared to get. So while the big family at Oak Hill—Mary Keith Marshall gave birth to her fifteenth and last child, Nancy, near the date of her eldest's twenty-sixth birthday—talked of their new home over the mountains, John Marshall laid his own plans for making a living in Richmond. He had yet to be entrusted with his first case, but for a young lawyer there was an occupation which did not involve the caprices of clients. Public office might be a pleasant alternative, and there was Thomas Marshall's seat in the House of Delegates, as the Burgesses now called themselves. The Colonel's son was popular, especially among the war veterans who, after Yorktown, were coming home in considerable numbers. They were prepared, as home-coming soldiers have always been, to give their suffrages to a deserving member of their order. Without inquiring too closely into the former Captain's theories and principles of government, Fauquier County elected him to the legislature, and as the session of 1782 opened on a gray November day, Marshall had a sound excuse for remaining in Richmond all the time.

He had been there for some weeks before the House could get itself organized. The difficulties of travel kept a quorum from reaching the capital until eighteen days after the session was supposed to start, but Delegate Marshall was on hand promptly. Polly was almost seventeen, and as soon as she reached that mature age, they were to be married.

[5]

State legislatures in the 1780's were a good deal more important bodies than their successors. They attracted a rather more distinguished type of candidate. John Marshall took his seat in a House which boasted of Jefferson, Patrick Henry, the portly Benjamin Harrison, Richard Henry Lee, one of the early revolutionaries, whose friends thought he and not Jefferson should have written the Declaration of Independence. Among the young unknowns was Marshall's old schoolfellow, James Monroe, gawky and a little shy.

While Jefferson's capitol was being planned for the top of Shockoe Hill, the legislature met in a rather inadequate building, which served for almost all other public functions as well. Richmond had been chartered as a city in May, and almost the first act of the new municipal government had been to license Mr. Ryan, the theatre manager. His house of entertainment was a mere shanty on lower Main Street, but it added considerably to the gayety of the legislative session. Marshall's first term was not much different from his second, and of that one a keen foreign observer, Johann David Schoepf, wrote:

"The Assembly had just now come together for its half-yearly winter session; a small frame building serves the purpose, used also on occasion, with change of scene, for balls and public banquets. It is said of the Assembly: It sits, but this is not a just expression, for these members show themselves in every possible position rather than that of sitting still . . .

"During the visit I made, I saw this estimable assembly quiet not 5 minutes together . . . At the open door of the hall stands a doorkeeper, who is almost incessantly and with a loud voice calling out for one member or another. In the ante-room . . . they amuse themselves zealously with talk of horse races, runaway negroes, yesterday's play, politics, or it may be, with trafficking . . . In the same clothes in which one goes hunting or tends his tobacco field, it is permissible to appear in the Senate or the Assembly. There are displayed boots, trowsers, stockings and Indian leggings; great coats, ordinary coats, and short jackets, according to each man's caprice or comfort, and all equally honorable."

This informality, much as it shocked Schoepf and many another foreign visitor, suited Marshall thoroughly. He himself favored the "trowsers" and short jacket, along with a disreputable slouch hat and loose-fitting linen. Slovenliness did not stand in the way of his rather remarkable and easy progress toward a position of leadership in the legislature. He was appointed to committees on Courts of Justice and national defense. Eleven days after he took his seat he was elected to the Council of State or Executive Council, which served in effect as the Governor's Cabinet.

In later years, the speedy inclusion of Marshall in this select and powerful body was attributed to some sort of aura of greatness which was supposed to have emanated from the rather uncouth young delegate. Actually his election was the result of far more prosaic and usual forces. Some of the members were under obligation to Thomas Marshall or were old friends and colleagues glad to oblige the son. More could be influenced by the amiable Jacquelin Ambler, and he was eager to push the fortunes of his prospective son-in-law. Even in that era of young men in high positions, the Council of State was thought to be a little rarefied for a youth of twenty-seven. Pendleton, from his eminence as head of the Virginia judiciary, complained to Madison:

"He is clever, but I think too young for that department, which he should rather have earned as a retirement and reward, by ten or twelve years hard service in the Assembly."

Judge Pendleton did not mention an even younger member of the Council, Monroe. He owed his election to the same sort of influence that had served Marshall, but he was the favorite nephew of Pendleton's colleague, Judge Jones.

As a Councillor of State, Marshall was ready to marry even though he had his first client still to find. His father was prepared to make over to him some of his unsold land in Fauquier County. His marriage to an Ambler would assure him position among the First Families of Virginia. He was very much in love, and so was Polly; therefore it seemed a little stiff and conventional to insist upon waiting for her seventeenth birthday, which would not take place until March 18. This seemed reasonable to Ambler, and on January 3, 1783, Polly and John were married.

They journeyed out to the estate of her cousin, John Ambler, for the ceremony. The bride's own home was a little cramped and mean for so important an occasion; in fact there was hardly a suitable edifice in all of Richmond for such nuptials as these, but John Ambler's country seat was a tasteful and roomy house adequately furnished and staffed.

Marshall took his bride straight to the house he had rented in

Richmond. This was a two-room dwelling hardly better than a shack, but not worse than other young couples had to accept in the housing shortage of that last year of war. Here the young couple were to start life. They had youth and health, love and a wide circle of friends, one guinea in cash after John paid the clergyman who performed the ceremony, one Negro slave and three horses, these last the wedding gift of the bridegroom's father.

V

Leader of the Bar

JOHN AND POLLY started their lives together almost at the same time that their country embarked upon its undisputed independence. The country faced even more hazardous odds than the couple. It was younger. It was poorer. It was much more friendless. The Marshalls, after all, had their guinea and fine prospects. The United States had only debts and what most impartial observers thought was a doubtful future. Shrewd men in the chancelleries of Europe believed that the new nation soon would face the choice between returning to the British fold and being absorbed by France.

News of peace had not reached Virginia by January 3, when the Marshalls were married, although a preliminary document had been signed in Paris on November 30. It was not to be effective until an Anglo-French treaty was concluded, but less than three weeks after the Marshall wedding, hostilities were ended formally by an armistice.

The peace, finally made definite in September, was a triumph for the diplomacy of Adams, Franklin, and John Jay, who had negotiated it with skill and judgment. But none of them were Virginians, so the exploit did not rank very high in the Commonwealth. Her citizens in 1783 were much more concerned with the troubles which victory had brought along with it than with the glorious fact that liberty had been won in spite of long odds. A young lawyer without clients was especially aware of the difficulties which crowded upon the average family in the backwash of war.

All through the years of fighting and sacrifice, of defeats and the slow struggle to regain the ground lost in those defeats, it had seemed that victory would solve all problems. Strangely enough, the stubborn problems not only remained but grew more burdensome than they had been when armies marched or fought or waited and the little substance of the public treasury was consumed in maintaining them. Trade was still stagnant, land titles insecure, travel difficult and dangerous, the West held by British garrisons. But the most disheartening feature of postwar life was inflation.

This was the era when the phrase "not worth a Continental" had real, bitter meaning as a synonym for utter worthlessness, and it referred to the currency of the country. One aspect of the inflation was the price Thomas Marshall got for his land. But another aspect showed when his son began to set up housekeeping. In the first year of his married life, John Marshall spent a pound for a pair of stockings, two shillings a bushel for oats and three pounds for a hat for his wife. Yet the whole fees from his law practice that year amounted to ten pounds nine shillings. This was due to a scarcity of clients, but it made the days of oats at threepence a bushel seem very attractive. Of course he had credit—he bought his furniture on the installment plan. He had some income from the land and stock his father had left when the family moved to Kentucky. He had his salary as a State Legislator. Yet, in spite of these revenues, he admitted in private correspondence to being "pressed for money."

He did not let it bother him. He was very gay and quite busy,

occupied with legislative duties, pitching quoits, attending Mr.
Ryan's playhouse. He was festive at whist and backgammon
parties, shopped for the household and at rare intervals prepared
a law case—he had four that year. But after the fashion of the
time and place, Polly had little share in the fun or in the duties. At
seventeen she was a staid matron who was supposed to be above or
beneath or at any rate apart from a husband's cavortings in the
society of his fellows. Marshall wrote a few gossipy letters which
have survived, especially to James Monroe, whose interests he represented while that youthful solon was away from Richmond. But
while the bridegroom chronicled the matrimonial prospects of
capital belles, he did not mention his bride. Perhaps it was natural
that weddings should have been especially interesting to him in
those months, and he wrote to Monroe:

"The excessive cold weather has operated like magic on our
youth. They feel the necessity of artificial heat & quite wearied
with lying alone are all treading the broad road to matrimony."

Gaily he reported the weddings, the pursuits, the escapes and
the stratagems of the young men and women of society, but of
his own domesticity he was (as were most of his contemporaries)
completely silent. The only evidence that he had any home life
is in his account book where items for whist and rum and wine are
crowded together with "stockings for P." and little sums "given
Polly," a thimble, a sugar pot, "Linnen for P.," milk, tea, gauze,
coal, and a Dutch oven. Only behind these prosaic items is it possible to catch a glimpse of Marshall's domestic felicity.

It is easier to follow the slow development of his political philosophy. As a lawyer virtually without clients, he had ample leisure
to devote to his legislative duties. He served diligently on a number of committees, and he was a keen critic of the debates and their
results. He found it "surprising that Gentlemen of character cannot dismiss their private animosities, but will bring them into the
Assembly." He noted how Patrick Henry dominated the House,
observing appreciatively the orator's trick of putting his oppo-

nents in the wrong. Henry was able, the younger man wrote, "when he altercates to appear to be drawn unwillingly into the contest and to throw, in the eyes of others, the whole blame on his adversary." Of course, as Marshall saw, Henry really plunged into controversy with delight.

Marshall's chief criticism of his colleagues was that they accomplished so little. This is such a common complaint against legislative bodies that it is hardly worth mentioning. In this case it is significant only because it reveals what seemed to Marshall at the outset of his career to be important.

"This long session," he wrote of the meeting of 1783, "has not produced a single bill of Public importance except that for the readmission of Commutables."

Commutables were those commodities which, by the act which Marshall opposed, citizens of Virginia were allowed to send to the public treasury up to the value of half their taxes. It had been made necessary—at least in the eyes of the majority—by the scarcity of the kind of money which the State considered acceptable for the payment of legal debts. Marshall objected to the measure because the State took a substantial loss on the items it received. He also objected to another clause in the act which postponed all tax payments until the following January. Young Mr. Marshall was a stickler for the letter of the law, but more important was his belief that the government could not afford to let its citizens get into the habit of regarding their payments to the State as of less consequence than their payments to each other. The Commutables Bill struck him as a measure to weaken government, and he opposed it.

He opposed it so vigorously that he was blind to other acts of that session which were considerably more important to the community. Perhaps the most important of all was the authorization to convey to the United States as a nation Virginia's claims—strong claims, too—to the Northwest Territory, out of which five States were one day to be carved. Marshall overlooked the law, also passed at this session, governing citizenship and immigration. He overlooked an act which barred British refugees from Virginia and one which authorized Congress to retaliate in trade regulations against any British discrimination on American commerce. He only knew that if the government had no money, it would have no strength. He liked a strong government.

[2]

Many years later he was at a loss to recall just how his principles became so firmly fixed. Perhaps he remembered his youthful emotions as being more revolutionary than they actually had been, but when well along in years he wrote:

"When I recollect the wild and enthusiastic notions with which my political opinions of that day were tinctured, I am disposed to ascribe my devotion to the Union, and to a government competent to its preservation, at least as much to casual circumstances as to judgment. I had grown up at a time when the love of the Union, and the resistance to the claims of Great Britain, were the inseparable inmates of the same bosom, when patriotism and a strong fellow-feeling with our fellow-citizens of Boston were identical, when the maxim 'United we stand, divided we fall' was the maxim of every orthodox American."

While that emotional basis for a love of Union existed, there were more practical reasons why a man might like a government of reasonable competence. In Marshall's case, perhaps one of the "casual circumstances" which swayed him was that, beginning in 1784, his law practice became a reality. Clients discovered that he had a great deal of common sense to make up for his lack of erudition. They learned that he argued a case or advised on a point of law as wisely as men who had their hair trimmed more regularly and dressed more becomingly. Men who go to law, even men who only consult lawyers, are likely to be men interested in property and its preservation or acquisition. They are more at ease in a community where government is strong and capable of protecting property. Their views could hardly be without influence on the young man they employed, for their views coincided with and protected his own interests.

His activities in the legislature during the months that his professional duties began to take some of his time were on practical measures. He took very little part in the debates or even in the voting on the measures which were establishing freedom of religion in Virginia, but he was eager to push measures which would strengthen the hands of Congress, settle the confused debt issues of the day, and improve the means of transportation.

Debts, especially debts owed to Englishmen, aroused great storms in the Virginia Assembly. Jefferson thought that Virginians owed at this time some ten or fifteen million dollars to British merchants. During the war, of course, payment to Englishmen had been suspended by law. But the peace treaty contained a clause providing that no obstacles would be put in the way of the collection of bona fide debts. Agents for the English creditors promptly put in an appearance to press their claims, but they found that the Virginia law still balked them. In fact a few new laws had been passed in 1783. A resolution to repeal all these measures was offered in 1784, and an impassioned debate began.

Feeling ran high on the issue, and the Assembly was rather sensitive when its motives were questioned. The argument chiefly advanced against debt collection was that the British had not lived up to the treaty either. British garrisons still held posts in the West in violation of the treaty, and the promised return of slaves seized during the war had not been so much as begun. At the same time, the British debts were a dark cloud on the horizon of prosperity for many a planter. British merchants before the war had been extremely generous with credit; they could afford to be because they made such big profits in the American trade. Planters had wiped out one debt by incurring another, and hardly bothered to keep books on them, for that was a tedious occupation which could be done just as well in London. Then came the war, and the debts seemed almost as if they had never been. Now it was proposed to revive them.

While this point of view was not frequently expressed in actual debate, it colored the thinking of a good many members. The resolution to repeal the laws which they regarded as protective was lost by twenty votes, with Marshall in the minority. That the House was not quite satisfied with its own reasoning was evident when a citizen sneered that some of the members who had voted against paying the debts had voted against paying for the coats on their backs. This truth was so offensive that the man only cleared himself of contempt by making a formal apology to the House.

In the meantime, Marshall was changing his status as a public servant. Apparently Judge Pendleton's discontent with so young a man's appointment to the Executive Council had communicated itself to other judges, and the young lawyer bowed to their views gracefully.

"I am no longer a member of the Executive, the opinion of the Judges with regard to a Councillor's standing at the bar determined me to retire from the Council board," he wrote to Monroe in April, 1784.

He had been on a visit to Fauquier County to get himself re-elected there, and perhaps to attend to a few law cases, for he had clients in his old home community. They returned him to office without too much exertion on his part, for he was a substantial property owner. His father had given him the remains of the Marshall plantation, and he was soon to buy several hundred acres more. Slaves and livestock were added, and by the time their first child was born on July 21, 1784, the John Marshalls were as secure economically as a young couple needed to be. The baby was named Thomas for his grandfather.

[3]

Eager as he had been to secure re-election in April, Marshall was weary of the legislature by the time the year closed, and he decided not to seek another term. The fate of most of the measures in which he took an interest did not inspire him to keep up the fight.

He was especially angry about the failure of the British debts resolution "because it affords a pretext to the British to retain possession of the posts on the lakes, but much more because I ever considered it as a measure to weaken the federal bonds which in my conception are too weak already."

He consoled himself with the growing interest and volume of his law practice, with the joys of Richmond society and with the pleasures of acquiring and moving into a new house. The house came after he had been married three years and had risen so high in his profession as to be an object of some envy and renown. He was generous of his time, however, so that for the most part he was well liked, and a young Swiss interpreter who spent several winters in Richmond during the eighties was struck mostly with the talents of only two of its inhabitants—Marshall and Henry—for in his old age Albert Gallatin noted:

"I was received with that old proverbial Virginia hospitality to which I know no parallel anywhere within the circle of my travels. It was not hospitality only that was shown me. I do not know how it came to pass, but everyone with whom I became acquainted appeared to take an interest in the young stranger. I was only the interpreter of a gentleman, the agent of a foreign house that had a large claim for advances to the State; and this made me known to all the officers of government and some of the most prominent members of the Legislature. . . .

"Everyone encouraged me and was disposed to promote my success in life. To name all those from whom I received offer of service would be to name all of the most distinguished residents at that time in Richmond. I will only mention two: John Marshall, who, though but a young lawyer in 1783, was almost at the head of the bar in 1786, offered to take me in his office without a fee, and assured me that I would become a distinguished lawyer. Patrick Henry advised me to go to the West."

Gallatin preferred Henry's advice to Marshall's offer, and grew up to become a stalwart of Republicanism after some years of surveying, storekeeping and land dealing on the Pennsylvania frontier. Association with Marshall might have turned him to another political camp, and deprived Jefferson of his best financial adviser. But then Henry was always the more persuasive speaker on any subject.

Leadership at the bar was acquired by the young man in so short a time because he won cases—the usual method of winning a reputation. In doing so, his greatest asset was a gift for going straight to the heart of an argument, reducing it to its essentials. That meant that the argument was reduced to simplicity also, and even judges had a sneaking fondness for the man who could put things so that they understood them without too much trouble. Appealing as he did to common sense, Marshall had the less need for a knowledge of those intricate pleadings which made up the learning of more profound scholars. In his arguments he was anything but flashy. Francis Gilmer put it perhaps in the most flattering light when he wrote of the Marshall of the eighties:

"So great a mind perhaps, like large bodies in the physical world, is with difficulty set in motion. That this is the case with Mr. Marshall is manifest from his mode of entering on an argument, both in conversation and in public debate. It is difficult to rouse his faculties. He begins with reluctance, hesitation and vacancy of eye. Presently his articulation becomes less broken, his eye more fixed, until finally his voice is full, clear and rapid, his manner bold, and his whole face lighted up with the mingled fires of genius and passion, and he pours forth the unbroken stream of eloquence in a current deep, majestic, smooth and strong. He reminds one of some great bird, which flounders on the earth for a while before it acquires impetus to sustain its soaring flight."

His eloquence, however, never reached anything like the impassioned frenzy of a Patrick Henry, nor did it ever soar beyond the comprehension of the average citizen who attended the courts and listened to the debates staged by public figures. It was above all else his ability to make himself understood that attracted people to him. It was exemplified in one of the legendary stories of his legal prowess.

A countryman with a law suit on his hands came into Richmond in these days to inquire where he might find the best lawyer to take his case. Marshall was recommended by one of his friends —the number of those friends was another element in his success —and the countryman had Marshall pointed out to him. The lawyer was even more crudely dressed than the prospective client, a good deal more careless in the way he wore his clothes, and was eating cherries out of his hat. This would never do, the man thought, so without inquiring further he selected a dignified and well-dressed man with powdered wig, a pompous manner, and snowy linen. This gentleman promptly relieved his client of $95 for the fee, and the man sat back to watch his champion in action until his own case should come up.

Before long, the dignified gentleman and the casual young fellow (who had finished eating his cherries) were opposed in argument. The man of the black coat and the powdered wig had nothing but words and a pompous manner to oppose to the younger lawyer's keen grasp of the case and the facts. As soon as the case was concluded, the countryman rushed over to Marshall, introduced himself and threw himself upon the young attorney's mercy. He explained why he had refused to employ Marshall in the first place, and timidly mentioned that he had only $5 left for a fee. It was typical of Marshall that he roared with laughter, accepted the fee, and won the case, but never was tempted to try dressing in a black coat and powdered wig.

Among his colleagues, the slovenly dress was beginning to be taken as the badge of eccentricity which goes with genius. Certainly no man at the bar was regarded with greater respect professionally, and in May of 1786 one of the big cases of his career linked his history again with the Fairfax name and estate. He was interested because his own lands in Fauquier County had come from that estate, but there was more at stake. There was a possibility that the whole Fairfax title to the Northern Neck would be overthrown.

Lord Fairfax had seen with dismay the conflict between his country and his neighbors. With much sympathy for the cause of the colonies, he could not see that outright armed resistance was anything less than treason. He had returned to England, and of course his estate had been sequestered. But the peace treaty restored the Fairfax title, whether the laws of Virginia did so or not. However, the question of which ranked higher, a treaty or a state law, was not easily answered in 1786. On the side of the state law were local pride, a feeling that the Fairfax grant had been much too big in the first place, a dislike of Englishmen, and a general feeling that the War of Independence had won a new deal for land titles as well as freedom from more objectionable British practices.

As so often happens in the courts of the land, the actual case in which so much was involved seemed to approach the matter by a rather roundabout route. On the docket it was entitled *Hite et al* vs. *Fairfax et al*. The Hite was one Joist Hite who had a claim based both on that of Fairfax and an independent grant from the Crown before the war. When he and some of the others had first received their grant and it was discovered that the land lay within the Fairfax empire, His Lordship had wisely agreed for the sake of continued good relations with London to confirm the titles if Hite and the others actually settled on the land. The legal question arising in 1786 was whether this was a good basis for a title. The purpose of the case was not so much to deprive the settlers of their land as to set a precedent on which their title could rest. It was possible that the validity of the whole Fairfax grant would be involved.

Marshall was retained to protect the Fairfax title. John Baker was looking to the lands immediately at stake. Opposed to them were John Taylor of Caroline, one of the most acute reasoners of his time, and the highly popular Edmund Randolph, then Attorney General of the State. Randolph, one of the handsomest men in Virginia, had the enormous influence which went with his name, reinforced by moderate abilities and unsurpassed charm. And in his arguments, he threw some keen barbs at the Fairfax title. Without going into the legal technicalities of land titles, Marshall impressed the court by a simple line of reasoning.

Marshall pointed out that it was immaterial whether the grant to His Lordship was wise or deserved, and he added that his opponents themselves were the best evidence of the validity of the title "for if he had not title, he could convey none, and the court would never have directed him to make the attempt."

Hite won his particular point in the case, but the decision did not question the Fairfax title to unsold lands in the Northern Neck. This was all that Marshall had been contending for, and he won more than his point. Six months later, when Randolph was elected Governor, he sent out a little notice that since he could not take cases any more, "I beg leave to inform my clients that John Marshall Esq. will succeed to my business." Randolph's business was one of the best in Richmond.

[4]

In winning reputation, clients, and friends, Marshall had suffered one personal tragedy. His Polly had fallen a victim to a rather obscure ailment, a nervous disorder which baffled the best physicians of Richmond—Marshall called in three of them during this year. Her illness, as much as the customs of the time, kept her from the society her husband most relished, but unlike other wives she was not able to enjoy the company of her sisters in matrimonial isolation.

"With a delicacy of frame and feeling that baffles all description," wrote her sister, Eliza, "she became, early after her marriage, a prey to an extreme nervous affliction which more or less has embittered her comfort thro' life."

Just what this affliction was, what caused it and how it might have been treated cannot be deduced from the prim and meager reports which, at the time, it was thought to deserve. It was not considered very polite to discuss these tragedies, yet a great many facts which the eighteenth century (although not so prudish as the next) would have considered unmentionable are necessary for a diagnosis of these ailments, let alone a cure. All that was known is that Polly did not go out very much. She had a phobia about sudden noises, so that her husband used to walk about the house in his stockings, shush the children and the servants, and even persuade the city fathers to miss ringing bells on her worst days. Yet no hint of martyrdom ever crept into his correspondence, and Eliza thought that her sister's illness "only served to increase his care and tenderness." He hired a housekeeper, but he continued to do most of the marketing, and he was genuinely glad to get back home after long trips.

Between 1784 and 1805, Polly bore her husband ten children, four of whom died before adolescence. Two of them, a daughter and a son, died within two weeks of each other, the boy's death being attended, Marshall wrote many years later, "by a circumstance we can never forget." He was writing to perhaps his dearest friend, Joseph Story, and he went on:

"When the child was supposed to be dying I tore the distracted mother from the bedside. We soon afterwards heard a voice in the room which we considered as indicating the death of the infant. We believed him to be dead."

Actually Marshall found the boy breathing a few minutes later, but being certain that he could not live "and as the pang of his death had been felt by his mother," he persuaded Polly to go to her own mother, who was living across the square.

"The child lived two days," he wrote, "during which I was agonized with its condition and the occasional hope, although the case was desperate, that I might enrapture his mother with the intelligence of his restoration to us. After the event had taken place his mother could not bear to return to the house she had left and remained with her mother for a fortnight.

"I then addressed to her a letter in verse in which our mutual loss was deplored, our lost children spoken of with the parental feeling which belonged to the occasion, her affection for those which survived was appealed to, and her religious confidence in the wisdom and goodness of Providence excited. The letter closed with a pressing invitation to return to me and her children."

The suggestion that she needed a pressing invitation to return and the line in an even later letter that she might enjoy his stories more when he wrote them than when he told them in person are the only two hints Marshall ever gave, or at least the only two surviving, to show that perhaps Polly's nerves were a trial to his, too. He bore himself so toward her that Eliza reported:

"He is always and under every circumstance an enthusiast in love."

It was inevitable that a friendly fellow like Marshall would have additional family responsibilities. Especially was this true of the eldest of fifteen, and he had gladly taken on additional cares when he married Polly. While most of his own brothers and sisters were with their parents in Kentucky, one of them, James, had remained in Virginia and was sometimes in need of financial aid as well as brotherly counsel. His sister Lucy was only two years younger than his wife, and when she was seventeen she came to live with them. Marshall was studiously attentive to the needs of a girl setting out in Richmond society, and she was launched with great success, thanks in part to the standing of Polly's relatives. Lucy continued to be a bright note in the Marshall household until she married Polly's wealthy cousin, John Ambler, in whose home the Marshalls had been married themselves. The Amblers called on Marshall for delicate family duties, such as the one that Eliza chronicled after the death of her first husband in 1785. Her father,

she wrote gratefully, had sent "my darling Brother Marshall" to
bring her back to Richmond, where in due course she married
one of his friends, Edward Carrington.

[5]

While the Marshalls had been prospering, the country as a whole
had been descending further and further into an economic depression, which reached its lowest levels in 1785. The States had
stopped issuing paper money for a short time, but that did not seem
to add any security to the old notes. Money grew scarce, and at a
time when a real expansion of credit was needed in order to catch
up on buildings neglected during the war, to enable veterans to
settle on the land, to build ships, and to start industries.

Commerce, although reviving somewhat in 1786, suffered so
much from mad rivalries of the States that some sort of concerted
action was obviously indicated. A convention to consider the
problems of interstate commerce was called at Annapolis for September, and two of the most thoughtful of Americans, Alexander
Hamilton from New York and James Madison from Virginia,
were hoping to accomplish a real reform. But only five states sent
representatives. Obviously nothing could be put through by such
a small number. However, Hamilton saw a chance to snatch a possible victory from the wreck of the conference. He proposed,
eagerly seconded by Madison, a report to Congress to the effect
that commercial problems were so bound up with general governmental matters, it was impossible for a convention restricted in
its discussions to make any progress. Therefore, it was suggested
that a general convention should be called "to take into consideration the situation of the United States, to devise such further provisions as shall appear to them [the delegates] necessary to render
the constitution of the federal government adequate to the exi-
gencies of the Union." Seldom has an invitation to revolution
been more politely worded.

Riding back to their homes, some of these delegates heard of
events which sounded much more revolutionary to them. The

farmers of Massachusetts had risen up against debts and taxes—
their outcry had strange echoing notes from 1775—and were terrifying the good people of Boston with the thought of civil war.
Angrily these farmers began to form mobs, and before long they
found a leader, one Daniel Shays. News of the rebellion went out
on the wings of terror. Congress was literally scared into calling
a convention to meet in Philadelphia the following May.

The actual riots staged by the men of western Massachusetts
were far less dangerous than the rumors of them. Shays's men had
little in the way of arms; the old soldiers had brought out their
muskets again, but just as before they were woefully lacking in
powder and shot. They were easily dispersed by the Massachusetts
militia.

"We are fast verging to anarchy," Washington wrote to Madison in November.

If Washington was depressed, Marshall was ready to give up
the last of his "wild and enthusiastic notions." While Jefferson in
Paris was recording his view, "God forbid we should ever be 20
years without such a rebellion," Marshall wrote about the doings
in Massachusetts:

"These violent, I fear bloody dissensions in a state I had thought
inferior in wisdom and virtue to no one in the union, added to the
strong tendency which the politics of many eminent characters
among ourselves have to promote private and public dishonesty,
cast a deep shade over the bright prospect which the revolution in
America and the establishment of our free governments had
opened to the votaries of liberty throughout the globe. I fear, and
there is no opinion more degrading to the dignity of man, that
those have truth on their side who say that man is incapable of
governing himself."

VI

☆ ☆ ☆

A Nation Is Born

A NEW NATION, conceived in liberty and dedicated to the proposition that all men are created free and equal, was tottering toward complete disintegration as the year 1786 went out amid a chorus of pessimism. While Jefferson, as Minister to France, was expounding the perfection of his government to admiring Frenchmen, his countrymen were finding the Articles of Confederation intolerable. Jefferson's enthusiasm was perhaps a diplomatic necessity; a Minister is supposed to speak well of the government he represents. But in addition, Jefferson the philosopher found features to admire in the Confederation. The theory of a group of brotherly States supporting a mutual agency which would serve but not oppress their people attracted more critical minds than his. It might have worked, too, if the States had provided enough material support to enable the government to serve anyone.

The Congress, wandering unhappily from place to place, was disliked by virtually everyone. Men who remembered that they had fought a war against taxes regarded a central government as an incubus hardly distinguishable from the British monarchy. They were not appeased by the irrelevant detail that nobody paid any taxes to it. On the other hand, men who saw the need for a single power to regulate commerce, build roads, improve waterways, and keep the balance between thirteen jealous sovereignties were disgusted with the impotence of the Confederation.

The struggle, then, was to be between those who wanted a moderately strong government for the thirteen states and those who wanted what in effect was no government at all. That last is what prevailed when the question began to be argued. Under the Articles of Confederation, incidents which were regarded as threats to the whole country—Shays's rebellion—were not proper objects for consideration by the central government. But few of those who wanted nothing more than slight changes in the status quo would go to the convention called to meet in Philadelphia.

Only those with a strong desire for reform would fail to be deterred by lack of pay, fairly high expenses, and a brutally exhausting journey for anyone who lived more than twenty miles from Independence Hall. The opposition might have been more numerously represented if it had been generally realized that the men who organized the convention were bent upon more than reform. They wanted a revolution.

The revolutionary aspect of the Philadelphia meeting was obscured because the members were so eminently respectable, because their methods were covered by a veneer of legality, because they were very quiet about it, and above all because they were unusually successful. There were fifty-five members, but they represented only twelve states because Rhode Island refused to send delegates. Within Independence Hall, however, could be counted the very cream of American brains, talent, and property.

Lawyers had a tidy majority of the fifty-five, for an even thirty were members of the bar, a rather smaller proportion than prevailed in most future American legislative assemblies. In addition there were eleven wealthy men who were engaged in commerce as their chief activity, seven planters, two men of no occupation but great means, two physicians, two land speculators and one printer-philosopher-inventor-statesman-diplomat, the venerable Franklin.

The combination of their intelligence and patriotism, prejudices and material interests made the Constitution of the United States. Furthermore, they were quite familiar with the methods of creating such documents. Since 1776 the States had given the world a new science or art or form of red tape (depending upon the point of view)—the written Constitution. They and their countrymen had grown up hearing about Constitutional principles, but they felt that the British model of a constitution by tradition and precedent had betrayed them. So since 1776, all the States except Rhode Island and Connecticut had drawn up quite elaborate Constitutions. These constitutions had two points in common. Every one of them had a bill of rights and strictly limited the power of the government. None of them abandoned the basic Whig republican doctrines of the people as sovereign. In fact, it was freely said that in limiting the power of government to do evil, the Americans had surrendered the power to do good.

Some of the men meeting in Independence Hall had helped draft their State Constitutions—Madison and Mason for Virginia. All of them were familiar with the process. All of them had ideas, from those who wished to do only a bit of tinkering with the Articles of Confederation to those who proposed a government little short of absolute. There were so many points of view so loquaciously represented that after less than two months Washington wrote:

"I *almost* despair of seeing a favorable issue to the proceedings of the Convention, and do, therefore, repent having any agency in the business."

Washington's position was especially trying. He had been elected to preside over the Convention, so it was his fate to listen to the debate and take no part in it. The notes taken at the time indicate that the theorizing was keen, the arguments brilliant, and the oratory repetitious.

The public at large heard little of this. The Convention sat in executive session, and perhaps it was just as well. Men engaged in revolution are wise to keep the beginnings of their work as quiet as possible, especially if they are aiming at a peaceful revolution. Besides, enough conflicting points of view were expressed in Independence Hall as it was without stirring up more from the outside.

[2]

While the Convention sweltered and argued its way through the summer, the country had to carry on as best it could in the old manner. In Richmond, that was not too unpleasant for successful young fellows like Marshall despite a fire early in the year which destroyed a considerable part of the town. The capital was being partly rebuilt in brick, which gave it a somewhat more permanent and very much more elegant appearance. The rising dignity of John Marshall was attested by the fact that in 1787 he was able to contribute, without sacrifice of his own comfort, the sum of twenty-one pounds for the relief of fire victims. This was nearly twice as much as his whole professional income only four years earlier.

An even more impressive mark of his importance was the "draft" that brought him back to the legislature. The still unknown work of the men in Philadelphia would have to run the gantlet of State conventions, and State conventions would have to be called by the legislatures. There were not too many men who could be counted upon to befriend a real central government of adequate powers, and the careful exponents of strength laid their plans well in advance, enlisting leadership for their cause with a keen sense of values.

Marshall was not eager for further service in the little frame Capitol. His previous experience in the House had "opened to my view the causes which had been chiefly instrumental in augmenting those sufferings," but had "convinced me that no safe and permanent remedy could be found but in a more efficient and better organized General Government." He was willing to take it on the word of Washington and Madison and Wythe that such a government had been outlined in Philadelphia. So in the early autumn of 1787 he announced his candidacy. He was elected to the session of the legislature which began in October to decide whether Virginia would call a convention to accept or reject the Constitution.

That document had not been signed until September 17. Sixteen of the delegates failed to affix their signatures, some of them, including Randolph and Mason of Virginia, because they thought it was too imperfect to merit their support. They were very far from subscribing to the stately opinion of Gladstone, uttered years after success had been proved by experience, that this was "the greatest work ever struck off at a given time by the brain and purpose of mankind." Many of the thirty-nine who did allow their names to be affixed would have disagreed profoundly with Gladstone's lavish phrases. Even Madison, who had seen more of his ideas adopted than any other delegate, was temperate in his endorsement of the final product. Hamilton could find no more enthusiastic term than a cool "better than nothing." His last words in the debate at Philadelphia were:

"No man's ideas are more remote from the plan than my own are known to be [he had offered the most highly centralized authoritarian system of all]; but is it possible to deliberate between anarchy and convulsion on one side, and the chance of good to be expected from the plan on the other?"

In the next twelve months, the country proved to him that such deliberation was not only possible but inevitable. Even before the text of the proposed Constitution, drafted in Gouverneur Morris's finest prose style, was very widely distributed, the arguments began. They ranged from disquisitions on the sovereign rights of states and the liberties of people to the cry that fellows like Madison were only slave owners trying to ensure a profitable market in other southern states.

The contest in Virginia started almost as soon as the legislature was organized. It was orderly and peaceful compared with that staged in Pennsylvania. There the supporters of a strong government found themselves in control of the legislature but in some doubt as to whether they could keep it in a fair test of electoral strength. So within a week of the signing of the Constitution and before legislators had so much as a chance to read the document, the majority pushed through a resolution calling for a ratification convention in five weeks. The majority were in such a hurry that members of the minority were dragged into the hall and held there forcibly to make a quorum while the ballot was taken, a process that involved torn clothes and scratched faces—and lacerated feelings which took even longer to mend. In the then state of communications, some of the more remote sections of Pennsylvania could not learn in so short a time as five weeks that an election had been called, let alone choose delegates. Since they would have elected enemies of the Constitution, the brevity of the interval between the call and the election was considered a shrewd stroke. Certainly it roused a deal of talk both before and after Pennsylvania ratified in December, the first State to do so.

Virginia more decorously debated a set of rival resolutions while four hundred miles to the north, Hamilton was sitting in the cabin of a Hudson River sloop writing the first number of *The Federalist*. There was no question that a convention would be called. The dispute in Virginia centered around the terms of the call. The party which was taking the name of those papers being born in young Mr. Hamilton's mind as his sloop coasted gently downstream from Albany wanted an assembly which would be empowered only to accept or reject the Constitution. Their enemies demanded that the convention be authorized to make reservations; that is, to adopt amendments as a condition of ratification. This was in part a sincere demand, in part a dodge to defeat the whole plan since it was recognized that amendments by one State would

have to be submitted for approval to all the others. The whole
program would be dropped before that process could be completed.

The absence of a Bill of Rights in the Constitution as drafted
was a powerful argument for this second course of procedure. It
lost nothing in the clever management of Patrick Henry, who
took the lead against the Constitution while protesting himself as
"truly federal." It was an argument which Virginians who had
been battling for freedom only a few years earlier found difficult
if not impossible to answer directly.

The indirect answer was given by Marshall after long days of
hot debate. The brusque demand for a yes or no decision, which
had been introduced by his party, smacked unpleasantly of the
high-handed Pennsylvania tactics which were being reported and
denounced with considerable effect on public opinion. On the
other hand, if a virtual invitation to amendment was issued, the effect on other states where ratification was being debated would
be bad. They would be tempted to hold off until they saw what
Virginia's reservations would be, or they would be encouraged
to adopt reservations of their own. Either course might easily
prove disastrous, offering victory to those who were suggesting
that a new constitutional convention from all the States be summoned to perfect the unworthy, incomplete job done in Philadelphia.

The proposal for a second convention was a very real peril because it sounded so sweetly reasonable and was so certain to fail.
At Philadelphia, conflicting interests and rival philosophies had
been brought to majority support of an acceptable plan only with
the greatest difficulty. To reopen all the old arguments and add
to them the new bones of contention which might be thought up
in a year of animated controversy was as certain a way as could be
devised to split any convention wide open.

Therefore, Marshall had a receptive audience when he offered
his compromise resolution. He proposed the simple solution of a
ratifying convention without any strings to it at all. The delegates

should be elected without restrictions, he urged, and "the new Constitution should be laid before them for their free and ample discussion."

Each side thought it had won when this phrasing was read. Marshall's own party were pleased not to have amendments specifically suggested, and they were equally pleased to escape from their ill-chosen all-or-nothing position. Henry and his friends were confident that they could dominate any "free and ample discussion" likely to arise. They had been doing it in Virginia for more than twenty years. So Marshall's resolution passed without a single adverse vote. A day in June was appointed for the meeting.

[3]

The solemnity of legislative debate was not unrelieved that session. Besides the usual gayety of the capital, the Marshalls enjoyed a great deal of family sociability, for the father of the clan was in Richmond that autumn and winter—and in the legislature, too, representing a Kentucky district. He had become a leading citizen of the new country across the mountains, and had sufficient influence to obtain for his eldest son the business of agent for that district. James was also a visitor, and there was a good deal of entertaining in a quiet way—Marshall's wine bills at least were modest —of the Amblers and their connections, the members of the legislature, and clients from near and far.

Polly, it is true, took little part in the festivities, even in the strictly family gatherings. Her melancholy illness kept her from participation in most of them, but in addition she was going to have her second child in December. (They named him Jacquelin Ambler for her father.)

As a man of family, Marshall was grateful for the fact that his professional activities were also increasing. He did not need to rely for clients upon his family connections any longer. As a recognized leader of the Richmond bar, he was sought out by men of large affairs to watch over their interests, so that before long he was looked to as an authority in questions of property—he did not try as many as half a dozen criminal cases in all his life. Robert Morris was one of his clients, and was sometimes in Virginia to exchange congenial political gossip and practical business information with his lawyer. Marshall was also becoming a favorite with members of his profession in other parts of the State, who entrusted him with appeals by or against their clients. This was a valuable part of the business of a lawyer in the capital, because travel was so wearisome that attorneys at a distance sometimes could not and sometimes would not brave the perils of a journey to Richmond. They preferred to relinquish their fees to a man who already lived there.

But not even the pressure of court work, not even the joy of adding another son to his little family could keep Marshall from preoccupation with the fate of the Constitution as the time for election of delegates to the Convention drew near. The credulous little newspapers and the full-throated orators—these latter reached a wider audience since the 3,000,000 Americans were 75 per cent illiterate—were giving plenty of attention to the Constitution now. They were making up for their silence while the document was being drafted, although frequently their remarks indicated as complete an ignorance of its contents as had prevailed of necessity during the previous summer of secrecy in Philadelphia.

With all the ranting, the moderation of the public comment was exceptional for that day. There were loud cries that failure to ratify would lead to an anarchy and terror which had had but a pale prelude in Shays's rebellion. There were equally loud cries that the Constitution spelled an end to all human liberty, that every American would become the slave of a power-crazed President backed by a Praetorian Guard of hundreds of thousands of reckless idle men seduced into the army by high pay and the prospect of looting their fellow citizens.

These ravings had their effect, of course, but there was a large amount of solid sense spoken on both sides in a reasonable manner.

At the head of this list, setting the tone for the country's writers and speakers, was *The Federalist*. Widely published in newspapers throughout the States, this series offered the friends of the Constitution their best ammunition. Composed by Hamilton, Madison, and John Jay of New York, the articles appeared every two or three days for more than six months. Marshall was only one of thousands who read them and admired. In some cases, doubters actually were won over, so powerful was the reasoning, and one of the converts was Hamilton himself. He decided that the Constitution was more than merely "better than nothing." As he wrote his share of the essays—the lion's share—he became convinced that there was plenty of latent power in the instrument.

However, it was not the strategy of the Federalists to dwell on the power potential of the proposed new government. They wished rather to allay the fears of citizens whose dread of power had been cultivated carefully throughout the War of Independence. In Virginia, the managers for the Constitution, led by Madison and with the prestige of Washington in the background, were looking for candidates who would be firm but would not alarm their constituents by a belligerent advocacy of strong government.

Marshall was an ideal nominee, and Henrico County (which included Richmond) was going to be hard to win for the Constitution. A substantial majority of the voters were opposed to ratification at this time. There was some question whether even ratification with reservations could have carried a popular referendum there. One of the County's two delegates was bound to be the handsome young Governor who had refused to sign in Philadelphia. (It was a well-kept secret that Washington and Madison were exhausting every resource to win him over. The opponents of the Constitution thought no candidate was put up to oppose him because everyone knew he could not be beaten.) Marshall was nominated for the other Henrico seat because he was the only man of his party who had a chance to win it.

The fact that he had a chance was due to personal rather than to political circumstances. His views were well known to the

electorate, which did not agree with them. But the firmness with
which he might be expected to maintain those views was not so
well known. Many a voter seems to have believed that because
the young lawyer was careless in dress and careless in casual conversation, he might be careless in his principles too. His friendli-
ness and good humor, his readiness to oblige anyone and everyone
led some of his fellow citizens to suppose that he would be an easy
convert to their opinions once they had honored him with their
suffrages.

On the positive side, Marshall attracted the war veterans because he had served in the army himself, because he had made a
point of providing legal advice to former soldiers at even more
modest fees than usual, because he was open-handed with small
loans to them, and because he was "one of the boys" when it came
to pitching quoits, playing cards, or passing the glass at a talkfest.
Also, he had been for a year Deputy Grand Master of the local
Masons, and members of the lodge remembered that he had obtained for them the lottery which provided funds to build Ma-
sonic Hall.

Thanks to a combination of these circumstances, men of greater
standing in the community than Marshall were not so well liked.
One of the secrets of his popularity, too, was his own genuine
fondness for people and the completely barbless nature of his wit.
He loved to tell stories, but never made anyone he knew the butt
of them. There was such a lack of malice in his ready gossip that
the fact aroused comment.

All these traits and mysteries of character fought for him when
he opposed Dr. William Foushee, one of Polly's physicians, for
the privilege of being Randolph's colleague in the Constitutional
Convention. The good doctor was not a popular figure fortunately, but the issue seemed so close that Randolph wrote to Madison on February 29:

"Marshall is in danger."

The Governor was needlessly alarmed. He was in a rather
nervous state just then, for he was in the process of yielding to the

blandishments of Washington and the flattering protestations of
Madison that only he could save the country. Randolph had decided to support that Constitution which he refused to sign, and
he knew the change of front would bring upon him the full wrath
of several of the greatest masters of invective then living. A sensitive man, intelligent rather than strong, he did not relish the prospect. Apprehension could not sway his decision, but it affected his
judgment. Marshall actually was elected two days later by a comfortable majority.

[4]

Richmond put on its best to welcome June, the annual meeting
of the Jockey Club, and the Constitutional Convention, all of
which arrived in the city together. Every kitchen was hot and
steamy and pleasantly odorous as cooks vied with each other to
impress the hungry guests. Every bed was taken, every stall filled,
and horses were tethered in every convenient place. The roses
were very fine that year, and the trees had been washed fresh and
green by recent showers. Whenever the noise and bustle of the
unaccustomed crowds died down a little, the muted roar of the
falls above the city provided a pleasant musical background.

The twin attraction of horse races and the greatest debate ever
held on the Constitution of the United States (although the Richmond crowds on this June day could not know that this would be
true) had drawn the curious from hundreds of miles. This was
greater tribute to the interest aroused by the Convention than a
generation accustomed to the ease and comfort of modern travel
can well imagine. Those who had come to Richmond by stage
from Williamsburg, only a little more than fifty miles as the road
twisted, had been jolting and tossing—and sometimes getting out
to walk or push—from eight in the morning until eleven at night.
Men from Kentucky had been days in the saddle, armed and alert
for Indians or robbers, spending their nights in filthy inns or
crowded farmhouses. A few elderly, ill, or wealthy gentlemen had
driven to the capital in their own vehicles, usually light gigs or

phaetons, but they had been only a little more comfortable. The spring rains had muddied the roads and swollen the streams to make travel more difficult, but in the last day or two the sun had shone hot and steady, so Richmond's streets were now deep in dust.

On the morning of June 2, the Jockey Club took second place to the Convention. Spectators jammed the galleries of Academy Hall, a new building finished just in time for this occasion. Marshall, taking his seat on the floor, could watch everyone who was much of anyone in Virginia (except two) getting settled around him. The two missing were Washington, whose influence in absentia was greater than that of any present, to the vocal chagrin of his opponents, and Jefferson, who was far away in France watching the preliminaries of a very different revolution than the one which was to be confirmed in the warm atmosphere of Academy Hall.

Marshall had been taken into the inner circle planning the strategy of ratification. Little Madison, neat, frail, and unimpressive in debate, was the chief organizer and floor leader. Pendleton, much aged and so crippled that he could not stand without the assistance of a pair of crutches, and the diminutive but energetic Wythe were the chief figures to inspire respect among the rank and file. Randolph would be used for his popularity but his conversion was not, in the minds of his colleagues, so certain that they dared admit him to their counsels. Their "brain trust," therefore, was completed with George Nicholas, a grossly fat man who hid a keen brain behind the rolls of flesh and whose oratorical talents were indicated in the bald brow and great hooked nose; James Innes, a giant of a man whose war record was imposing and who had succeeded Randolph as Attorney General, and Henry Lee, the beautiful and dashing "Light Horse Harry."

At the head of the party which confidently looked upon itself as the majority was the redoubtable Patrick Henry. He gave the impression of being a very old man although he was only fifty-two. He had difficulty keeping his red wig on straight and his shoulders were bent, but when he shoved his spectacles up from his dark eyes, opened his thin mouth and began to talk, he was again the Henry of "If this be treason" and "Give me liberty or death." White-haired George Mason was at hand to tell why he had refused to sign, and as the author of Virginia's constitution and bill of rights, his words carried weight. Aristocratic Benjamin Harrison, perhaps a little surprised to find himself on the same side as Henry, was old-fashioned in dress but keen in mind.

The struggle beginning on this dusty June morning, however, was not an ordinary debate. The supporters of the Constitution were a compact group in firm agreement as to their objective and how to reach it. Their opponents were a band of individualists held together mainly by dislike of the Constitution. They were by no means in complete accord even in objections. So, as the 170 delegates gathered for the opening of the Convention, the men with the affirmative program had the advantage of initiative and organization.

They promptly set out to make the most of these assets. Before their foes could learn their own strength, Pendleton had been elected president of the Convention and Wythe Chairman of the Committee of the Whole. In the ensuing weeks, the Federalists were to have the support of the presiding officers. Marshall was on the board of strategy, but he was not one of his party's heavy guns. He had the privilege, therefore, of listening without being too distracted by other considerations to the debate which more than any other argument except *The Federalist* went deeply into the real meaning of the Constitution.

The whole country was as breathlessly interested as he. Pennsylvania's hasty ratification had been followed by that of Delaware, Connecticut, Georgia, New Jersey, Massachusetts, Maryland and South Carolina—eight in all. The Constitution was to go into effect if nine States ratified, but the Union could hardly survive if its biggest member, Virginia, and its most strategically located member, New York, held aloof. So while New Hampshire actually assured the Constitution's ratification by a ninth State, news of her action did not reach Richmond before the Convention ended, and it would not have been of great effect if it had. Supporters of the proposed system of government were much more concerned about New York, whose convention was to meet in Poughkeepsie on June 17. More than two-thirds of the members opposed the Constitution, and Virginia's example would be needed to convert them because New York could not hold out against all the rest of the Union.

[5]

If in addition to his other talents, Marshall had possessed the gift of clairvoyance, he might have seen most of the rest of his life unrolling before him in the Convention debate. Also, he might have refrained from the most important speech he made before that body.

The Virginia debate lasted for three weeks. It was a long show, but it held its audience to the end. In a day which has seen the attention once concentrated on speech-making diverted to the radio, the screen, and the juke box, the absorption with which the men of 1788 followed the words of their leaders seems a little fanatical. But it was recorded at the time that the galleries were so delighted with the quality of the speaking that they paid the speakers the tribute of respectful silence. On the floor, Marshall was for a long time as silent as the spectators, and like them he was organizing in his mind the strengths and weaknesses of the points which were made both for and against the Constitution.

One big question, which Washington thought was in the minds of many of the delegates, was not actually brought out into the open. This was a fear—and a well-grounded one, too—that if the central government became really effective, offices in the State governments would lose much of their prestige and their importance. For the rest, the speakers dealt with the realities of eighteenth century politics, and in Marshall's orderly mind, the objections and their answers were presented like this:

1.   Patrick Henry thundered that the Constitution usurped the

power of the States and Congress and the name of "We the People" to set up a consolidated government which was never authorized by the States or by Congress or by the People. Randolph replied with a recital of the intolerable weaknesses of the Confederation, explained why there was no longer time to amend the document as he had once hoped, and wanted to know why the name of the people should not be used since the Constitution was for their benefit as much as for that of the States.

2. Mason raised the specter (never laid since that day and not always so insubstantial) of a tax-hungry central government devouring the substance of thrifty men. Mason expected rank discrimination as between various classes of taxpayers. He saw an "exciseman to every farmer's house who distills a little brandy where he may search and ransack as he pleases." Henry too built up the revenue collectors as "unfeeling blood-suckers" and "harpies" who would derive their greatest delight from seizing and selling up the lands of poor but honest men. Descending to cases, he said it was a certainty that the only way the Confederation's war debts could be paid was by taxation. Young James Monroe urged with Henry that Congress could not be trusted to levy taxes, since it would be too far removed from the people. Marshall himself gave as good an answer as the Convention heard. He pointed out that gentlemen seemed to be afraid only of abuse of power, in this case the taxing power. But such an argument could be used to destroy any government of any kind, for power might always be abused. Certainly, he said, taxation was necessary to protect the whole country from foreign dangers, and surely no one was any longer fatuous enough to believe that the States would obey Congressional requisitions even in an emergency, when there had never yet been a single example of such obedience. Marshall failed to see why Congress should be any more likely to betray the people than State legislatures because both were elected by the same voters. Outrageously high taxes, abusive regulations would be repealed promptly, he said, because the people simply would not re-elect usurpers.

3. The absence of a Bill of Rights was as ubiquitous as King Charles's head in the writings of Mr. Dick. Despite the fact that every one of the 170 members professed the strongest attachment to such a bulwark of liberty, no one could leave the subject for long. One side insisted that the Constitution should not be ratified until the liberties of the individual and the States were protected. The other side promised speedy amendments after ratification but held that if the Constitution should be delayed until all the States accepted Virginia's reservations, there would be no government and no liberties for any individuals.

4. Henry and his friends were very much alarmed by the powers to be conferred upon the President. They saw an inevitable despotism based on command of the army, the conduct of foreign affairs, the appointing and veto powers. They hinted that the friends of the Constitution were creeping toward a stronger form of government than was being avowed in the Convention. Since this last charge was quite true, it was answered feebly or not at all.

5. One of the great talking points of the Opposition was the danger which would follow the deeding of supreme authority over a tract of land ten miles square to the central government. The purpose, of course, was to build a permanent capital outside the boundaries of any one State. But orators described this as if it were bound to become a fortified camp offering refuge to evildoers of every description and harboring hordes of bandits and ruffians who would sally forth at intervals to plunder and kill. Orators on the other side poked a little fun at this fear. Marshall, for example, wondered what would have become of the intrepid American spirit to which Henry referred so often in his purple periods. "Will no one stay there but the tools and officers of the government?" he asked.

6. Linked to the fear of the ten miles square was the fear of standing armies, something which had not been eradicated from English consciousness. States saw themselves robbed of their precious militias to form what the Henrys and Masons regarded as the

army of a foreign power. Indeed, their whole argument was based on the theory that the proposed government would be at least as alien to Virginia as that of King, Lords, and Commons in London had been. In the course of this section of the debate, the Convention came close to a little fighting of its own. Randolph, resenting Henry's sneers at his change of front, indulged in a few reflections on the great patriot's motives. That night Henry sent a "friend" with the usual demand for explanations, but a duel was averted by disclaimers of personal insults on both sides. Meanwhile the fear of a standing army was countered by a warning that the Thirteen States, unless firmly united, would be easy victims to any determined aggressor. Marshall was one who argued in this vein and showed himself somewhat in advance of his time by saying of European powers: "Sir, the sea makes them neighbors to us. Though an immense ocean divides us, we may speedily see them with us."

7.   Considering the uproar which debts, foreign and domestic, were to create in the politics of the country within a few years, the Opposition made very little of the debt issue. Henry did point out that Virginia had paid off her own war debt and would now be taxed for those of the Continental Congress and other States. He also painted a dark picture of free men who had escaped from British creditors being flung back into bondage by having to pay up. Mason described the evils of paper money speculation, and charged that it was already beginning—an offensively true remark. He protested bitterly the likelihood that "we may be taxed for centuries to give advantage to . . . a number of rapacious speculators." Madison retorted somewhat disingenuously that the Constitution changed nothing in respect to the debt and currency —words he would have to eat one day.

8.   The development of the West, the Opposition asserted, would be stopped forever under the Constitution because Massachusetts, Rhode Island, Connecticut, New Hampshire, New York, New Jersey, and Delaware would form a majority of seven to block expansion and so save themselves the trouble and expense of defending larger territory. The Federalists replied hotly that

in the absence of a central government which could be respected, the Spaniards, Frenchmen, Britishers and Indians by whom the country was surrounded would bar Americans from their manifest destiny. The men of the West apparently believed Henry and his friends, for ten of the fourteen delegates from Kentucky voted against ratification.

9. "Liberty" and "monarchy" were two words which recurred again and again. Perhaps they were inevitable in an argument in which Patrick Henry took part, but the hopes and fears they induced were very real. They were met by stressing with equally dogged repetition that the proposed government was one of very limited powers—Madison made them sound more limited than they really were—and that all final authority rested with the people.

[6]

One other subject of first importance was taken up at some length in the Convention. It was a subject which had its implications in many other sections of the debate. This was the role of the proposed Federal courts. The Opposition felt that the Constitution was purposely vague in the few paragraphs it devoted to this part of the new system. The grim prospect of being hauled hundreds of miles at the mercy of autocrats of the bench was dangled before the Convention as a virtual certainty. Judges secure for life from the salutary force of public opinion, said these speakers, might well be the tyrants who would realize all the public's fears about debts, search and seizure of property, the extinction of State authority, even, according to the gloomy prediction of Henry, torture and murder by judicial process.

At first glance it would not have been supposed that Marshall was the best equipped man present to deal with such a thesis. Pendleton and Judge Paul Carrington were two of the principal jurists of the Commonwealth, accustomed to saying the last word on legal questions. Wythe's professional learning was unsurpassed in America. Randolph and Innes were leading gladiators of the bar who had the added advantage of high public office. But the floor leaders preferred Marshall to any of them for the big speech in defense of Federal Courts.

Many years later, when Marshall headed those Courts, it was customary to say (and believe) that already his great grasp of constitutional principles was so firm that he towered over his contemporaries. It was said that Pendleton (who only a few years before thought him too young for the Executive Council) now recognized his master in Marshall, and that Wythe (who best knew the gaps in his former pupil's education) felt that the younger man's instinct was a more powerful weapon than a lifetime of study. The little circle gathered around Madison were much more astute than that. They put Marshall up because they wanted a plain man to utter some plain truths. They wanted a man whose learning would not be discounted, whose position as a judge would not lead to any suspicion of special pleading. They wanted to appeal to a jury, not a court. Finally, they wanted a popular, easy speaker to discuss an unpopular, traditionally dry subject.

Of course, they knew, too, that Marshall had exceptional powers of reasoning and that he possessed a certain eloquence, respectable if not inspiring. He already had made his start in the Convention discussions, when on June 18 the judiciary became the specific topic of debate. Talking on the army and taxes, he had achieved the running start which was to lift him off the ground. But before he spoke, he had to listen to some sound predictions uttered by Mason and Henry.

In somewhat more detail than they had done before, these shrewd men pointed out just how the Constitution could lead step by step to that really all-powerful central government which they feared and which the Federalists disclaimed. The courts would be the medium by which the advocates of what Mason called "one national, consolidated government" would have their way with the helpless country. The word "consolidated" carried horrid implications as these men used it, much as "appeasement" and "totalitarian," once so innocent, became terms of opprobrium to a later generation. Mason foresaw "consolidation" through the Federal Courts because, he said:

(a) The Constitution and laws of the United States as well as treaties made by the United States were to be the supreme law of the land, binding upon State courts regardless of their own constitutions.

(b) The Federal courts were allowed to try disputes between citizens of different states and between a State and the citizens of another State. It was intolerable to think that a Pennsylvanian, for example, could hale the sovereign state of Virginia before a foreign tribunal.

(c) Even if a man won a judgment in the lower courts, he might be ruined by being forced to travel hundreds of miles with witnesses and papers to defend himself on appeal.

(d) No provision was made for juries, so Mason said that meant there would be no juries and an accused man would not be able to challenge for cause.

(e) The Federal courts would be the arbiters of British debts and claims. Mason objected to this on two counts. First, the debtors would get shorter shrift in these courts than in their own state tribunals, he thought. Second, the state laws which had confiscated British property such as the estate of Lord Fairfax might be set aside. Thirty thousand Virginians had bought Fairfax land, so Mason feared the State would have to pay Fairfax's heirs or see 30,000 worthy husbandmen put off their land.

(f) There was no limit on the number of courts which the new government might create, so to Mason it was inevitable that an army of unscrupulous toadies to the President, masquerading as judges, would be foisted for life upon the backs of the taxpayers.

Henry reinforced Mason's arguments, so that in effect Marshall was taking on the two principal champions of the Opposition when he rose to reply. One hopes for Polly's sake that he was wearing the new coat he had bought on the opening day of the Convention. One wishes, also for her sake, that it had not been quite such a cheap garment—he paid his tailor only one pound for it, and one pound did not buy what gentlemen considered appropriate coats. He should have looked his best, for while he did not pack the galleries to the bursting point, as Henry did whenever he spoke, there was a very respectable audience indeed to hear him.

He did not make a complete answer to all the objections raised, and some of the things he did say this day were to rise up and plague him later. But the speech served its purpose of quieting the fears which Mason and Henry had roused with their terrifying pictures of oppression and fraud.

Mason, he declared, should set his mind at rest about the supremacy of Federal laws and Federal courts because the United States would be able to make laws on such a limited number of topics. Marshall, all his life a great devotee of the rhetorical question, added:

"Can they make laws affecting the mode of transferring property or contracts or claims between citizens of the same State? Can they go beyond the delegated powers? If they were to make a law not warranted by any of the powers . . . the judges . . . would declare it void."

If the Marshall of 1788 had answered these questions as the Chief Justice of twenty years later did, he could have lost the Convention for his party. But no one at the time had any suspicion that he had any other replies in his mind than a ringing unqualified "no."

The fear that citizens of one state would be able to sue another state in the Federal courts was brushed lightly aside as "not rational" and quite unthinkable. Madison had used this argument too, but in a little more than four years the Supreme Court was hearing as one of its first cases just such a suit. In 1788, however, Marshall's flat statements had a most reassuring ring.

The objection that men would be dragged great distances to foreign courts and the cry that the new government might establish an unlimited number of courts were cleverly used to answer each other. If there were many courts, Marshall explained, a man would not be forced to go very far for justice. Furthermore, he said, the unjust man would be deterred from seeking to force an opponent to a distant city by the fact that the loser would have to pay the costs. Despite this ingenious reasoning, the expense of Federal justice (and sometimes of State justice, too) was to be a recurring source of complaint.

Marshall speedily demolished the argument based on the absence of a clause providing for the jury system. He could not understand why gentlemen supposed juries would not be used just because they were not mentioned. The Virginia constitution, which Mason had written and which was extolled as a model, made no specific provision for juries either.

He grew a little confused when he reached the question of debts and land titles. Mason had exposed with sharp insight the probable course of constitutional development. Marshall's difficulty was that he thought it a fine thing that a creditor might have access to a tribunal which would give his honest claims a fair hearing. Although he himself owned land whose title derived from that of Lord Fairfax, he was not at all afraid of permitting the rights of such a claim to be decided by a Federal court. However, it would be poor tactics to admit his beliefs. Lamely, he urged his hearers from the Northern Neck to repose their faith in the State confiscation law. This may have been good advice, but it was small answer to Mason's charge that it was this very law which the Constitution permitted the Federal courts to review.

Marshall was not content merely to answer objections. He made a few positive points as well. One was that Federal courts would relieve the State dockets, which were then "crowded with suits which the life of man will not see determined." Another telling point was that a Federal judiciary would provide tribunals for the many disputes which could not be settled at all or not settled properly because no other courts had jurisdiction over them. He also thought that the Federal bench, appointed by a President and confirmed by a Senate, would be filled with men at least as able and honest as those elected in Virginia by the Assembly. Finally, in the courts Marshall saw the surest barrier to dictatorship and tyranny.

"To what quarter will you look for protection from an infringement of the Constitution, if you will not give the power to the judiciary?" he demanded. "There is no other body which can afford such a protection."

[7]

The great debate was drawing to a close. By June 22 the question of the courts had been disposed of if not settled, and Madison that day wrote to Hamilton:

"The Judiciary Department has been on the anvil for several days . . . The attacks on it have apparently made less impression than was feared."

Three days later the vote was taken, after Henry had closed the debate with a speech which had the violence of nature added to the violence of his personality. In the midst of his final sulphurous indictment of the Constitution as the probable forerunner of terrible miseries, the skies darkened and a summer storm began to crash and blaze so close to Academy Hall that nervous spectators fled for other shelter. Inside the room grew dark. Henry could be seen in intermittent flashes and heard between deafening roars which shook the building. Members had some difficulty in distinguishing between him and the rumblings of the thunder as it receded in the distance after each shattering shock. But as he subsided, so did the storm. Just before the vote was taken, the weary orator, still the patriot of '65 and '75, told the Convention in what for him were restrained and quiet tones:

"I will be a peaceable citizen. My head, my hand and my heart shall be at liberty to retrieve the loss of liberty and remove the defects of that system in a constitutional way."

Then, with four delegates absent or not voting, the Constitution was ratified by 88 to 78. The news was immediately rushed northward to win the adherence of New York, while in Academy Hall the weary delegates set themselves the task of drafting amendments for a Bill of Rights which, as a sop to the Opposition, Virginia would forward to the First Congress of the United States.

VII

☆ ☆ ☆

The Making of a Federalist

MARSHALL WAS little more than an observer of the early struggles of the government which he had helped to bring into the family of nations, and he did most of his observing at a safe distance from the principal events. The country had been started on its way to greatness; the world was about to embark upon a generation of revolution and war, but Lawyer Marshall was entering the years of his greatest personal peace and comfort.

Most of the other leaders in the great struggle for independence and good government were moving to the front. Hamilton as Secretary of the Treasury was preparing to establish his country's credit and saw himself as a sort of Prime Minister. Jefferson was coming home to take what by some then and by nearly everyone now is regarded as first place in the Cabinet. Madison had defeated Monroe in a close contest for one of Virginia's seats in the House of Representatives. Randolph was Attorney General. Jay, offered his choice of any post he wished, had selected the Chief Justiceship.

Marshall remained in Richmond, even refusing Washington's offer to become United States Attorney in his home district, and the year that the government was formed he bought a city block in what was becoming the fashionable part of town for a new home. He did consent to stand for the legislature again in the election of 1789, for this would not take much time from his practice, his family, and his pleasures. Also, it enabled him without much sacrifice to do a little rear-guard activity in defense of Federalism —mostly fighting a losing battle for resolutions to support the Administration. It was a losing battle because the majority remained solidly opposed to the principles which had led Marshall to support the Constitution.

Throughout these years, he was busier than ever professionally. Hardly a case of importance involving property came to trial without his appearance on one side or the other. When other lawyers were employed on the same side, Marshall nearly always was chosen to close the argument. He never acquired a very profound acquaintance with precedents, partly because he had learned very few during his brief education but also because they did not seem to him to be the most impressive part of legal knowledge. So he would leave precedents to be introduced by his colleagues while he concentrated on the case at issue. If he had no colleague, he very often dispensed with precedents altogether and did quite well without them. In fact, a good deal of his strength in practice was due to his absorbed concentration on the problem before the court rather than on what some other court had decided in some other case.

Marshall could resist an active part in affairs outside Richmond, but he maintained an active interest in them. He observed with keen attention the growth of a new nation in a world heading rapidly into completely strange and uncharted seas. The administration of Washington and the French Revolution were combining to present one of history's most absorbing dramas. Marshall followed it through the increasingly articulate, and increasingly abusive, press of the country, through letters and through talks with friends and clients in high places. He managed to be much better informed than most Americans on the events which were changing all of Western civilization.

The man who had seen that the Atlantic made Europe his neighbor, was not likely to underestimate the influence of the highly dramatic developments overseas. In this he could not be said to be in advance of his time. Leaders of all parties knew that they were by no means isolated from European storms, even if news of them might be weeks or months in arriving. Foreign affairs were an accepted ingredient in domestic politics.

The French Revolution actually was watched more eagerly and greeted more enthusiastically in America than the first steps taken by the new government in New York. It was happily supposed that a wartime ally and friend was following the American example. There was just enough truth in the supposition to make it convincing. But as the revolution, in the way that revolutions have, proceeded to make sweeping and even violent changes, unanimity of opinion in America became as impossible as it was in France.

As Jefferson's successor as Minister to France, Washington sent Gouverneur Morris. Morris had rather less sympathy with the revolution than had Marie Antoinette for, like Pooh-Bah, he was born sneering. Dazzled by his titled friends, flattered by the acquisition of an aristocratic mistress, and temperamentally a cynic, the American Minister was an eager partisan of the old regime. The aspirations of French peasants and artisans were ridiculous in his eyes. Marshall was exposed to a good deal of his point of view because the envoy wrote frequently to Robert Morris, no kinsman but admired as much as if he had been one. The financier sometimes repeated the best bits to his lawyer, and they helped mould Marshall's opinion of events in France then and later. On the other hand, Jeffersonians retained a temperamental sympathy with the Revolution. They could tolerate even the terror and keep their eyes steadily on the struggle of a great people to be free, to choose their own government, to select their own leaders and measures, even if foreigners did regard those measures as nothing short of atheism and murder, anarchy and plunder. A little of the French revolutionary sentiment, it was said, might be a very excellent importation, wiping out a deal of American privilege and corruption.

Thus, fairly early in the struggle and before it had risen to the proportions of a world war, American politics were split by a European conflict. As usual, too, the difference over foreign affairs engendered more heat and bitterness than even the most controversial of domestic issues. Somehow, when Jefferson called Hamilton an "Anglomaniac," it was much more insulting than the epithet "monocrat." When Hamilton referred to Jefferson as a "Jacobin" he meant to be much more scathing than when he merely said his great rival was a fanatic. The domestic achievements of Washington's administration broke up political alliances; the doings of the French sans-culottes ended private friendships.

[2]

During Marshall's service in the legislature which met in 1790, the disputes still centered around domestic issues. Hamilton had won passage of a law by which the Federal government assumed the remaining war debts of states, and it had roused Patrick Henry's full fury, for he had warned against this and been brushed lightly aside by Madison as a man who was seeing things under a bed. Now he introduced a resolution which branded the measure as a violation of the Constitution because it exercised a power which the Constitution did not grant in so many words.

Marshall and his friends were beaten by nearly two to one in their efforts to block this resolution. Marshall in particular saw that a Federal authority rigidly limited to those powers actually named in the Constitution would never be strong enough to provide the kind of national government he wanted. If Henry's view should prevail—and resolutions passed by the legislature of the biggest State in the Union might influence many votes—then Marshall had fought in vain in the Convention.

Passage of Henry's resolution drove Marshall out of the legislature, for he thought his services were useless against the tide of the majority. But he remained an unofficial adviser to Washington, consulted on appointments in Virginia and making occasional speeches in support of an Administration which was becoming more and more unpopular, largely because of its foreign politics.

In the first years of the nineties it was possible for a friendly even-tempered man like Marshall to take part in political discussions without losing his friends. Mason, for example, was a close companion despite their differences in public matters. Henry was always cordial, but as the years passed, the old patriot's politics changed. He grew very rich, and as his wealth increased, he found unexpected charms in Federalism. At Farmicola's Tavern, one of Marshall's favorite spots for a leisurely glass and chat, it was not unusual for him to exchange good-humored jests and speculations with political enemies.

Marshall's lanky figure and undistinguished costume were familiar to every corner of Richmond, for he liked to walk around the city. He was seen at the markets, gravely shopping for the family larder. He strolled up the hill to look in at the Capitol which Jefferson had designed on the model of a Greek temple. He drifted along the river front admiring the ocean-going ships whose tall masts swayed gracefully, and he exchanged gossip with masters and mates of the little coastal schooners. He watched the big wagons from the Blue Ridge crossing the pontoon bridge over the James, their bearded drivers in buckskins and fur caps yelling like Indians as they cracked their whips. The better class of driver always adorned the canvas top of his wagon and the harness of his horses with bearskins and gay rosettes before entering Richmond, and made quite a show.

If Marshall turned up Main Street, perhaps accompanied by Polly on one of the rare occasions when she felt well enough to brave the bustle of the city, they might drop in at Richard Denny's store. In the winter of 1791 they might have been served by Denny's new clerk, a bright and eager lad of fourteen from the

backwoods of Hanover County named Henry Clay. The young
fellow was working there to get money to go further west. The
Marshalls could pay in tobacco receipts—a common form of currency—or if they had cash it was likely to be any one of a dozen
varieties of coin still current in Virginia, Spanish or French or
Dutch pieces, even Arabian sequins. But trade was brisk and Main
Street was very fine these days, except for the mud. It was sometimes called Brick Row, because so many solid buildings had replaced the flimsy frame construction of Marshall's earlier days in
the city.

Everywhere he went, men were glad to exchange a bit of gossip or a joke with Lawyer Marshall. But the days of easy com-
radeship with all and sundry were drawing to a close. Political
differences, far from being eased after the adoption of Hamilton's
program and the increasing prosperity of the country as a whole,
were becoming more embittered. The French Revolution was
bursting the borders of France itself. As a coalition of Kings
moved ponderously to crush what they called republican madness, Americans found themselves drawn ever more strongly into
an intense partisanship.

The country tended to take its cue from Washington's Cabinet,
which was setting an example of anything but harmony. Hamilton
and Knox, the Secretary of War, were increasingly at odds with
Jefferson and Randolph. The two chief Secretaries for a time
worked together well enough, but soon their rivalry grew so keen
that Jefferson himself distastefully described their relationship in
the Cabinet as that of "cocks in a pit." Out of it two great political
parties were being formed. In the election of 1792 the two had the
same candidate for President, Washington, but contested virtually
every other place. Jefferson, worried by Marshall's popularity in
Virginia, even suggested to Madison that the Richmond lawyer
ought to be made a judge to keep him from running for Congress.
Marshall had no intention of doing so, but there were plenty of
candidates for all places, and both sides took to the hustings and
the newspapers with loud whoops of assorted invective.

The leading party organs of the day were the *Gazette of the United States*, edited by John Fenno, a former Boston schoolteacher, and the *National Gazette*, presided over by Philip Freneau, a poet of some distinction who had roomed with Madison at Princeton and developed a gift for caustic criticism during the war, a large part of which he spent in a British prisoner-of-war hulk. Federalists thought it monstrous that Freneau should be patronized by Jefferson and Madison and subsidized by employment as a translator in the State Department. Republicans thought it monstrous that Fenno should be patronized by Hamilton and Senator Rufus King and subsidized by a contract for Congressional printing.

Washington himself was unable to reconcile the two "cocks in a pit." He tried hard, warning them that internal dissension was "most alarming" and more dangerous than differences of foreign policy. He asked "why should either of you be so tenacious of your opinions as to make no allowance for those of the other?" But his mediation failed, and he had to let them fight it out in the elections. The Federalists made the fight on the issue of peace and prosperity—the latter point answered by Freneau in jingle:

> Whales on our shores have run aground,
> Sturgeons are in our rivers found—
> Nay—ships have on the Delaware sailed,
> A sight most new.
> Wheat has been sown—
> Harvests have grown—
> On coaches now, gay coats of arms are borne
> By some who hardly had a cent before—
> Silk gowns, instead of homespun, now are seen,
> Instead of native straw, the Leghorn hat,
> And, Sir, 'tis true
> ('Twixt me and you)
> That some have grown prodigious fat,
> And some prodigious lean.

The Federalists won that struggle, in the polling place if not in the press, but with a reduced margin in the House. The gulf between the parties deepened and widened that winter as details of French events in September, 1792, trickled belatedly across the country. Marshall, the interested observer, could tell a man's politics by his reaction to the name of the month. If he broke into spontaneous panegyrics on the magnificent victory of tattered, untrained republican heroes who had sent the proudest armies of Europe reeling back from the French frontier in retreat and disgrace—why then he was a Republican. If he spoke in hushed tones of the Paris gutters running full with the blood of all that was noblest in France—why then he was a Federalist. Marshall was a Federalist. He was an advocate, too, of what he once called "those slow and cautious steps which gradually introduce reform without ruin."

In the midst of this emotional conflict, the French republic added to the excitement by declaring war on England and by sending a new Minister to the United States. The twin measures were new fuel for American political fires. All the old denunciations of British tyranny were revived, and popular enthusiasm for the French rose to new heights. America, it was said, would now repay her debt to France by rushing to her defense. That sort of gratitude is marvellously difficult to inspire in any kind of government. Help from one nation to another is usually selfish no matter how generously or gracefully done, and that fact apparently is the first—sometimes the only one—that diplomats learn. In this case, the usually divided American Cabinet agreed upon a neutrality proclamation which was so severely neutral that all the friends of France screamed with rage.

Meanwhile the new French Minister had landed in Charleston, and as he made his way northward, political animosities flamed so hotly that they burned away ties of friendship in Richmond. Marshall, for instance, could no longer avow his support of Hamilton's measures and his loyalty to Washington without getting his fingers burned. But he was as ardent a disputant as any American when it came to foreign affairs, and he held out his hands gladly in the blaze.

[3]

Citizen Edmond Charles Genêt, the bellows to these flames, was a handsome young man, a matured child prodigy who had been the darling of Queens and commoners but never saw so much adulation as the enthusiasts of French republicanism showed on the east coast of America. Stronger heads than his might have been turned by the demonstrations, the dinners, the songs, and parades. Stalwart men were wearing liberty caps over one ear in his honor and kissing each other in what was said to be the true French fashion. Little children were singing "Ça ira" and the "Marseillaise" for him in newly learned French. Ladies were waving to him from windows and smiling on him and throwing flowers and calling one another "Citizeness" to show their genuine republicanism.

Citizen Genêt, a Girondist of even higher and more impractical ideals than most of his party, replied with enthusiasm and not a little bombast. The irony of his situation was that in the very days he was treating himself as a conqueror, his Girondist friends were losing their last struggle for moderation and within a month were hiding in cornfields or waiting in jail for the tumbrils to take them to the guillotine.

Marshall was trying to rally a little Virginia sentiment against the Minister, Monroe reported to Jefferson. He did not succeed. Only Genêt was strong enough to dissipate his own popularity, and he managed to do it with two indiscretions. Haughtily, he refused to sit down to dinner in Philadelphia with an *émigré*, the Vicomte de Noailles, who had been one of the distinguished French volunteers in the American War of Independence, and Americans still had a soft spot for those heroes. Equally haughtily, the Minister fitted out a privateer, and sent her to sea in defiance of the American government and of Washington's proclamation— a bit of highhandedness which even Jefferson could not stomach.

Genêt's recall was demanded, but by then he knew what had happened to his friends. Recapturing prudence, he retired from public life, married an heiress and became an American citizen.

But if he had found peace for himself, he had ended the repose of a good many Americans, including John Marshall. Richmond's leading lawyer found himself for the first time in his life under personal attack for his defense of the Administration. Nobody except Polly and her sisters had ever complained of his dress and deportment. But now Jefferson took note of him—perhaps it was a compliment—and suspected that Marshall's "lax, lounging manners" were really put on to curry favor with the populace. Jefferson would not have liked the fact that later commentators were to find that the distant cousins had much in common in their carelessness as to clothing and posture.

More public if anonymous attacks were being made upon Marshall's habits. His fond sister-in-law, Eliza, was consumed with indignation because his "slanderous enemies . . . would catch at the most trifling circumstances to throw a shade over his fair name." In that age of gargantuan potations, a man had to be dissipated indeed before his drinking attracted attention, and even then charges of drunkenness were usually made in the absence of proof of more heinous offenses. But now it was being whispered that Marshall both gambled and drank. Eliza exclaimed that she knew for a fact that "Mr. M———ll always played for amusement and never, never for gain, and that he was, of all men, the most temperate."

More damaging, although not written for publication, Madison was hinting that Marshall's latest speculation was based upon "an absolute confidence in the monied interests which will explain him to everyone that reflects in the active character he is assuming."

The speculation was Marshall's final intimacy with the Fairfax grant. Through him, his brother James had met Robert Morris. James not only won the affections of the financier's daughter, Hester—they were married two years later—but had conceived the plan of buying up the remnants of the Fairfax estate, something under 200,000 acres of the most valuable land in the Northern Neck, as Morris's partner. John Marshall went into the purchase with them, and for years was harassed by lawsuits concerning it and money to pay for it. In 1793, however, such troubles seemed remote, not to say improbable, for Morris had agreed to finance the deal, and many supposed him to be the richest man in the country.

Marshall himself was more concerned in these months with building his new home in Richmond. He was putting up a comfortable brick house of nine rooms on his city block, and he moved into it that year. The neighborhood was a stronghold of Federalism and of Ambler in-laws. On adjoining squares lived Polly's parents and her three brothers-in-law—Colonel Edward Carrington, friend of Washington and a double officeholder under the Federal government, who had won the fair Eliza after losing her temporarily to her first husband; Daniel Call, a leading member of the Richmond bar, and George Fisher, one of the principal merchants of the booming little city.

[4]

Marshall's own family connections were impressive—and thoroughly Federalist. James's marriage to Hester Morris would link them with the national powers of the party. Old Thomas Marshall, active in politics in the West as he had been before he crossed the mountains, held an important post in the revenue department. Two of his daughters had married sound Federalist politicians— Senator Humphrey Marshall of the new State of Kentucky, soon to lose his seat because of his Federalist opinions, and Alexander Daviess, the United States Attorney there. Daviess so greatly admired the leader of the party that he had given himself the middle name of Hamilton.

With all this array of talent married into the family, Marshall was sure of ample support whenever he was attacked, but he did not get used to slander. Even his appointment as a Brigadier General of the militia did not soothe his feelings, and in a rare mood of anger he wrote:

"Seriously there appears to me every day to be more folly, envy, malice, and damn rascality in the world than there was the day before and I do verily begin to think that plain downright honesty and unintriguing integrity will be kicked out of doors."

That is a common complaint in times when the institutions men live by are being suddenly and even violently remodeled, for then stupidities and wickednesses are much more apparent than wisdom. In 1794, the war in Europe was reaching the stage of all world wars when the rights (if any) of neutrals begin to get in the way of the belligerents. In the United States, a domestic crisis was in the making over the excise, the farmers of the West and South having a legitimate but unheard grievance that the tax on whisky was discriminatory, outrageous, and ruinous.

Marshall was interested in both, and both called for his services as a militia general. In the summer, the international situation brought Marshall into the field as a soldier for the last time.

In a little port near Norfolk, a vessel named the *Unicorn* was being fitted out as a privateer in defiance of the neutrality proclamation. The United States Marshal wanted to seize the ship in accordance with his orders, but he could not find more than a handful of men willing to help him use force. A much larger number were ensconced in a house overlooking the *Unicorn* with several cannon and a number of muskets to protect the privateer. The Marshal appealed to the Governor—at this moment Marshall's old comrade "Light Horse Harry" Lee—who called on the Richmond brigadier to help carry out the law. No shots were fired. General Marshall had only to show himself at the head of his little army, peacefully confiscate the arms in the house overlooking the port and report that local officials could have done as much if they had wished or dared.

He got home to find that Washington had called the militia for a more arduous task. In the backwoods of Pennsylvania, the farmers had decided that another war against taxes was in order. Virtually every farm had a distillery; the only reasonable way to transport grain to market was in the form of liquor, and they could not see why it should be taxed just because it had been reduced to transportable proportions. So tax collectors were run out of the district, law violators rescued from jail, the barns of tax informers burned. It sounded like a most formidable uprising, this Whisky Insurrection, and a formidable force was called up to meet it. The whole might of the nation was to be used—Hamilton himself took the field—but there is no record that Marshall's brigade actually went out through the rain and mud (which were the worst enemy the troops encountered) to bring back the few poor farmers who were to be an example to their fellows to pay their taxes.

Meanwhile, the foreign situation had become complicated by the inevitable British interference with free trade. The British always had their own interpretation of their rights at sea when they were at war. They were now asserting with their usual blunt force a supposed right to stop American ships, impress American seamen into their navy and seize cargoes bound for France.

"The man does not live who wishes for peace more than I do," wrote Marshall, "but the outrages committed upon us are beyond human bearing."

When even men like Marshall, soon to be accused of pro-British leanings, could write in this vein, it was inevitable that the popular sympathy for France, allied to English oppression, would cause the war fever to spread across the land faster than the plague. But leaders of both parties remained strong for peace. As a last resort, Washington borrowed John Jay from the Supreme Court to seek a new treaty with England. Jay had done much of the skillful diplomacy which won the highly favorable peace of 1783; perhaps he could do it again. As a sop to the Republicans, who denounced the Jay mission as a timid, pro-British move, their rising young star Monroe was sent to replace Gouverneur Morris as Minister to France. Then, for a short time after the elections of 1794, which

showed the temper of the time by returning a Republican majority to the House as a protest against harshness to Whisky *Insur-
rectos* and failure to aid France, there was a lull in the political
storm.

[5]

Jay left New York in May, 1794. The Senate confirmed his treaty
thirteen months later, and the public learned the terms only after
the vote had been taken. They would not have known at all if the
Federalist majority could have had its way. The treaty was so
humiliating to American pride and so destructive of American
interests that the Senate had voted not to publish it. A Republican
Senator refused to be bound by the decision, and carried a copy
to the newspaper owned by Benjamin Franklin's grandson, Bache.

Anger and disgust swept virtually the whole country. For once
Hamilton and Jefferson (both had left the Cabinet) agreed about
something, each of them using the adjective "execrable" to describe the treaty. But they were not in accord as to the desired
course of action. Jefferson would have rejected the treaty out of
hand. Hamilton's influence alone had rallied Federalist Senators
to confirm it, for he thought it was not too high a price to pay for
peace.

The country's reaction was unexampled, even in that age of
unbridled invective. Washington was denounced this time, accused of overdrawing his salary, and the negotiator of the treaty
was burned in effigy all across the country. Half the male population seems to have got drunk toasting: "Clipped wings, lame legs,
the pip and an empty crop to all Jays." Hamilton was stoned in
Broad Street when he tried to defend the treaty. Jefferson thought
the humiliating terms had ended Federalist power in Virginia.
Washington found the outcry like that "against a mad dog." Virginians were especially indignant because everything they had
hoped to gain from England had been surrendered by Jay—no
payment for sequestered slaves, no speedy evacuation of the Western posts held by the British, no relinquishment of British claims

for debts owed her citizens. Instead the envoy had yielded to the British in pledging enforced payment of debts owed to Britishers, free rights for Englishmen to take part in the trade of the West without any compensating gain for Americans. All in all, the treaty constituted a surrender of more rights than had been abused by the British before the Chief Justice started on his mission.

In the midst of the controversy, Marshall received from Washington an invitation to join the Cabinet as Attorney General. The salary of the Attorney General of the United States was $1,500 a year, less than a third of the sum Marshall was making at the bar although he did not charge high fees. The same day he received the letter he turned the offer down because his Fairfax and family commitments would not permit him to take it.

"While the business I have undertaken to complete in Richmond forbids me to change my situation tho for one infinitely more eligible," he wrote, "permit me Sir to express my sincere acknowledgments for the offer your letter contains & the real pride & gratification I feel at the favorable opinion it indicates.

"I respect too highly the offices of the present government of the United States to permit it to be suspected that I have declined one of them."

Marshall also refused the commissionership of debts set up under the Jay Treaty. But he was still willing to help the administration by working in Richmond. For the Attorney Generalship he proposed Patrick Henry, now believed by Marshall to be wholly on the side of the Federalists. He attempted to persuade the aging orator, but Henry was cool.

More practical aid to Washington was Marshall's decision to let himself be returned to the legislature again so he could try to moderate the language which that body was sure to use in denouncing the Jay Treaty. He spent weeks in leading the debate—he and Charles Lee carried the burden for the badly outnumbered Federalists—but they could not prevent the legislature of Washington's own State from passing a resolution of censure by about two to one. When they tried to retrieve the insult with a little

resolution of their own in praise of the President's general conduct, they could not get members to vote for the proposition that
George Washington had at any time displayed either wisdom or
integrity.

After that, Marshall had to solace himself with domestic joys—
a daughter, Mary, was born to him in September—and with loyal
Federalist friends. He could also be grateful that long ago the
Barbecue Club, his favorite resort of relaxation, had absolutely
barred any political discussion. The meetings every Saturday at
Parson Buchanan's farm were dedicated wholly to jesting and
feasting and quoits. Here Marshall could take off his coat, pick up
his personal set of quoits—a great heavy pair of rough iron instead
of the new-fangled polished brass affected by other members—
and forget the vicissitudes of politics. The talk over the punch or
occasional baskets of champagne was confined to the game, to
sports, jokes, farming, and business.

[6]

Then one day in July, 1796, Marshall came home to find a letter
from Washington. Relations with France were going from bad to
worse, as Revolution degenerated into dictatorship with a small
Corsican General looming very large on the political horizon.
Furthermore, Monroe had not been altogether discreet. Washington wrote in confidence "that it has become indispensably necessary to recall our minister at Paris & to send one in his place who
will explain faithfully the views of this government & ascertain
those of France." The President added:

"Nothing would be more pleasing to me than that you should
be this organ, if it were only for a temporary absence of a few
months; but it being feared that even this could not be made to
comport with your present pursuits, I have in order that as little
delay as possible may be incurred put the enclosed letter under
cover to be forwarded to its address if you decline the present
offer or to be returned to me if you accept it. Your own correct
knowledge of circumstances renders details unnecessary."

The enclosure was addressed to Charles Cotesworth Pinckney in South Carolina, who was willing.

At this time Marshall was one of a little group of Federalists who were trying to get Patrick Henry to run for President. None of them was too sure of John Adams, whom Marshall did not know at this time, and the Richmond lawyer wasted a good deal of time trying to persuade his colleague to make the race. So far had they drifted together since the days seven years ago when they faced each other in sharp debate on the floor of the Virginia Convention. But Henry was too wary a bird to get himself into the kind of fight he would have to make to win the Presidency from Adams and Jefferson. He politely declined, "from an apprehension," Marshall thought, "of the difficulties to be encountered by those who shall fill high Executive offices." The Federalist leaders reluctantly resumed their support of Adams. Some of them hoped and even plotted that Thomas Pinckney, the Paris envoy's brother, who had been put up ostensibly for Vice President, would get more votes and win first place. The Constitution at this time provided that each presidential elector vote for two men. The candidate who got most was President, the next Vice President.

Marshall owed his better acquaintance with Federalist leaders in the North to his only appearance before the Supreme Court as a pleader. During the February term he had gone to Philadelphia to argue the case of *Ware* vs. *Hylton*, on which the collection of a great many debts owed by Americans to Britishers depended. The debtors claimed the protection of the State law suspending collection of debts. The creditors claimed the protection of the treaty under which collection was guaranteed.

Ironically enough, Marshall had been employed to defend the debtors, a position which was in direct contradiction to his own political and philosophical principles, as well as to his personal interests in the Fairfax deal. He did such a good job of it that he had won in the lower court, where his associates were Henry, Innes, and Alexander Campbell. For the appeal only Campbell and Marshall went to Philadelphia.

The arguments of counsel consumed six days before the Supreme Court. Marshall's own effort was in direct contradiction to the opinions which he maintained and defended all his life. But as a lawyer, he was a paid gladiator for his client, bound, once he had taken the assignment, to use his best efforts for a cause which he believed to be wrong. (Of course there was no compulsion to accept the retainer.) In this case, he spoke with apparent feeling of "those who wish to impair the sovereignty of Virginia" —words which sound strange coming from him. He also argued that "there cannot be a creditor where there is not a debt"—and that Virginia had abolished the debt, a line of reasoning which would get short shift from an older John Marshall. His plea attracted much attention. Rufus King, Senator from New York, concluded from Marshall's speech: "His head is one of the best organized of any one that I have known." Marshall himself noted:

"I then became acquainted with Mr. Cabot, Mr. Ames, Mr. Dexter and Mr. Sedgwick of Massachusetts, Mr. Wadsworth of Connecticut, and Mr. King of New York. I was delighted with these gentlemen. The particular subject which introduced me to their notice was at that time so interesting, and a Virginian who supported, with any sort of reputation, the measures of the government, was such a *rara avis*, that I was received by them all with a degree of kindness which I had not anticipated."

The praise and the kindness were not enough to win his case. The Justices ruled against him, and Marshall silently rejoiced. He lingered in Philadelphia only one more day, to hear Hamilton argue as special counsel for the government in the first case brought before the Supreme Court to test an Act of Congress. The argument impressed him tremendously; he did not wait to hear the decision, which upheld the taxing power of Congress.

Marshall returned to Virginia to find that his personal affairs had fallen into some difficulty. As the year wore on, the great financier, Morris, was encountering the problems which generally overtake the too optimistic speculator. Morris had the means to gratify a passion for land but he went even beyond those means. He had sent James Marshall to England to negotiate with Fairfax's heir and borrow money, and early in 1797 James succeeded in raising 7,700 pounds sterling for the purpose. He paid it over to Denny Fairfax, the clergyman to whom the nobleman's estate had passed, but the financing of the loan proved too much for Morris's over-burdened affairs. John Marshall was called upon, and his law practice did not meet sudden demands of this nature. The need for ready money, therefore, drove him out of Richmond into a new field, diplomacy, since extraordinary missions at that time were handsomely rewarded.

VIII

A Mission to Paris

MARSHALL GOT the money he needed, nearly $20,-
000, in return for eleven months' expenditure of time
and some sacrifice of comfort—"oh God, how much
time and how much happiness have I thrown away!" he himself
exclaimed before his mission was half over. Furthermore, he never
got back to private life again.

While it was the money that tempted him, he gave full value
for it because he was a good advocate. Besides, he was advocating
his own principles.

The immediate background of his mission dated to the day
when he had forwarded Washington's offer of the French embassy to C. C. Pinckney. France, angered by the Jay Treaty and
the recall of Monroe and proud in the victories of her invincible
armies, insultingly refused to receive the new envoy. Pinckney
was ordered out of the country on pain of arrest, and withdrew to
Amsterdam. His report of his reception, or lack of it, reached
Philadelphia only after Adams had been inaugurated.

At the same time, inflammatory versions of a speech which

Barras, head of the French Directory, had made to Monroe in taking affectionate leave of that dull and tactless gentleman reached Philadelphia. In it the Frenchman called upon Americans to rise against domestic tyrants and join their sister republic. The Cabinet which Washington had left behind him thought that these remarks provided ample cause for war. The new President, who could be as belligerent as the next man over trifles but kept his head in real emergencies, preferred peace. Although he made an indignant speech refuting Barras, he proposed an extraordinary mission of three to iron out all difficulties. Knowing that Marshall had been Washington's choice for the Paris assignment in the first place, he urged the lawyer to become one of the three. Pinckney of course was to be another and the third was Elbridge Gerry, Adams's old friend from Massachusetts—still a friend although he had become a Jeffersonian.

With Morris heading into bankruptcy, Marshall could not refuse. The mission would pay several times as much as he could hope to earn in a year at the bar, so July 4, 1797, found him in Philadelphia at a celebration given by a number of Senators and Representatives.

"I experienced from them the most flattering attention," he wrote Polly.

He had dined on the previous Saturday with the President, "a sensible, plain, candid, good tempered man," he thought. He had been at the playhouse to see *Romeo and Juliet*. He had spent an evening at the capital's fashionable resort, the Vauxhall, "a most elaborate place," where he hobnobbed with society, listened to the music, entered into the conversation of the strollers in the formal gardens, sipped punch and devoured ices. He also dined once with Morris, who still lived "what we should call most elegantly," but in some isolation. The throngs once seen at his home had deserted his declining fortunes as it became known that he could not redeem his paper.

Marshall's Philadelphia sojourn, however, was not altogether devoted to amusement and talk about the Fairfax purchase. He was there to get his instructions and learn some of the problems he would be expected to solve. For nearly three weeks he remained in the capital. He listened carefully while Adams poured forth his wisdom. "His Rotundity" had a wealth of experience and knowledge to communicate from his years of highly successful diplomacy in Europe and observation of affairs at home. He was an excellent pedagogue when humored, and only his ungovernable temper and inordinate vanity prevented his contemporaries from realizing that as a political philosopher he was the peer of Jefferson or Hamilton. Marshall's respectful attention won his regard instantly.

"He is a plain man, very sensible, cautious, guarded, and learned in the law of nations," Adams commented.

Marshall must have been very guarded indeed to give so suspicious a man the impression that he was learned in the law of nations. He made no such pretensions himself, but he had even better qualifications for diplomacy than many an authority on Grotius and Puffendorf. First of all, Marshall knew his own limitations; he knew he was unfamiliar with precedents. So he had to rely on something stronger, his ability to analyze an argument, determine its strong points, seize upon its weaknesses. To reinforce that ability he had patience, humor, an easy temper, a quite sufficient command of English to state his own case forcefully, and much too much common sense to engage in another man's game, whether of intrigue or craft or deception.

The instructions to the embassy were long and sought to cover every possible contingency. Since an exchange of letters between Philadelphia and Paris would take months, the home government had to anticipate as many phases of the negotiation as possible, all of which took time and space. The orders to Marshall and his colleagues consisted for the most part of things not to do. The envoys were not to agree to any aid to France during the war, for that would be violating the spirit of neutrality and probably lead to war with England. They were not to agree to the sacrifice of any American trade anywhere in the world. They were not to accept any clause in a treaty which would imply that their own government was at fault in the coolness which had arisen between the two republics. Finally, the envoys were not to permit the treaty to abrogate the validity of any existing American agreements, a usual provision in such agreements.

For three weeks, Marshall conferred, talked and dined at the homes of Philadelphia's leading families. He received gratefully letters of introduction from Washington to useful persons in Europe. He had a conversation with Hamilton, probably illuminating, since Talleyrand considered the Federalist chieftain as the best mind of his time and added: "He divined Europe." Certainly he had an uncanny facility for predicting European events, and at this time he foresaw dictatorship in France. All this was highly instructive and interesting to an inexperienced diplomat. But if we may believe Marshall's letters to his wife, he was "beyond expression impatient to set out on the embassy." One reason, he confided to Polly, was that the fare of the Philadelphia nabobs was too rich for him.

"I like it very well for a day or two, but I begin to require a frugal repast with good cool water," he confessed.

At last the conferences and the instructions, the dinners and receptions were over. The brig *Grace*, carrying one Envoy Extraordinary and Minister Plenipotentiary of the United States, dropped down the river and sailed slowly before a light breeze into Delaware Bay. Like any other traveller, the diplomat rushed into his cabin to write last minute letters for the pilot to take ashore. In one he assured Polly that his cabin was neat and clean, that the provisions were ample, that "I have taken care to provide myself with a plenty of excellent porter, wine & brandy," that the Captain was a fine fellow and that the other passengers seemed most agreeable. He ended in the tone on which he closed virtually all of his letters to her through nearly fifty years:

"Do not I entreat you omit to write. Some of your letters may miscarry, but some will reach me & my heart can feel till my return no pleasure comparable to what will be given it by a line from you telling me that all remains well. Farewell my dearest wife. Your happiness will ever be the first prayer of your unceasingly affectionate

"J. Marshall"

[2]

Behind him the political storm raged without cessation. It is not in the nature of politicians to profess much optimism, and this summer all of them saw disaster coming hard on the heels of one or another policy—the other fellow's, of course. The rage of partisan conflict had grown to such heat that Jefferson, presiding over the Senate with that silence which is expected of a Vice President, wrote:

"Men who have been intimate all their lives cross the street to avoid meeting, and turn their heads another way lest they be obliged to touch their hats."

The extreme Federalists were screaming for war with France. Even the more moderate ones were proposing preparedness—the beginnings of a navy, enlistment of a regular army, and the arming of merchantmen, that answer to outrage which several times has been the prelude to war. The Republicans denounced these proposals as leading inevitably to actual hostilities. Their favorite gesture to peace consisted of drinking toasts such as: "May the Irish harp be speedily torn from the British willow." They continued to talk about the Jay Treaty as a base surrender to insults which should have been wiped out in blood. But unkind remarks about France were denounced as war-mongering.

Marshall, well out of the debate, was moving from a continent which only talked of war to one which was actually engaged in it. The voyage of seven weeks was enlivened by meetings with three British warships, each of which sent boarding parties to the *Grace*, and Marshall was impressed by "the entire dominion which one nation at present possesses over the seas." This was soon to be erased by experience of another nation's dominion over the land. He landed at The Hague on September 6, two days after one of those post-revolutionary *coups d'état* which seemed at the time to have changed the course of history. This one had established Barras as a virtual dictator in Paris, so long as he remained on good terms with General Bonaparte. As Marshall saw the European situation—he wrote of it briefly to Polly and at great length to Washington—this is what had happened:

A legislature of moderates having been elected by the good people of France, the three most unscrupulous members of the Directory got rid of their two colleagues, called in the army to support them against the will of the people, arrested the majority members of the legislature, gagged the press, forcibly removed local officials hostile to them and in general violated the Constitution "in so many instances that it wou'd require a pamphlet to detail them."

Marshall's report was not too inaccurate as to facts, although he wrote it nine days after his first glimpse of Europe and without seeing France or talking to anyone except Americans and a few English-speaking foreigners. But a newcomer more sympathetic to the French republic might have found a different interpretation for those facts. Jefferson, for example, would have learned that the real popular base of the *coup d'état* was the army, that vast mass of citizen-soldiers who had been fighting for their revolution all over Europe. While they were away, deprived of their votes, their enemies had stolen an election from them and were preparing to betray the principles of liberty, equality, and fraternity.

Truth perhaps lay somewhere in between these partisan views, but Marshall's preconceived antagonism to the rulers of France was not going to make him any more pliable in negotiation with them. His conviction of their villainy was not the best possible preparation for a peace mission. He seemed to realize that himself, and was in a pessimistic frame of mind. He wrote to Polly that he dreamed about her every night, but that in the daytime he heard about events in France which his informants said made failure so certain that he would be back in Richmond before the autumn was over.

On September 18, he and Pinckney started for Paris, travelling slowly in the hope that Gerry would catch up with them, for his ship had been due the end of August. They spent a short time in Antwerp, and at the end of September rode into Paris. Pinckney had been there before, but Marshall marvelled at the maze of narrow streets, the jumbled houses, the palaces, squares, churches, and gardens. Soon afterward Gerry arrived, and the three went together to wait upon M. Talleyrand, the Minister of Foreign Affairs.

They found a man as tall as Marshall but painfully thin, the almost startling ugliness of his face distracting the attention of those who met him for the first time from his awkward limp. The excommunicated Bishop of Autun had a genius for betrayal and was so faithful to it all through a long life that he did more than any other diplomat in history to foster the belief that his profession is the practice of deceit. He fancied himself as an expert on America because he had spent more than two years of his exile in the United States, travelling restlessly and making acid comments on men, customs, and beliefs. During his stay in Boston, he had met and been on friendly terms with Gerry.

Receiving the envoys in his ornate office, Talleyrand saw three oddly assorted Americans. The tallest, ungainly but with a pleasant dark face and black hair, looked like a modestly superior countryman. Pinckney, portly and yet faintly military in manner, had a rather cosmopolitan air which oddly enough seemed to suit his simplicity and broad friendly countenance. Gerry was a sparrow of a man, standing very straight to make up for his small stature, and glancing about quickly, his sharp features and long nose emphasizing his birdlike quality.

No business was attempted at that meeting. Talleyrand discouraged business with an offhand remark that he was much preoccupied with large affairs but would advise the envoys as to their future procedure. Talleyrand did not propose to waste his precious talents on three inconsequential representatives of a country which could do little to advance his career. He had marked them for the routine treatment which the victorious republic had established for third-rate powers.

[3]

France already was using the diplomacy of dictatorship. This saved a great deal of time and trouble—for the dictator. The French Foreign Office merely informed the hapless governments of countries within reach of French armies that they would be permitted to enjoy peace upon the payment of a subsidy and loan. The illusory prosperity of France at this time was based upon the cash and loot extorted from the richest trading areas of the Continent—Portugal, the Netherlands, and the German city-states. In the course of this diplomacy, it was customary for a substantial share of the plunder to stick to the fingers of members of the Directory and their ministers.

Talleyrand saw no reason why this procedure should be varied in the case of the United States. But he did realize that Americans had not had the benefit of a close view of the invincible French armies in action. Therefore, he arranged for a few preliminaries to create the same impression.

The first step was to keep the envoys waiting. The next was to alarm them by having their own compatriots tell them of the frightful depredations which were being committed upon defenseless American ships and crews by French privateers. The three saw quite a procession of sorrowful merchants and shipowners come to lament the loss of valuable vessels and cargoes and tell of crews mistreated. Their stories were all the more impressive for being perfectly true. Then Talleyrand's secretary advised the envoys through their consulate that while it was too much to expect the Directory or the Foreign Minister to begin negotiations, the three would hear from persons appointed to treat with them.

The first of these persons appeared a few evenings later and set forth the French peace terms, which never varied through all the ensuing months of E. Phillips Oppenheim diplomacy. The visitor was a gentleman of Swiss extraction named Hottenguer who had been one of the agents through whom Robert Morris had tried to raise money for the Fairfax purchase. Marshall might be expected to display gratitude; Talleyrand always displayed a keen discrimination in his selection of tools.

In the best tradition of the worst fiction, Hottenguer actually whispered when he imparted the information that he had a message from the Foreign Minister himself. The message, stated in a normal tone of voice, was that the first condition for a treaty would be $250,000 to be turned over to Talleyrand and spent to put the members of the Directory into a sufficiently friendly frame of mind to listen to reason. The terms they would then accept would be an apology for Adams's harsh words about the government of France, a substantial loan to the French republic and a guarantee that the American government would pay off all claims by Americans for debts or for damage done to commerce by privateers.

Marshall favored a brusque rejection, but his colleagues thought they ought to see where this line of talk was leading them. It led to another quite unofficial character, one Bellamy, who professed himself to be a trusted friend of Talleyrand anxious to give the Americans good advice. His advice was the same as that of Hottenguer. The envoys handed him a letter which Gerry had signed reluctantly because he did not wish to rush matters or offend the French. Yet the missive merely said that they had no power to make a loan, but if the request came officially, one of them could go home for new instructions. No bribe was mentioned.

Talleyrand, a little surprised by this show of resistance, now received a reinforcement. Bonaparte's victories had permitted him to impose a peace of his own terms on Austria, and the whole weight of France could be thrown against England. A bribe to the Directory was all that could save America from sharing the doom of the British, Hottenguer warned, and the haughty Pinckney lost his temper.

"No, not a sixpence!" he cried.

[4]

The Frenchmen were patient. They tried to explain the facts of life to these stubborn Americans, and went so far as to introduce a man from their own side of the Atlantic into the negotiations. This was M. Hauteval, who had made his fortune in the French West Indies. He added little substance to the discussion.

Then at the end of October came a new hint. England was to be invaded and the last defense between the United States and an all-powerful France would be brushed aside. The danger would be two-fold, Bellamy pointed out, because Americans were not united at home for effective resistance. Marshall quotes him as saying:

"Perhaps you believe that in returning and exposing to your countrymen the unreasonableness of the demands of this government, you will unite them in their resistance to those demands. You are mistaken; you ought to know that the diplomatic skill of France and the means she possesses in your country are sufficient to enable her, with the French party in America, to throw the blame which will attend the rupture of the negotiations on the federalists, as you term yourselves, but on the British party as France terms you. And you may assure yourselves that this will be done."

The words were Bellamy's; the thought was Talleyrand's. He meant the Republicans, and he was repeating his mistake of judging the United States by his experience in Europe where a minority party was so often willing to accept the help of a foreign enemy against domestic rivals.

As another means of impressing the Americans with the hopelessness of holding out, Talleyrand let them know of the great preparations being made for the invasion of England—"immense" Marshall called them in a letter to Washington, adding:

"It is perhaps justly believed that on this issue is stak'd the independence of Europe and America."

However, Marshall was shrewd enough to see the dangers involved in striking across the Channel at England while she still held dominion of the seas. He was inclined to believe that the elaborate, ostentatious preparations were a colossal bluff designed to cover secret negotiations for peace.

At this time Talleyrand already had become the satellite of Bonaparte's rising star. On December 10, Marshall was among the foreign diplomats who watched Paris go happily and picturesquely mad in welcome to the hero. Marshall, looking across the splendid array of uniforms, noted that the central figure, his pale chiseled features not yet marred by fat, was ostentatiously simple in his gray riding coat. He also noticed that the General had his hand on Talleyrand's arm.

The next diversion was a new emissary, much more charming than Messrs. Hottenguer, Bellamy, and Hauteval. This was Madame de Villette, a lady who had known Voltaire and was still personable, witty, and gracious. She made life a good deal more pleasant for the envoys, hinting prettily that they should yield to French importunities.

After she had failed, Talleyrand produced a still more theatrical figure, Pierre Augustin Caron de Beaumarchais, author of *The Barber of Seville* and *The Marriage of Figaro*, but also agent through whom several million dollars' worth of war supplies went from France to America after 1776. Beaumarchais had sued several years before to recover some of the money. Marshall had been his lawyer and the suit was still pending. He and the envoys now exchanged dinners, and after the second one Bellamy suggested that Beaumarchais be allowed to win his case, in which event he was willing to allot $250,000 of the award to Talleyrand's bribe so that American face could be saved. There was some difficulty in explaining to these gentlemen the scruples which prevented the envoys from accepting this offer.

By the beginning of the new year, lack of success was beginning to fray the nerves of the envoys. Since Gerry disagreed with Pinckney and Marshall, it was usually the Bostonian who quarreled with one or both of the others. He thought they were needlessly provoking a war. They thought he was attempting some sort of pro-French skulduggery behind their backs, for he saw Talleyrand occasionally alone as a friend. Marshall admitted losing his temper with the little man, and Pinckney wrote to King that he had "warmly remonstrated" with his Boston colleague.

A feeling of isolation, to which in those days of slow communications veteran diplomats became accustomed, had added to the acerbity with which the meetings of the three were conducted. Marshall was not accustomed to being cut off from family and friends, especially the family. His domestic feelings were not soothed by the fact that four months after he left Philadelphia he had not received a line from home. Nevertheless, he and Pinckney managed to get along very well, exhausting their irritation on their colleague. Marshall admired the South Carolinian, and Pinckney wrote of him:

"General Marshall is a man of extensive ability, of manly candor and an honest heart."

After several candid conversations, these two persuaded Gerry to join them in a letter to the Foreign Minister which Marshall drafted. It was a ponderously lengthy, logically acute statement of the case for neutrality. After more than 130 years it seemed to a great Scots jurist, Lord Craigmyle, to have been put "with a clearness and a strength and simplicity which no other author has excelled." Talleyrand, however, did not read it. One of his secretaries told Gerry it was too long for anyone in the Ministry to read.

This was not much of a disappointment. Both sides were considering home consumption much more than any actual approach toward sincere negotiations. Only the naïve Gerry stubbornly clung to the idea that the Foreign Minister, and through him the Directory, could be persuaded. To the others it was clear Talleyrand wanted his money or a chance to blame failure on the two Federalists. They themselves had given up hope of success.

After Marshall's letter had been lying in his office unread for a month, Talleyrand condescended to see all three envoys together. They met three times within a week, and except for the exercise of repeating themselves, it might have been their first hearing of and reply to the French terms in October. But by now it was March, and on the eighteenth Talleyrand finally replied to the unread letter. His remarks were designed quite as much as Marshall's for publication in America. The main point, after rehashing French complaints of unfriendly actions, was that Adams had sent as envoys two "persons whose opinions and connections are too well known to hope from them dispositions sincerely conciliatory." He proposed that these persons, obviously Marshall and Pinckney, go back to America and leave the third to negotiate a treaty.

Marshall again drafted the reply in which the three pointed out that they were not permitted to entrust their mission to any one of their number. The letter then went on to explain the whole American case again, ably but interminably. Gerry, although he signed, was willing to remain in Paris; in fact he did remain. The others started packing at once, Marshall for home and Pinckney for the south of France where he planned to spend a season in the hope of benefiting a sick daughter. There was some bickering with Talleyrand's office over passports, while the Paris spring put forth its best efforts of young foliage, flowers, and balmy airs to charm the visitors. Marshall, however, was anything but charmed. As he embarked from Bordeaux on April 24 on a vessel named the *Alexander Hamilton*, he felt that he had earned his $20,000 the hard way.

[5]

As the *Alexander Hamilton* rolled and tacked and sometimes even ran before the wind on a fifty-three-day crossing to New York, the United States was working itself into a war hysteria. The mails in winter were not likely to make very good time, and the dispatch from Paris dated October 22, 1797, did not reach the State Department until March 4, 1798. Adams spent his first anniversary as President reading the demand for a bribe, a loan and an apology for his speech. "His Rotundity" was not the man to read these things unmoved. He spent two weeks preparing a suitably restrained message to Congress. He announced that the mission had failed, and called on Congress to build up the army and navy and arm the merchantmen.

Republicans were sure this was all a trick. While Hamilton, who had seen the dispatch, was wondering how it might be accorded the widest possible circulation, his enemies solved the problem for him. They proposed a resolution in the House calling upon the Executive to produce "the papers."

"The Jacobins want them," exulted Jonathan Mason, Boston Federalist, "and in the name of God let them be gratified."

Adams fanned Republican suspicion by hesitating. He said he was afraid that the envoys might be subjected to violence if the dispatch was published before they got out of France. The Republicans were sure he wanted to avoid publication because the documents would show that his message was unjustified, that French overtures had been rebuffed. Thus urged by the opposition to do what he most wanted, Adams graciously sent the file over to Congress.

Those who believed that Americans would not easily catch war fever were amazed by the reaction. After all, a corrupt government's corrupt officials had made corrupt proposals to a set of honorable men. The real American grievances against France were exactly those against which Federalists had been trying in vain to inflame the people for two years. Now an insult had done the trick, and Adams with a rare stroke of propagandist genius had made just one slight change in the papers which gave them a far spicier flavor than the originals. He decided to confer anonymity upon Hottenguer, Bellamy, and Hauteval, so in the documents as published these gentlemen appeared under the designations of X, Y, and Z. As the XYZ Papers, the dispatches from Paris attained immortality, but what was of more immediate importance, they whipped the whole country into a frenzy which apparently nothing but war could allay.

The usual catalogue of wildly improbable stories went rocketing across the land with a speed surprising in view of the slowness of communications. William Cobbett, the newest English master of journalistic sensation and invective, was printing fantastic stories in his *Porcupine's Gazette* about French invasions and slave insurrections armed and led by Frenchmen. Preachers were assuring their congregations that the conflict with infidel Jacobins (it had been several years since a Jacobin dared show his head in Paris) was a holy war. Grave New England elders prayed for war. Even Jefferson, who could see that there really was no genuine *casus belli* in the XYZ Papers, gloomily predicted that war was "almost inevitable." Every day more Americans were convinced that war also could be noble and glorious, and in street and tavern and theatre they were singing a song by Joseph Hopkinson. He had called it "The President's March," but it got a new name during the spring of 1798 as the crowds chanted:

> Hail Columbia! happy land!
> Hail ye heroes, heaven-born band!

[6]

Marshall was quite unaware of all this excitement when he landed in New York on June 15, rested and refreshed from the voyage. He got only the barest inkling of the state of popular opinion even there, for he passed through the city on his way to Philadelphia so quickly that Hamilton's ardent cohorts, eager as they were to boom the war spirit, had no time to organize a demonstration. Their new hero was heartily sick of his mission. Writing of it ten years afterwards he was as bitter as on the day he left France, saying:

"History will scarcely furnish the example of a nation, not absolutely degraded, which has experienced from a foreign power such open contumely and undisguised insult."

Bitter as he was, the degree to which the country shared that bitterness amazed him. When he reached Frankford on the road to Philadelphia—he made it in three days—he "seemed to be rather disconcerted at the unexpected honor of his Reception." Such at least was the view of Elias Boudinot, a New Jersey Congressman who was one of a considerable party who rode out to meet him. Marshall was more disconcerted by the pardonable exaggeration of this escort in the Federalist press. There he could read that never had anyone seen "so prompt and general a muster of cavalry." Fleets of carriages and armies of horsemen were in the writer's imagination. On the road itself, Boudinot reported, were about 150 troops and fifty or sixty civilians.

Even this was quite a show for a man whose travels had hitherto been quite unnoticed. But it was as nothing compared to the reception in the capital. All the bells rang and all the people cheered and "every female in the city whose face is worth looking at" smiled from the windows, so *Porcupine's Gazette* reported. Marshall could hardly get a moment's rest at O'Eller's tavern from the distinguished citizens who came to see him. One he missed. The Vice President called twice and left a card regretting he "was so unlucky" as to find that Marshall was out. By a slip which might interest a psychologist, Jefferson had omitted the "un" when he wrote "lucky" and had to pencil it in above the line. In reply "J. Marshall" was "extremely sensible" to the honor of the call, and "would with pleasure charge himself with any commands of Mr. Jefferson" to his part of Virginia.

The Vice President had also mentioned his "regret that a pre-engagement" kept him from the dinner that night. He was fortunate, for he would have been miserable. No such Federalist feast of joy had been held since the party stalwarts had met to toast the triumphs of Hamilton. The distinguished gathering included the leaders of Congress, the Cabinet, and the Supreme Court—Marshall and Jefferson between them had not yet eliminated the Federal bench from active party politics. There was song and gladness and above all the great feature of any social or political or business celebration—the toasts. On this occasion, glasses were filled—and emptied—seventeen times, and the thirteenth removed from the lips of the people Pinckney's not quite immortal phrase, "No, not a sixpence!" which had been a favorite ever since its publication in the XYZ Papers. For the thirteenth toast this night was:

"Millions for Defense but not a cent for Tribute."

Unfortunately, by this time the reporter of the scene was not quite able to remember who coined the phrase. He may be forgiven, for no doubt he already had drunk to these sentiments: The United States, the people and government, the President, George Washington, General Pinckney, the Army, the Navy, the Militia, American youth, the heroes of the last war, the American eagle, and union and valor. After it, he drank also to the duties of a citizen, agriculture and commerce, the Constitution and finally "General Marshall— The man whom his country delights to honor."

IX

From Congress to Cabinet

MARSHALL WAS impatient to be gone. The frenzy of
the Federalist politicians, enjoying their first and last
taste of genuine popularity, did not go down well with
a man who was temperamentally incapable of such mental antics.
Least of all did he relish being the central figure in the physical
manifestations of their hysteria.

He had good personal reasons for wishing to get back to Virginia. Polly's illness had been aggravated in his absence, and she
was avoiding the annoyances of a household by visiting in Winchester. In January, she had borne him a son, who had been chris-
tened John. Marshall was quite impatient to see this interesting
addition to the family. On the business side, he needed to earn
some more money. The French mission would take care of immediate obligations, but Morris no longer could be counted upon
as an asset in the Fairfax deal. "The Bubble of speculation is burst,"
as Theodore Sedgwick put it, and the financier had been for some
months in debtors' prison. The Marshalls and their brother-in-law,
Raleigh Colston, who was a partner in the purchase, would have
to meet the payments themselves.

In a mood of paternal and economic anxiety, Marshall hurriedly completed his reports to Adams and the Secretary of State, Timothy Pickering, a spectacled soldierly New Englander who had been elevated to this post by Washington in despair after most of the eligible men and a few not so eligible had refused. The returned envoy also rejected an appointment to the Supreme Court and set out for Winchester to be greeted by demonstrations at intervals on the way.

He found Polly suffering from an unusually warm summer and with her nerves insufficiently quieted to return to Richmond. He had to go on without her, and there, in the midst of a notable heat wave, his children and his friends (and a good many strangers) welcomed him with a warmth which matched the weather. Marshall even was sure that little John recognized him—from pictures, he presumed—but it is not quite certain whether the little fellow's expression which called forth this belief was caused by heat or teething.

While Marshall entertained constant streams of visitors come to hear a first-hand account of the XYZ affair, the Federalist party in Philadelphia had decided to commit suicide. Popularity is a perilous ingredient to mix with the delusions of grandeur which normally go with the principle that some higher power has meant a small class of men to rule their fellows. The Federalists held this principle, and in the temporary enthusiasm of the crowd they thought they saw an opportunity. They had been so successful in passing a law for a standing army and in the creation of a Navy Department with a Secretary in the Cabinet that they thought they could carry anything.

Several extraordinary pieces of legislation known as the Alien and Sedition Laws were the result of this blunder. Crazed by the unaccustomed plaudits of the people, the party stalwarts in Congress broke the very tight rein which Hamilton had kept upon them and bolted recklessly into oppression. While he warned them against cruelty and tyranny—"Energy is a very different thing from violence," he admonished the unheeding legislators—

they decided to make a new crime, and with it they launched the first witch hunt of the independent United States.

Yellow fever was seeping through most of the big cities that summer and was especially virulent in Philadelphia. But the terror inspired by the plague could not compete with the terror roused in Federalist bosoms by the prospect of losing control of the government. So, goaded by their fears and the exultation of their popularity, they ignored the advice of their wisest man.

The Alien Act authorized the President to expel undesirable foreigners without trial; his definition of undesirability was to be accepted, for their only appeal was to him. This law was aimed at two classes of recent immigrants. First were the French and their sympathizers—Englishmen like Dr. James Priestley, the eminent scientist, and Thomas Cooper, newspaper publisher and college president; popular leaders like Gallatin, who was chief of the Republicans in the House; Frenchmen like Volney and Victor du Pont, son of Jefferson's friend. Adams was unexpectedly intolerant and wrote from his home in Quincy to the Secretary of State:

"I shall not be guilty of so much affectation of regard to science, as to be very willing to grant passports to Dupont de Nemours, or any other French philosophers, in the present situation of our Country. We have had too many French philosophers already."

The second group against whom the Alien Act was aimed were the Irish, fleeing in increasing numbers from the suppression of the revolt of '98. Most of them became ardent Republicans the day they landed on American shores. The law aimed at them resulted in no deportations at all, but two shiploads of Frenchmen did depart immediately after passage of the bill, and most of them were agents of the French government.

The Sedition Act was an even greater blunder, for it struck at citizens. It created the crime of opposition to the government. It also established some unobjectionable penalties for the sort of conspiracy which most men regard as seditious, but one clause provided the same jail sentences for criticism of Congress or the

President if that criticism could be construed "to bring them or either of them into contempt or disrepute, or to excite against them or either of them the hatred of the good people of the United States." Contempt for politicians of another party was already part of American custom. Even more polite political opposition than was then common would have fallen under the ban, and the Federalists thought they had been very clever. They believed that they had silenced the Republican press and the Republican leaders, and their own newspapers sang happily:

> Each factious alien shrinks with dread
> And hides his hemp-devoted head;
> While Slander's foul seditious crew
> With gnashing teeth retires from view.

Aside from the fact that Slander's crew was just as numerous among the Federalists as among the Republicans, this was nonsense. The Sedition Act led to twenty-five arrests and ten convictions, mostly of Republican editors. Their remaining colleagues, far from retiring, gnashed their teeth in the open with greater noise and effect than ever, for they won public support. Americans of that day were a good deal more violent than their descendants in asserting the rights of free men to say what they pleased about the government and its policies. The brief popularity of the Federalists vanished like smoke, and in Virginia the party fell into such speedy disrepute that Washington was moved to intervene. He summoned Marshall to Mount Vernon to enlist him as a candidate for Congress, since it seemed that he alone could carry the Richmond district.

[2]

Washington himself had accepted command of the new army. He doubted that the French actually would invade America, even in case of war, but he lent the weight of his prestige to the government. In this crisis, he refused to admit the right of anyone to put his private affairs before the public welfare.

The idea that the Father of his country was above or beyond politics has been fostered by men who failed to understand that their hero was both human and a realist. He deplored the rise of political parties—so did everyone else from Jefferson down—but he had never hesitated as to which one merited his support. It was to strengthen Federalism that he had consented to come out of retirement, and for the same reason he had invited Marshall to pay him a visit.

He took the precaution of sending an emissary to see to it that his guest actually took to the road. This envoy was his lawyer-nephew, Bushrod Washington, a small man, thin and sharp of feature but learned. He refrained from the imposing dignity which became his tall uncle but which would have been absurd in a little figure of undistinguished appearance. He and Marshall pooled their luggage in one pair of saddle bags for the ride from Richmond, where Bushrod had established himself in practice. In a tavern along the road, they picked up the wrong pair by mistake, so that on his arrival in Washington's stately home, Marshall found himself equipped with a big black bottle of whisky, a twist of tobacco, a chunk of corn bread and the worn working clothes of a wagon driver. His host laughed immoderately at the appearance of his guests, fitted them out more appropriately and got down to business at once. He told Marshall it was his "most sacred duty" to run for Congress.

"I told him," Marshall recorded, "that I had made large pecuniary engagements which required close attention to my profession and which would distress me should the emoluments derived from it be abandoned."

Washington had no patience with this mercenary view. He cited his own sacrifice of repose, and Marshall finally gave in, or as he put it:

"My resolution yielded to this representation."

He got home to find that he would have to refuse the Supreme Court appointment again. Adams had not taken his rejection in

Philadelphia as final, and on September 26 the President wrote to Pickering that the choice had narrowed to Marshall or Bushrod Washington, adding:

"I still think that General Marshall ought to be preferred. Of the three envoys, the conduct of Marshall alone has been entirely satisfactory, and ought to be marked by the most decided approbation of the public."

Marshall declined, and Bushrod Washington was duly appointed. With all respect for the new Justice's uncle, Marshall could have wished himself out of his other chance of public office as easily. Lamenting his lot to Pickering, he reported that he had "as a punishment for some unknown sins, consented to be nam'd a candidate for the ensuing election to Congress."

[3]

The punishment was severe because the contest was hot and without any holds barred. The Republicans saw clearly enough that there was only a small step from the witch hunt to the sort of dictatorship they always suspected the Federalists of seeking. Furthermore, it was plain to the Republican leaders that if this sort of legislation should be enforced for a few years, with or without dictatorship, their party would disintegrate or be forced to secret plots and eventual rebellion. Therefore, the Congressional elections were fought with unusual bitterness.

Marshall succeeded in exposing himself to the attacks of both extremes. The big issue of the year was support or repeal of the Alien and Sedition Laws. Marshall was in the uncomfortable position of disliking both the laws and the attacks on them. He was neither slow nor vague in expressing himself, and he was not shy about disagreeing with Washington on a subject of some delicacy. The General had no hesitation in declaring the laws necessary, even desirable, and he sent Marshall printed arguments in support of his view. The more intemperate of these had been spoken from the bench in the form of charges to grand juries—a favorite electioneering method of the judges of the day—and an unfriendly newspaper described this set as "brimstone and saltpetre, assafoetida and train oil."

Marshall burst into print on his own account. In answer to questions propounded to him in an open letter—some of his biographers think he wrote the questions himself—he asserted that if he had been in Congress at the time of their passage he would have voted against the Alien and Sedition Laws, that he would if elected vote to repeal them and would oppose their renewal, although he did not think them quite as harmful as others supposed them. By this time, October, 1798, many of Marshall's party endowed the Alien and Sedition Acts with a sanctity which Holy Writ no longer possessed for them. In Massachusetts, Fisher Ames used phrases like "meanest of cowards, falsest of hypocrites" to describe Marshall. Theodore Sedgwick, Speaker of the House to which Marshall was seeking election, called the candidate's letter "unpardonable" and "pitiful electioneering." Republicans, giving some praise to Marshall's words, were inclined to regard them as insincere.

The campaign opening in this vein in October grew ever more heated until the actual election in April. In the meantime, a new issue was introduced by twin statements from the legislatures of two states, known as the Kentucky and Virginia Resolutions. Written by Jefferson and Madison, and adopted by overwhelming majorities, they asserted the unconstitutionality of the Alien and Sedition Laws. They went further, and suggested that it was the duty of States to pass upon such measures. This last point became of more interest years later; at the time the resolutions centered on seeking repeal of the obnoxious statutes. Marshall was one of the few who tried to swerve the debate to the Constitutional issue, where his party was right, away from the free speech argument, where they were in the wrong.

Meanwhile Adams was adding to the difficulties of Federalist candidates by the wisest and bravest act of his career. The party which was reluctantly supporting him for re-election counted upon turning the unofficial fighting into formal war. Their new navy, fourteen ships strong, was about to put to sea, and some two hundred merchantmen had been armed and commissioned with letters of marque and reprisal. In these circumstances, France had nothing to gain by a declaration of war, and Talleyrand let it be known that he would welcome another mission and receive it properly.

Adams decided for peace, and the warmongers of his party cried out that he was as bad as Jefferson. They had a long time to abuse him for his peaceful intentions, since the mission, first discussed in October, 1798, actually set out under the leadership of Chief Justice Oliver Ellsworth a year later. Meanwhile, Marshall, who was counted upon to oppose the scheme because of his own experience and his knowledge of the situation, further inflamed Federalist extremists by agreeing that the effort to avert war should be made.

Because of Adams's belligerent pursuit of peace, the Federalists could not even capitalize as much as they would have liked upon the successes of the infant navy. They celebrated and cheered when Commodore Truxtun captured the French frigate *L'Insurgente*, but their cheering was changed to jeers, for in less than a month after that glorious event, Adams nominated his peace mission.

All this made hard going for a Federalist candidate in Virginia, and as the April election day neared, Marshall was in some doubt as to his prospects. He had been campaigning hard, making speeches and shaking hands and being generally agreeable to the constituency as befits a candidate, but even his stand against the Alien and Sedition Laws might not be enough. Then, in their desire to clinch his defeat, the Republicans overstepped the bounds of prudence. They reported that the great patriot, Patrick Henry, opposed Marshall, and they failed to inquire if that really was true. Henry no longer had any affection for the principles espoused by Jefferson or the men who surrounded the sage of Monticello. He promptly wrote a long letter to one of Marshall's friends asserting that he would rather vote for Marshall than for any man in Virginia except Washington and added:

"Tell Marshall I love him, because he felt and acted as a republican, as an American."

Marshall's friends nearly wore the letter out showing it to voters, and as the long tables were placed on the green in front of the courthouse for the voting in April, they felt some slight confidence. The secret ballot was a long way off then, and every voter came up to the tables, at which the candidates sat with the election judges, and announced his choice. He rated a bow and a smile from the man whose name he gave before he retreated into the crowd, where he might find himself engaged in a fist fight with a friend of different political persuasion. Such fights were plentiful this day, and there were more of them as the balloting wore on, because a barrel of whisky had been provided for the electorate. When it was all over, Marshall had won by 108 votes.

"With infinite pleasure I received the news of your Election," Washington wrote. "For the honor of the District I wish the majority had been greater; but let us be content, and hope, as the tide is turning, the current will soon run strong in your favor."

And to Bushrod, the aging hero commented after riding ten miles to help elect "Light Horse Harry":

"The election of Generals Lee and Marshall is grateful to my feelings. I wish, however, both of them had been elected by greater majorities; but they are elected, and that alone is pleasing. As the tide is turned I hope it will come in with a full flow, but this will not happen if there is any relaxation on the part of the Federalists."

Really, it was becoming difficult to pretend that His Excellency was not a partisan.

[4]

Marshall had a little more than seven months to wait between his election and the next meeting of Congress. Meanwhile he found himself driven into an increasingly independent position as regards Federalist policies. He was not happy at the manner in which men like Ames and Sedgwick raged against the President's desire for peace. Nor could he share their blood-thirstiness in domestic issues.

That spring the Federalists were ravening for the life of a Pennsylvania militia captain, a German immigrant named John Fries, who had led an armed resistance to the collection of a new Federal tax on houses, which had been levied to pay for the army. In a trial at which Justice Samuel Chase of the Supreme Court had presided in his usual bullying way, Fries had been found guilty of sedition and treason and sentenced to death. Adams had a sneaking sympathy for men who did not like the growing militarism.

"This damned army will be the ruin of the country," he had remarked.

As an old revolutionary, too, Adams had not the same reverence for tax laws which most of his party had acquired. So he pardoned Fries, and the Federalist comments could not have been more severe if Adams had loosed the devil himself.

Fries was safely home in Pennsylvania and the Ellsworth mission was on the high seas bound for France when Congress assembled for its last session in Philadelphia on December 2, 1799. In later years it became rather difficult for a new member to become the leader of his party. Marshall assumed that position from the start, partly because he was one of the few able Federalists in the House and partly because he was the only one who thoroughly supported the President. Against him was the Republican chieftain, Gallatin, who had been urged fifteen years before by Lawyer Marshall to study law in his office.

But leadership did not always mean that his party followed. The New Englanders were suspicious, and more than one of them feared that the new member's politics had a "Virginia taint." (George Cabot thought the Virginia air made men "incredibly credulous.") This was partly due to the fact that they found him out of sympathy with their desire to elect some other Federalist than Adams to the Presidency, a move which Marshall detected before he had been in the capital a fortnight.

He was an active Congressman, seldom missing a roll-call, but his first serious business was to report to the House the death of Washington. His next was to carry out his pre-election pledge and vote for repeal of the Sedition Act. The strength of the parties was so even that his vote carried the resolution—50 to 48—since if he had voted with his party the tie would have been resolved against the repealer by the vote of the Speaker. The Senate refused to concur, and the laws were left to the next Congress.

On the next important matter before the House, Marshall again found himself in opposition to most Federalists. Senators had evolved a plan which they hoped might save them from Jefferson even if he should be the choice of the voters later in the year 1800. They proposed a committee of six Senators, six Representatives, and the Chief Justice to decide whether electoral votes as sent in to Congress should be counted, or whether there had been fraud or other reasons for throwing out certain ones. The report of this committee was to be final. Marshall angered his colleagues again by speaking and voting against the measure, which was defeated at last.

The other business of the House that session found Marshall more regular as a party man. He supported the maintenance of the army in spite of Republican efforts to reduce it on the ground that peace with France was in the offing. He took the leading part in drafting the National Bankruptcy Act, under which his friend Morris was at last released from prison. Finally he made a great speech in defense of Adams, one of those samples of Congressional oratory which for many years—until the development of more sprightly forms of entertainment—were reprinted and re-delivered as model oratorical exercises.

A British sailor named Thomas Nash had been arrested in Charleston and his extradition was requested as one of a band of men who had murdered the officers of their ship and sold it in a Spanish port. Nash's only defense was that of mistaken identity.

He claimed to be an American, Jonathan Robins, a native of Danbury. Connecticut officials reported that there was no record of such a man and no family named Robins ever had lived in the town. A British officer identified Nash, and he was duly turned over to British justice and in time hanged. The Republicans made a great to-do about this case, first accusing Adams of surrendering an American to be murdered, then arguing that he should have permitted the man to have a jury trial. Marshall's argument for living up to an extradition treaty was so powerful that it dismayed at least one opponent. Gallatin had been making notes for a reply, then he paced up and down and finally, as his colleagues urged him to deal with Marshall's argument, he snapped:

"Answer it yourself, for my part I think it unanswerable."

In the midst of these works, Marshall heard that Polly had given birth to another son, James, and the father mingled pride with regret that he had been unable to come home for the occasion. But at last the session was over, and with it Marshall's Congressional service. For early in May, Adams discovered that two of his principal advisers, Pickering and Secretary of War McHenry, were secretly consulting Hamilton first and then passing off that elder statesman's suggestions as their own. The President did not learn that Secretary of the Treasury Wolcott was doing the same. In a burst of rage he dismissed the disloyal Pickering and McHenry and called upon Marshall to become Secretary of State.

Marshall hesitated for two weeks, as well he might. The job was not likely to last, for with the Federalists split even more disastrously by this Cabinet break, the re-election of Adams was more than doubtful. But finally he yielded, for it was obvious that all hope would be gone if the government had to stagger along without men of some reputation in the Cabinet during the heat of an election year. While he felt that he could not afford it—first place in the Cabinet was compensated at the rate of $3,500 a year—he did not think it would be for very long.

[5]

The new Secretary of State went to Richmond for a brief vacation before he assumed his new duties. He arrived in time to witness a trial which was one of the bitter Federalist fruits of the Sedition Act, and Marshall's first glimpse of that legislation in actual operation.

The defendant was James Thompson Callender, a Jeffersonian hack writer who had composed some of the more exaggerated and abusive party diatribes. He had made some unpleasant remarks about Adams, accusing the President of warmongering, tyranny, and a few other misdeeds including the execution of Thomas Nash. Some of it was maliciously false, but none of it was seditious by the usual definitions of the word. However, Callender's judge was to be Chase, and Chase had boasted that he would teach the Virginia lawyers a thing or two. At the peak of his form, Chase was a terrifying fellow. He looked a good deal like Samuel Johnson, and some of the lawyers who practiced in his court called him "Old Bacon Face." Marshall was one of the lawyers who learned something new, for while he had no part in the case, he attended some of the sessions and thought that Chase's rulings were very strange.

Perhaps one of the strangest was Chase's refusal to hear a witness testify as to the truth of part of Callender's allegedly libelous writings. The Judge ruled that only witnesses who could prove the truth of all of the statements made by the defendant could be heard. He broke up the arguments of counsel with sarcasm and sneering jibes at their ignorance of law. Callender was promptly convicted, and it did not allay Marshall's forebodings to note that the jury had been drawn from a panel containing only three Republicans—one sick, one out of the district, and one excused on the intercession of Marshall himself—or that the panel had been selected by his brother, William, recently appointed clerk of the court.

A few days later Marshall was back in the capital, but this capital was the city of Washington. Teeming with malaria, a vast untrimmed clearing in the wilderness along the Potomac, there were a few scattered buildings—the 3,000 inhabitants of the District of Columbia shared 109 brick and 263 frame structures—including an incomplete Capitol and President's Mansion. The most gifted letter writers of the time never did justice to the mud, the dust, the heat, the mosquitoes, the discomforts of living in worse than barracks cut off from normal society since no man of sense would bring his wife or children to that city in the swamp.

Marshall was a pioneer of the Washington hardships, for a good many of the government leaders were not yet there. Adams remained at home in Quincy; Congress would not meet again until December, and the Secretary of State was virtually the acting head of what administration there was. Throughout the rest of the country the Presidential campaign was warming up as Republicans took heart from a great victory which Burr had engineered over Hamilton in the spring elections in New York, while Federalists intrigued and fought and bickered, and the slight chance they might have had slipped through their fingers.

Adams was still popular although the cost of government had nearly doubled during his administration—from $5,800,000 in 1796 to $10,800,000 in 1800. His positive ways, his tactless remarks and his passion for peace were a great deal more distasteful to the politicians than to the people. But when Hamilton himself wrote a semi-private vitriolic attack upon the President—discovered by Burr and published widely to the discomfiture of Federalists and the delight of all Republicans—the last hope went glimmering.

Fortunately, the duties of a Secretary of State were not very arduous. Correspondence with the embassies abroad, the formal letters to foreign powers, occasional talks with the diplomats accredited to the United States (most of whom kept out of Washington that summer) were a routine which permitted Marshall to make one visit home to argue a law suit. The most trying part of his position was waiting for news from the men who were succeeding in Paris where he had failed.

Their success consisted in keeping out of war, not in winning very many concessions from the French. But that is the price of neutrality, and even the shipowners and sailors who lost most by it were content to accept. Questions of war and peace were being settled in Paris now by First Consul Bonaparte himself, and war with the United States did not fit into his program. He drove a hard bargain, but in October Marshall received a treaty. He did not like it, yet he advised ratification for it meant peace. There was no compensation for damage to American commerce, although French ships captured by the new American navy were to be returned. On the other hand, Bonaparte withdrew the most obnoxious decrees against United States trade, demanded no loan and no bribes.

While the political campaign moved to its frenzied climax, Marshall sat in aloof contemplation writing a message for Adams to deliver to Congress in December. Federalists were accusing Jefferson of madness, of plotting a real September Terror against his enemies and all sorts of egalitarian excesses. The Republicans retorted with charges of pro-British treason and pointed to their martyrs languishing in confinement for their devotion to free speech. But Marshall was penning calm, dignified words on the importance of keeping up the navy in a world at war and arguing that the national judiciary needed expansion.

Autumn was well advanced when the President drove reluctantly into the new capital to take up with Abigail a brief and uneasy residence in the unfinished President's Mansion. The last session of a Federalist Congress was preparing to assemble on December 3, and would seek to save what it could from the wreck of party hopes.

The obvious remnant on which the Federalists could fasten was the judiciary. No Republican as yet had been a Federal judge, and the courts were as active as they could be in partisan politics. From the bench, violent political harangues were delivered under the guise of charges to grand juries, and were duly printed. In the missions of Jay and Ellsworth, the precedent of using the Chief Justice of the United States for political purposes had been established. If the judicial system could be expanded, Federalist control might be consolidated in the three months of power which remained.

A bill to grasp this opportunity was introduced early in the session, and it is certain that the Secretary of State must have been consulted. Sixteen new circuit judges were to be appointed to relieve the Supreme Court Justices from circuit duty. The Supreme Court was to be reduced from six to five members after the next vacancy so that a Republican appointment could be avoided or at least postponed. New district courts and justices of the peace were provided, ostensibly to bring the courts nearer to the people.

Before this bill could be debated, there came a vacancy in the Supreme Court which must be filled hastily before the number was reduced. On December 16, Adams wrote to Jay, serving then as Governor of New York:

"Mr. Ellsworth, afflicted with the gravel and the gout, and intending to pass the winter in the south of France, after a few weeks in England, has resigned his office of Chief Justice, and I have nominated you for your old station."

But Jay, disgusted with the Jeffersonian victory and with only unpleasant memories of his previous service on the Court, replied that he did not care to be associated again with such a faulty judicial system.

"Such was the temper of the times," he explained, "that the Act to establish the Judicial Courts of the United States was in some respects more accommodated to certain prejudices and sensibilities, than to the great and obvious principles of sound policy. . . . The efforts repeatedly made to place the judicial department on a proper footing have proved fruitless.

"I left the bench perfectly convinced that under a system so defective it would not obtain the energy, weight, and dignity which are essential to its affording due support to the national government, nor acquire the public confidence and respect which, as the last resort of the justice of the nation, it should possess. Hence I am induced to doubt both the propriety and the expediency of my returning to the bench under the present system; especially as it would give some countenance to the neglect and indifference with which the opinions and remonstrances of the judges on this important subject have been treated."

As an afterthought, he mentioned that the state of his health would also preclude his acceptance.

Adams had not asked Jay in advance, and he had to withdraw the nomination. But the President did not ask his next nominee either. Marshall had suggested that Justice Paterson be promoted, but on January 2, 1801, the day the House passed the new Judiciary Bill, the name of Marshall himself was sent to the Senate. Twenty-five years later, Adams wrote:

"My gift of John Marshall to the people of the United States was the proudest act of my life."

[6]

The new Chief Justice was confirmed within a week, only five days before the opening of the February term of the court. But Adams had insisted he remain as Secretary of State also for the few remaining weeks of the Federalist administration. Fortunately, there was no business coming before the Court, because its new head was too busy with last minute details of the State Department to attend. Not a single newspaper of the day so much as chronicled the fact that the Court met.

The papers were busy with a much more exciting piece of news. Jefferson and Burr had exactly the same number of votes in the electoral college—seventy-three—and since balloting for President and Vice President were not yet separate, the choice between them fell to the Federalist-dominated House of Representatives

where each State had one vote. To the beaten party this seemed
an opportunity sent by heaven to throw dissension into the ranks
of the enemy by electing Burr. They made every effort to enlist
his co-operation. Jefferson as Vice President was on the ground,
living uncomfortably at Conrad's boardinghouse and marshalling
his forces. Burr was in New York arranging for his daughter's
wedding, a far more significant event to him than any presidential
election, but he made one statement and retired into silence. The
statement to one of his friends in Washington was:

"It is highly improbable that I shall have an equal number of
votes with Mr. Jefferson; but, if such should be the result, every
man who knows me ought to know that I would utterly disclaim
all competition. Be assured that the federal party can entertain no
wish for such an exchange. As to my friends, they would dishon-
our my views and insult my feelings by a suspicion that I would
submit to be instrumental in counteracting the wishes and expectations of the United States, and I now constitute you my proxy to
declare these sentiments if the occasion should require."

Hamilton was almost the only Federalist who did not wish to
put Burr over Jefferson. He spent weeks writing impassioned and
singularly venomous letters attacking Burr on every ground both
public and private. Marshall was the recipient of one of them, and
replied:

"Being no longer in the House of Representatives, and, con-
sequently, being compelled by no duty to decide between them,
my own mind had scarcely determined to which of these gentlemen the preference was due. To Mr. Jefferson, whose political
character is better known than that of Mr. Burr, I have felt almost insuperable objections. His foreign prejudices seem to me
totally to unfit him for the chief magistracy of a nation which
cannot indulge those prejudices without sustaining deep and permanent injury.

"In addition to this solid and immovable objection, Mr. Jefferson appears to me to be a man who will embody himself with the

House of Representatives, and, by weakening the office of President, sap the fundamental principles of the government, and become the leader of that party which is about to constitute the majority of the legislature. . . . With these impressions concerning Mr. Jefferson, I was, in some degree, disposed to view with less apprehension any other characters, and to consider the alternative now offered us as a circumstance not to be entirely neglected.

"Your representation of Mr. Burr, with whom I am entirely unacquainted, shows that from him still greater danger than from Mr. Jefferson may be apprehended. Such a man as you describe is more to be feared, and may do more immediate if not greater mischief. Believing that you know him well and are impartial, my preference would certainly not be for him; but I can take no part in this business. I cannot bring myself to aid Mr. Jefferson. Perhaps respect for myself should, in my present situation, deter me from using any influence—if indeed I possess any—in support of either gentleman. Although no consideration could induce me to be the secretary of state while there was a President whose political system I believed to be at variance with my own, yet this cannot be so well known to others, and it might be suspected that a desire to be well with the successful candidate had in some degree governed my conduct."

This letter was written before his nomination as Chief Justice, and that even strengthened his determination to keep his hands off the contest in the House. No one else heeded Hamilton's pleas, and the Federalists balloted unanimously thirty-five times in six days for Aaron Burr. Their numerical majority of 55 to 51 did not give them a majority of States, however, and so on the thirty-five ballots the vote stood: Jefferson, eight; Burr, six; two deadlocked by ties. At last Burr's refusal to advance his own cause wore down the willingness of Federalists to start a revolution by electing him. On the thirty-sixth ballot the House awarded to Jefferson the office to which the people had elected him.

The last work of the Federalist administration remained. On

February 4, the Senate had passed the Judiciary Bill, and Adams began busily to fill up the new places. With Marshall's aid, he did it so speedily that by March 2 the whole lot of judges and justices of the peace had been named and confirmed by the Senate. It was the day that Jefferson wrote to Marshall:

"May I hope the favor of your attendance to administer the oath?"

The Chief Justice consented, but for the remaining two days Marshall spent most of his time as Secretary of State, filling out and signing commissions to the new jurists. Not until nine o'clock on the night of the third was this task completed. Then Adams returned to the Presidential Mansion to set out on his journey to Massachusetts, for he had decided not to attend his successful rival's triumph, and Marshall sought his lodgings to rest and wake in the morning only a Chief Justice, no longer Secretary of State as well.

At noon in the Senate Chamber, the two lanky Virginians faced each other before an attentive crowd. The red-haired Jefferson placed his hand on the Book held by his black-haired cousin and repeated:

"I do solemnly swear that I will faithfully execute the office of President of the United States, and will, to the best of my ability, preserve, protect, and defend the Constitution of the United States."

Gazing at each other steadily, the two minds held but a single thought: The Constitution, that is *my* responsibility now!

X

☆ ☆ ☆

The Highest Court

IN THE TWELVE years of its existence, the Supreme Court
had been by far the most insignificant of the three co-ordinate
branches of government. It was so little regarded that the
builders of Washington had forgotten all about it. The Capitol
had been planned on what was regarded as a magnificent scale for
the use of Congress. The President's Mansion was usually called a
Palace. But the day that Marshall was nominated Chief Justice,
the District Commissioners wrote to Congress:

"As no house has been provided for the Judiciary of the United
States, we hope the Supreme Court may be accommodated with a
room in the Capitol to hold its sessions until further provisions
shall be made."

The Act of Congress creating the judiciary, defining its jurisdiction, fixing the number of members of the Supreme Court, the
times of sessions and the subordinate Federal courts, had been
drawn up in the First Congress by a committee headed by Senator
Oliver Ellsworth of Connecticut. He was a shrewd man of busi-

ness as well as a successful lawyer. He arranged for a judiciary which would be most convenient for the merchants and financiers who probably would use it most.

Under this Judiciary Act, the Supreme Court was to consist of six members and hold two terms a year, in February and August. This, however, was the lightest part of their work, for the law provided that in addition they must in pairs hold circuit courts once a year in every district in the country, the district judge sitting with them to make a court of three. Not only did this mean that they would receive in the Supreme Court cases on which they had ruled in the lower courts, but it put an almost intolerable physical strain upon them. "Travelling postboys," Justice James Iredell called himself and his colleagues, and the job killed him in nine years although he was not yet fifty.

The first court met on February 1, 1790, in what had been the Royal Exchange, Broad Street, New York City. This and the succeeding few sessions were devoted to establishing rules and admitting lawyers to practice before the Supreme Court when any cases requiring their attention might arise. The longest of these sessions lasted ten days.

In these years, the Justices did their work on circuit, and set some interesting precedents. In May, 1791, for instance, Jay and his colleague from Massachusetts, William Cushing, held that a Connecticut law was invalid because it did not conform to the peace treaty. In June, 1792, these two and District Judge Henry Marchant declared a Rhode Island statute unconstitutional and void because it impaired the obligation of a contract. Neither of these decisions attracted much attention. Politics centered around the Hamiltonian fiscal policies and the French Revolution. The enormous possibilities inherent in the contract clause of the Constitution—"No State shall . . . pass any . . . law impairing the obligation of contracts"—had not yet been grasped.

Then the Supreme Court was called upon to decide its first Constitutional issue, and by a curious irony it was just such a case as Madison and Marshall had assured the Virginia Constitutional

Convention could never happen. A sovereign state was "dragged" before the Federal bar in the matter of *Chisholm* vs. *Georgia*. The Court, led by Jay, decided that Madison and Marshall had been mistaken in their interpretation. The case involved the claim of heirs of a British creditor against the State of Georgia. The uproar against this insult to State sovereignty resulted in the Eleventh Amendment, which bars citizens of any State or foreign country from suing a State in the Federal courts.

The Court's next important ruling on a Constitutional matter was the case Marshall lost in his only appearance before it as a lawyer. This decision established the rule that the Constitution meant what it said in the words: ". . . all Treaties . . . shall be the supreme Law of the Land, . . . any thing in the Constitution or Laws of any State to the Contrary notwithstanding."

The very next day, the Court heard one of the most obviously cooked up cases ever brought before it. Congress had imposed a tax on carriages, and it was known that Republicans would assert that this was a direct tax. Therefore, they argued, it could only be imposed in proportion to population, not in proportion to carriages. To anticipate genuine litigation, the Treasury prepared *Hylton* vs. *the U.S.*, in which the government paid the fees for lawyers on both sides. In assessing Hylton, the government solemnly charged that he kept 125 carriages exclusively for his private use and not for hire. This ridiculous assertion was thrown in to get the case into the money bracket required before the Federal courts could deign to handle a dispute.

Marshall stayed over for the argument, the first in which the constitutionality of an Act of Congress was involved. He heard Hamilton make his Supreme Court debut as special counsel for the government, but he did not wait for the decision, which upheld the Act. There was some criticism that only three Justices took part, but very little because the Court had presumed to consider whether or not Congress had acted within its powers.

[2]

Except for these cases, and their routine work on circuit, the members of the Supreme Court had been engaged chiefly in politics. As politics became increasingly partisan, so did the judges, and they all belonged to one party. It did not occur to Washington or Adams to name a Republican to fill a vacancy anywhere in the judicial system. There was no suggestion from any Federalist leader that perhaps the bench was a place for judicial calm and impartial summation. Washington himself had circulated with approval some highly charged political pronouncements from the bench.

The judges were very proud of their independent status, but so long as they remained tied by passion or interest to the Administration, their independence was a matter of brag rather than reality.

The first three Chief Justices did not regard their lofty position as setting them apart from the general run of officeholders who were expected to help influence public opinion. Jay was by nature reserved and shunned the common controversies of the day, whether on or off the bench. But he made himself the most controversial of contemporary politicians when he negotiated his treaty with England. He resigned soon after, not because he thought his partisan position handicapped him as a judge but because he preferred to be Governor of New York.

The man named to succeed him, John Rutledge of South Carolina, thought it not incompatible with his new office to make a ringing political speech in Charleston against the treaty negotiated by his predecessor. That was on July 16, 1795, and the August session of the Court was the only one over which he presided. Washington had designated him after the adjournment of Congress, and as soon as it met in December, the Senate took up his nomination. On purely political grounds, and by a purely partisan vote, 10 to 14, confirmation was refused. The fourteen Senators did not object to the fact that Rutledge had made a political speech. They were furious because he had made it on the wrong side.

Ellsworth could be relied upon not to fall into Rutledge's apostasy. He was one of the most unbending of men and of Federalists, a traditional compound of New England piety, learning, and business acumen. He was a scholarly and upright judge by his own lights, but these did not prevent him from making political speeches on the bench. In one of his judicial harangues he referred to Jefferson and his followers as "the apostles of anarchy, bloodshed and atheism."

The best—or worst—examples of judicial temperament were those of Chase. Contemporaries of Republican persuasion were constantly comparing him to Jeffreys, the bloodiest and most corruptly ruthless of British judges. With Chase, politics always came before his judicial duties. In 1800, while Ellsworth was abroad and two other justices were ill, the August term had to be adjourned from day to day because Chase was too busy making campaign speeches in Maryland to get to Washington. As an example of his fair-mindedness, he remarked on his way to preside at the trial of Callender:

"It is a pity that they had not hanged the rascal."

District Judge Peters, himself a bitter partisan and eager prosecutor of the Sedition Act from the bench, still could not stomach the extent to which Chase indulged his passions. Recording his dislike of being associated with him in circuit court, Peters wrote:

"I never sat with him without pain as he was forever getting into some intemperate and unnecessary squabble."

The officers of the court took their cue from the bench. William Marshall's action in summoning a jury panel containing only three Republicans for a political trial was standard procedure in many districts. Some of William's colleagues would not have included the three Republicans.

[3]

The political activities of his new associates did not upset Marshall, except as he always deplored intemperate abuse. The Justices themselves were a pleasant, happy family on their semi-annual meetings, which were strictly stag affairs since the terms did not last long enough for them to bring their wives. In the acrimonious atmosphere of that February when the new Chief Justice took over the presidency of a court with nothing on its docket, it was a satisfaction to be thrown with politically harmonious colleagues.

As the Supreme Court goes, it was young. Only one member was in his sixties, two in their fifties, two in the forties and one, the boyish-looking Bushrod Washington, thirty-eight. They came of necessity and law from all parts of the Union. The tradition of having the various sections represented, which resulted in some curious omissions and appointments to the Court in later years, grew up as a result of the practical difficulties of circuit court attendance. This arduous duty would be performed only by men who lived somewhere in the circuit; it was the only way they could manage to see their families once in a while.

Oldest in years and service in 1801 was William Cushing, the sole remaining Justice of Washington's original six. A staunch old Federalist, at this time sixty-seven, he was far less rancorous than most of his earlier brethren, but when he died ten years later, Jefferson's comment was:

"The event is a fortunate one, and so timed as to be a Godsend to me."

Cushing was a modest man, a hawk-nosed Yankee whose erudition was considerable and who cut an imposing figure in his carefully curled wig. In 1795 he had refused promotion to Jay's place, and remained happy serving under younger men.

William Paterson, a former Senator from his State, and a man of considerable means, was mild and amiable, smooth of manner but capable of harsh language. He was one of the most scholarly of

American judges, and in the Constitutional Convention he had played a big part in safeguarding the rights of small States through the device of equal representation in the Senate.

Chase, at this time nearly sixty and a sufferer from gout as well as rage, had notably coarse manners but was cherished by his boon companions over the wine for his wit. Beginning his public life as a red hot patriot, he was one of the chief factors in Maryland's adherence to the cause of Independence. Then he had become one of the busiest of Congressional speculators, earning in the dark days of the war a blast from young Hamilton:

"It is your lot to have the peculiar privilege of being universally despised. Were I inclined to make a satire upon the species, I would attempt a faithful description of your heart."

But Chase was an able lawyer and had served as Chief Justice of his State before he was named to the Supreme Court by Washington in '96. His whole career had been founded upon aggressiveness, and he never learned to curb it.

Alfred Moore of North Carolina was the same age as Marshall, forty-five, and had been appointed to the Court just a little more than a year earlier. His trim figure topped by a bald head made him not the least impressive on the bench, although he had the least influence.

Bushrod Washington in everything but looks was older than his years. As his uncle's heir, he enjoyed a prestige which he had never sought to capitalize. He remained a pleasant, unaffected gentleman all his life, much addicted to snuff and conversation, but with less party spirit than any of his colleagues. His temper was genuinely judicial; it was the law and not the political effect that interested him. On any other subject he was naïve, credulous, almost always incompetent. Marshall knew him best of all the Justices, for they were joined at this time in an odd literary-financial venture which both believed would make them rich.

[4]

This venture was nothing less than the official biography of George Washington. Bushrod, custodian of his uncle's papers, had suggested that Marshall write the "definitive" life from these documents with Bushrod's help, and that they would share the proceeds. The proposal was made while Marshall was still in Congress, and he had accepted for two sufficiently good reasons. He rather fancied himself as the man to put Washington in proper perspective before the world, and he thought that the profits would more than finish the payments for the Fairfax estate.

By 1801 he and Bushrod had infected each other with the most optimistic delusions. Marshall, like many another man of superior talents, was modest enough about his real ability but prided himself on his mediocre accomplishments. In this case, he was confident that he could turn out a finished literary work on a difficult subject without much expenditure of time or effort. Although he knew little history and had never written anything except speeches, briefs, and diplomatic papers, he was not at all timid about undertaking one of the most desirable biographical assignments ever offered to a writer.

It is more difficult to understand why Bushrod should have offered than why Marshall should have accepted. Probably the little Justice was moved by admiration for the statesmanship of the XYZ hero. He also knew Marshall's talent for getting at the kernel of fact in a great mass of discussion. He was satisfied that Marshall would not be as violently partisan or insulting as most Federalists in comments on events which were still controversial. He remembered his uncle's high opinion of the man he had pushed into Congress.

Washington had been dead only a few weeks when Bushrod began to be besieged by prospective publishers. He selected the house of C. P. Wayne, in Philadelphia, and negotiations dragged on with all the sluggishness of a foreign treaty, month after month. One difficulty was that both partners in the writing of the biography had extravagant notions of the value of their property. They expected to be paid one dollar for every volume sold; they had calculated that there would be four or five volumes; they thought that the publisher could sell 30,000 subscriptions. At one dollar a volume for five volumes, that would net the authors $150,000, but they were willing to settle in advance for $100,000 for the United States rights.

These rosy dreams were not dissipated by Wayne's refusal to consider $100,000 nor by his attempts to explain the facts of life in the book business. The highest price any copyright had ever brought, he said, was $30,000 and no book had attracted up to then more than two thousand subscribers in America. Marshall and Bushrod brushed these precedents aside. This was to be a book which would be more exciting to the reading public than anything ever written before, they thought.

To Marshall, the Chief Justiceship fitted ideally into his writing plans. The new Judiciary Act had turned the circuit courts over to sixteen judges especially appointed to preside over them. His own judicial duties, therefore, need extend only to two terms of a few weeks each, set in the new law for June and December. The rest of his time could be devoted to the Washington biography.

His essential unfitness for the task he had undertaken was indicated by his estimate of the time he would need. He had not yet examined any of Washington's papers, although he knew they were voluminous. He had made no tentative outline of the subject matter. Yet he expected to produce four or five volumes of four or five hundred pages each. With the optimism of ignorance, he said he would be able to complete the work in less than a year. Apparently even his arithmetic had deserted him. Without allowing any time for research or co-ordination of the material, he had blithely proposed to commit himself to writing in his neat penmanship an average of forty or more printed pages, revised and corrected, every week.

Fortunately for Marshall, Wayne was still holding out on the price. Negotiations dragged on, each party to them convinced that the other was wasting valuable time. Before they were completed, Marshall's lawyer caution came to his rescue. He did not set a definite time for the delivery of his manuscript and even in making an estimate, he doubled his original figure of a year. But by then, too, his hopes of almost infinite leisure had been dispelled by the changes in his life wrought by that apostle of change, Thomas Jefferson.

XI

☆ ☆ ☆

Last Stronghold of a Party

"WE ARE ALL Republicans; we are all Federalists." Marshall was one of the few men who actually heard Jefferson's voice pronounce this keynote of his inaugural address on March 4, 1801. The Senate Chamber was small, for the membership of that august body was only thirty-three, including the Vice President. But Jefferson's voice was smaller still; public speaking was the least of his accomplishments, and few of those who packed the room could hear him. However, Marshall sat at his left hand—on the right was the trim little figure of Aaron Burr—and as the Chief Justice listened, he almost approved.

That morning he had started a letter to his old XYZ colleague, Pinckney, and had used the term "Democrat" in referring to Jefferson. This was a word the Republicans disliked almost as much as they did the epithet "Jacobin." Gloomily Marshall had written:

"I wish, however, more than I hope that the public prosperity & happiness will sustain no diminution under Democratic guidance. The Democrats are divided into speculative theorists & absolute terrorists. With the latter I am disposed to class Mr. Jefferson."

At this point he interrupted himself to attend the inauguration, and on his return he was inclined to modify his morning judgment. Picking up his pen at four o'clock that afternoon, he added in his letter to Pinckney:

"I have administered the oath to the Presdt. His inauguration speech . . . well judged and conciliatory . . . is in direct terms giving the lie to the violent party declamation which has elected him, but it is strongly characteristic of the general cast of this political theory."

Since the heavens did not fall, since life went on pretty much as usual, the Federalists were relatively calm in the early months of Jefferson's administration. Their dread predictions had been so ridiculously exaggerated that in the absence of bloody proscriptions and universal anarchy, they enjoyed a pleasant feeling of relief.

Republicans were more angry than Federalists in these early days of their party's power. Many of them deeply resented Jefferson's calm refusal to turn out all the underlings of government to make room for those who had voted for him. They raged, too, against the sudden increase in the judicial establishment. "Midnight judges" they called the jurists confirmed in the closing days of the session, and invented a story that Marshall went on signing commissions right up to midnight on March 3 when Levi Lincoln, who was to be Attorney General for Jefferson, came in and stopped him with watch in hand and stern look in eye.

[2]

In Marshall's first year on the Supreme Court, free from circuit duties, he had leisure to observe and reflect upon the new President's policies and theories. He also had leisure to consider the

proprieties which a Chief Justice should observe toward an administration whose politics he disliked and distrusted. The net result was a profound silence on public affairs.

This silence was an interesting departure from the judicial practice up to that time. Marshall never cast any reflection upon the
conduct of his predecessors or colleagues, and there is no evidence
that he disapproved of active political campaigning by judges. But
he was sufficiently cool in his judgment to know that silence was
the better strategy. Whether he kept out of controversy from
principle or expediency, he set the precedent that a Chief Justice is
above taking part in the dusty strife of the political arena—at least
ostensibly and openly.

Marshall was much concerned with strengthening the Court's
position against the attacks which duller men than he foresaw. The
popular Republican press was saying that the Federalists had retired into the Judiciary like the remnants of a beaten army into a
fortress. It took little gift of clairvoyance to predict that the victors would not permit the stronghold to remain undisturbed, especially as it commanded the positions they had won. The assault
probably would be delayed only so long as it took to recruit the
necessary forces.

Marshall, so often at odds with his party, differed from them in
his estimate of Jefferson's character. Most Federalists believed the
new President to be wicked and depraved but also a theorist avid
for popularity. Marshall recognized that Jefferson could be a man
of action too, appraising him in the same way but not so kindly
as did the next great philosopher-president of Jefferson's party,
Woodrow Wilson, who wrote:

"He stickled for a strict construction of the Constitution only
when he thought that a strict construction would safeguard the
rights of common men and keep the Federalist theories of government at arm's length; not because he disliked to see the country
have power as a Nation, but because he dreaded to see it put in
bondage to an autocratic government."

Now that he had succeeded to the executive power, Jefferson would not be anxious to see that power diminished, but he had no such feelings about the courts, held in hands unanimously hostile to him. Backed by a handsome majority in the House and a bare one in the Senate, he expected to make the courts even less important than they had been under Washington and Adams.

Marshall's first act of defense was to strengthen his own authority in the Supreme Court. It had been the custom for the Justices to read opinions in turn. The Chief Justice had been only a great man among equals. Marshall changed that. He calmly assumed the function of delivering nearly all opinions himself. Another Justice's voice was heard only when he dissented or when the Chief disqualified himself.

The Court had been accommodated with the loan of one of the Senate Committee rooms on the main floor of the Capitol, an apartment of some twenty-four by thirty feet with a high ceiling and a rounded end. These "temporary" quarters were to be the home of the tribunal for seven years. Here in June, 1801, Marshall heard his first case as a judge. It was a pleasantly romantic one, too, involving adventure and booty on the high seas, and it was entered on the docket as *Talbot* vs. *Seeman*.

Captain Silas Talbot commanded the U.S. frigate *Constitution* and during the undeclared naval war with France had encountered the *Amelia* flying French colors and armed as for battle. The *Constitution* easily overpowered her, and Talbot then found that the *Amelia* was really a German merchantman captured by the French on her way home from Calcutta. The French had taken off the Germans, put their own prize crew aboard and ordered the vessel to what is now Haiti to be formally confiscated. Talbot interfered with that plan and brought her to New York.

The gallant Captain found that the German owners were disinclined to pay him for his trouble. At that time a naval officer was entitled to such perquisites as a share in the value of his prizes, and Talbot sued for salvage. The owners argued that he had not saved either ship or cargo from any of the normal perils of the sea

for which salvage is paid, and perhaps the French would have returned the *Amelia* unharmed. Marshall's first opinion was a common sense adjudication of the dispute. He held that under the
French decrees prevailing at the time the *Amelia* was captured or
rescued, the owners would never have seen either ship, cargo, or
compensation. Talbot actually had salvaged her in the real meaning of the word, and was entitled to his reward.

A few other cases completed the docket, and Marshall was able
to return to his home and to his and Bushrod Washington's negotiations with Publisher Wayne. These dragged on in desultory
fashion—Marshall still not doing any work on the biography except for random readings in other histories of the period—until
the two jurists returned to the capital for the December term of
court. Then their correspondence with Wayne took on a note of
urgency; they were groping toward a definite agreement. And
just at this time, four men who asserted that they were entitled to
be justices of the peace for the District of Columbia appeared in
the Supreme Court with an interesting point of law.

[3]

The four were William Marbury, Dennis Ramsay, Robert Hooe,
and William Harper. They were among forty-two men appointed
as District of Columbia justices of the peace by Adams in the
"midnight" naming of judges. They had been confirmed by the
Senate on March 2, and Marshall had signed their commissions as
Secretary of State.

The need for forty-two such functionaries for the muddy village of Washington and its surrounding ten miles square was obviously remote. Republicans properly regarded the Act of Congress authorizing them as a patronage grab by defeated politicians.
Madison found the commissions in Marshall's old office when he
succeeded to the State Department portfolio, and saw an opportunity to eliminate some sinecures and some Federalists. He obtained Jefferson's authority to issue only twenty-six of the commissions. Marbury and his three associates were among the other

seventeen, and they sued for their rights. They asked the Supreme Court to issue a writ of mandamus against the Secretary of State, an order to compel Madison to give them their commissions.

The suit was obviously a bit of Federalist animosity designed to embarrass the administration and perhaps to forestall the attack on the judiciary which all observers could see in the offing. The office of justice of the peace was not in itself worth all this trouble and expense. In fact, half a dozen of those to whom Madison sent commissions either resigned or neglected to qualify because the post was of so little account. Marbury, Ramsay, Hooe, and Harper were politicians enough to want a fight, and on receiving their plea, Marshall issued a routine order (routine except that it was directed against the Secretary of State) calling upon Madison to show cause why the writ should not be granted.

If it was hoped that the case which went down in history as *Marbury* vs. *Madison* would divert the Republicans from their attempt to remodel the judicial system, that hope must have been dispelled by Jefferson's first message to Congress on December 8. It was notable as the first occasion on which a President had failed to address Congress in person, and it set a fashion which persisted until Woodrow Wilson reverted to the older custom 112 years later. At the time, judges were more interested in what he had to say than in how he said it. For Jefferson desired to call particular attention to the Judiciary Act of the previous winter, and he offered evidence to show that there was not sufficient business before the courts to warrant the Act's extravagant increase in judges and courts.

Marshall and his colleagues would have been at least as keenly interested in another passage, which was cut out only at the last minute, and after the message had been signed. This was a clear explanation of Jefferson's views on the power to declare acts of Congress unconstitutional. Before he became President he had written one of the most forceful arguments why each State was entitled to pass on the constitutionality of Federal laws for itself. Now he had written that each of the Federal government departments must be its own judge, "according to its own judgment and uncontrolled by the opinion of any other department." Holding this view, he said of the Sedition Law:

"I do declare that I hold that act to be in palpable and unqualified contradiction to the Constitution. Considering it then as a nullity, I have relieved from oppression under it those of my fellow citizens who were within reach of the functions confided to me."

Jefferson omitted this passage from the message as finally sent, he explained, because he was afraid that "the public might be made to misunderstand." He recognized that confusion would follow general adoption of his principle that each State and government department was its own interpreter of the Constitution. But he could see no alternative save tyranny of the courts. Perhaps he did not see either that in the Federal government at least, his system would make the President a more absolute ruler than even most Federalists wanted. The Executive must carry out decisions of the courts and acts of Congress. The courts and Congress have virtually no power of action themselves. So if the Executive could decide what is valid or invalid in the work of the other two branches, the President would become a dictator curbed only by the doubtful and difficult process of impeachment.

[4]

Since the Seventh Congress was deprived of the knowledge of this theory, its members went to work with a good will on Jefferson's suggestion to consider the state of the judiciary. They elected to try their strength first in the Senate, where they were weakest, and on January 6, 1802, John Breckinridge of Kentucky moved the repeal of the Judiciary Act of 1801. Two days later he opened the debate. Tall and handsome, just past forty, he was a seasoned legislator of more than twenty years' experience, for he had been a member of the Virginia House when he was nineteen. He had moved to Kentucky, acquired a large plantation and a big political

following. For this occasion he had been primed by a long letter
of advice from the one man of his party who was Madison's peer
as a constitutional thinker, John Taylor of Caroline.

The Senator's reasoning was sound even if his prophecies were
speedily proven quaint. He declared that the power to create a
court must carry with it the power to abolish that court. He anticipated the Federalist argument that judges held their places
under the Constitution "during good behavior." He pointed out
that this rule was borrowed from England where it was instituted
to prevent removal of judges for political reasons. It did not mean
that useless courts and useless judges had to be perpetuated. The
Judiciary Act of 1801, he insisted, had created far too many courts,
and he launched into his prophecy.

"The time never will arrive when America will stand in need
of thirty-eight Federal Judges," he thundered.

On the constitutional argument, the Federalists had by far the
worst of it, but, as Senators will, they talked longer to make up
for the weakness of their case. Gouverneur Morris made the most
imposing effort, described by Hamilton's *New York Evening Post*
as "an elegant specimen." He won the hearts of Marshall and his
colleagues by arguing that the extra judges would make it possible
to employ "the learning of a judge [rather] than the agility of a
postboy." This had considerable appeal to men who suffered the
tortures of contemporary travel in getting to and from the capital,
much less slogging through the mud on circuit. But Republicans
could work up little sympathy for Federalists, and the judges were
all Federalists.

Breckinridge had neglected the most telling point written to
him by Taylor, and Senator Mason of Virginia picked it up. Em-
bellishing his remarks with a good deal of cogent sarcasm, he
quoted Section 24 of the law which the Federalists were defending
with so much passion:

"The district courts of Kentucky and Tennessee shall be and
hereby are abolished." Then he asked: "Where were these guard-
ians of the Constitution—these vigilant sentinels of our liberties—

when this law was passed? Were they asleep at their posts?"
The debate drifted off into a discussion of the power of the
courts to declare Acts of Congress unconstitutional, and here the
Federalists had all the better of it. But unfortunately for them that
was not the direct issue. On the power of Congress to abolish useless courts, the Republicans were virtually unanswerable, and on
February 3, the vote finally was taken. It was strictly a party ballot—the weeks of talk might have been saved—and repeal of the
Judiciary Act of 1801 was passed by 16 to 15.

The House for once did as much talking as the Senate. The
same arguments were asserted by both parties, and a month after
the Senate had acted, the House leaders decided to force the issue.
They kept the session going until midnight—that never had happened before—and again a strict party vote passed the bill, 59 to
32. With the despair in which a defeated party views the acts of
its enemies, the *Washington Federalist* predicted that the next
move would be to repeal the law creating the Supreme Court,
which not even the most rabid Republican suggested. "Farewell,
a Long Farewell, to All Our Greatness," was the title of the paper's article. But it did hope that the Supreme Court would find
the repeal unconstitutional.

This the Republicans feared, too. While Federalists raged in
letter and newspaper editorial, a bill was passed to relieve the Justices from the wide extent of their travels by assigning them singly
instead of in pairs to their circuits, so each would have less territory to cover. As a further lightening of their burden, the new
law reduced the Supreme Court terms to one a year, to open the
second Monday in February. Marshall and his colleagues were
never sufficiently grateful to their enemies for sparing them sum-
mers in Washington. In fact, all good Federalists were in a great
rage against the arrangement, for it abolished the June term of
court, and so no decision on the constitutionality of the repeal law
would be possible for nearly a year.

The constitutional question Marshall wanted to raise was the
new law which sent him riding circuit, away from his family and

Washington's biography. He questioned the power of Congress to order Supreme Court Justices to do other work than came to their high court. Since the six would not meet again until 1803, he wrote in April to inquire what his "brethren" thought about obeying the new law. He thought it only right to issue a practical warning that all previous Justices under Federalist administrations had performed these services without question, a fact which "will detract very much, in the public estimation, from the merit or opinion of the sincerity of a determination not now to act under it." Cushing, Paterson, and Washington favored compliance with the law; Chase thought the demand unconstitutional, and the six should consult about it; Moore's reply has not survived.

The result, of course, was that all six obeyed the law, and Marshall with a slave named Peter to take care of him, set off in his gig, to perform his district duties. He must have been extremely bitter against Jefferson and the Republicans, for the negotiations with Wayne were nearly completed, and district courts were going to interfere seriously with the biography.

Bushrod Washington signed the contract on September 22, 1802. He and Marshall were to divide one dollar for every volume sold; the work was to run to four or five volumes; the price to the public was to be three dollars per volume, and it was "supposed" that the manuscript would be delivered in less than two years.

If Marshall was annoyed with Jefferson, the President was equally angry with the Chief Justice. Jefferson was quite sure that the biography, word of which was circulating in well-informed quarters many months before the signing of the contract, would be a partisan political document. As early as May, 1802, Jefferson was writing to Joel Barlow to urge him to take up his pen to anticipate Marshall's "electioneering" effort by a sound "history of the United States, from the close of the War downwards."

Jefferson, however, was more immediately concerned with preliminaries to the Louisiana purchase. For a time he was too busy making history to worry about a man who was merely writing it. Nor was there any indication save the signing of the contract that

writing was being done, for Marshall was out on his circuit as
winter came. Also riding through the countryside was the incredible inventor of the Washington cherry tree myth, Mason
Locke Weems, an itinerant preacher, lecturer, writer, fiddler, and
book peddler. It was in the last capacity that he showed true genius, and Wayne had employed him to solicit subscriptions for the
Washington biography. By December he was showering Wayne
with letters, some reporting such good progress as an average of
twelve subscriptions a day, others urging that Marshall be warned
because people feared his book "will be prostituted to party purposes," others doubting that postmasters would be good agents for
this particular work.

As men who could write free letters and knew individuals who
could read, the twelve hundred or so postmasters of the country
were generally employed by publishers for work of this kind. But
Wayne was to find that they were less than enthusiastic about
helping sell what seemed to them likely to be a Federalist publication. Bushrod Washington could deny any party sentiment, but
Jefferson had indicated his beliefs. The result was that in one
Virginia town, Parson Weems reported that the postmaster got
only one subscription in six months, whereas he got thirteen in half
a day.

[5]

Driving through woods and swamps in his battered gig, Marshall
planned his great work on a scale which terrified poor Wayne
when he found out about it. The demand for the biography was
due to interest in the words and deeds of its hero. But Marshall
had decided to take a long running start. He had decided that it
was impossible to understand Washington's life without an understanding of colonial history, so he was going all the way back to
the founding of Jamestown and the Pilgrim fathers by way of introduction.

Perhaps it was while brooding on these events that he fell in the way of incidents which inspired far more sprightly writing than anything he ever put on paper about Washington. For instance, he had spent New Year's Day, 1803, driving down to North Carolina to hold court, and on January 2 he wrote from "Rawleigh":

"My Dearest Polly,

"You will laugh at my vexation when you hear the various calamities that have befallen me. In the first place when I came to review my funds, I had the mortification to discover that I had lost 15 silver dollars out of my waist coat pocket. They had worn through the various mendings the pocket had sustained and sought their liberty in the sands of Carolina.

"I determined not to vex myself with what could not be remedied & ordered Peter to take out my cloaths that I might dress for court when to my astonishment & grief after fumbling several minutes in the portmanteau staring at vacancy & sweating most profusely he turned to me with the doleful tidings that I had no pair of breeches. You may be sure this piece of intelligence was not very graciously received; however, after a little scolding, I determined to make the best of my situation & immediately set out to get a pair made.

"I thought I should be a sans-culotte only one day & that for the residue of the term I might be well enough dressed for the appearance of the first day to be forgotten.

"But, the greatest of evils, I found, was followed by a still greater. . . . Not a taylor in town could be prevailed on to work for me. They were all so busy that it was impossible to attend to my wants however pressing they might be, & I have the extreme mortification to pass the whole time without that important article of dress I have mentioned. I have no alleviation for this misfortune but the hope that I shall be enabled in four or five days to commence my journey homeward & that I shall have the pleasure of seeing you & our dear children in eight or nine days after this reaches you.

"In the meantime, I flatter myself that you are well and happy.
"Adieu my dearest Polly,
          "I am your own affectionate,

                                              "J. Marshall."

Raleigh, its bench and bar, managed to survive the sight of a
Chief Justice clad in trousers instead of breeches. For as his fame
increased, his carelessness in dress became almost as much a matter
of gossip and reminiscence as that of Jefferson, and with more reason. Marshall was not only as untidy as his cousin, he was frequently guilty of downright slovenliness. Even admirers commented on the frequency with which he appeared in soiled linen,
unbrushed coats, muddy boots, uncombed hair. After a time, however, men who were not admirers acknowledged that the easy
charm of his manner and conversation erased the unfavorable first
impression.

Actually this neglect of personal appearance played a big part
in Marshall's personal popularity. Indifference to dress and even
to cleanliness was thought by many to be a virtue, a symbol of
virility and independence. Only those who had never seen the
Chief Justice, dusty and a bit ragged, jogging out to his farm with
his thumb in a jug of whisky because he had lost the cork could
speak of him as a horrid aristocrat—and mean it. Richmond
chuckled for generations over the youthful dandy who hired a
seedy individual for a quarter to carry a turkey home, how meekly
the older man walked behind with the squawking bird over his
shoulder, how the dandy was covered with confusion to learn
that his attendant was the Chief Justice of the United States.
Strangers who met Marshall on the road or in the towns where he
held court were constantly amazed by the flow of language—
jokes or political argument or philosophical discourse—which
proceeded from one they had taken for a tavern loafer. Marshall
mingled happily but quite simply and easily with any society in
which he found himself, whether with tavern loafers or with the

cream of the Virginia bar at the "lawyer dinners" which he gave in his own home.

But of all society, he preferred his family. He always left with regret and returned with delight. For him there was no place so pleasant as Richmond, simply because his family lived there. All his life, of course, he had been accustomed to a large family, and he had the qualities of mind and heart to enjoy it. His only regret was that so few of his brothers and sisters lived near enough to see frequently. But he made up for it by adopting the whole Ambler connection, and became a great one to give sage advice to his brothers-in-law, lend a helping hand in their business affairs, run on little errands for their wives. He performed these chores, furthermore, as if he really enjoyed being helpful, and no doubt he did. Easygoing, generous with money, and genuinely sympathetic, he was the oak upon which the whole family leaned. When an Ambler in-law needed an introduction or a Marshall brother needed a loan, he was the man to whom they turned.

His second youngest sister, Jane, who was twenty-four years his junior, spent much time with him, and his own view of his position as the eldest of fifteen was perhaps best exemplified by his attempt to prevent her marriage. Marshall played a combination heavy father and meddling big brother with the appropriate results—Jane married the young man promptly and lived with him happily ever after.

On a visit to her brother, Jane had met, fallen in love with and actually "manifested some partiality for" Major George Keith Taylor, a young lawyer with no more fortune than Marshall had possessed when he courted Mary Ambler. That Marshall was stern if kind was shown by the fact that Jane did not confide in him, and he learned of the state of her affections only after she had gone on to visit their brother James. The elder was quite indignant not only that Jane had encouraged Major Taylor but that the affair had been kept from him. He explained to James that his only objection to Taylor was lack of funds, and that their sister should have known just what her suitor's circumstances were.

"Had I conjectured that Mr. Taylor was contemplated in the character of a lover, I shou'd certainly have made to her all proper communications," he complained.

Stuffy as this sounds, Marshall was good-natured enough to accept having been in the wrong and to rejoice when his new brother-in-law rose to the dignity of the Federal bench himself.

Marshall's own marriage was the wonder of his friends and relatives. They could not understand how he could live so long and happily with a neurotic semi-invalid. They saw only the querulous, unhappy woman. He saw only the lovely, adoring girl whom he had married. A more substantial reason for their happiness was the prosaic fact that they shared laughs. When she was in the mood, Polly had a gift for mimicry. Her husband's humor was tickled by her imitations of their friends and Richmond's notables. In her conversation, he once fondly recorded, she displayed also "a good deal of delicate and playful wit."

Although they had ten children, four of whom died young, Polly never seemed to grow up. Shortly after the birth of the tenth, her illness took the form of spells of anguish whenever she heard loud noises. These spells also often coincided with spring housecleaning. There is no recorded instance that her husband ever lost his patience or neglected any effort to soothe her nerves. He managed to keep the children quiet or out of doors when her attacks came. He himself walked about in his stocking feet.

To spare her domestic details, Marshall not only did the marketing but took charge of the household when it threatened to become as untidy as its master. Tenderly he would carry Polly out to her carriage, send her off for a long drive or a visit to a sister and return to the house himself. There with sleeves rolled up, he would wield broom and mop, leading the household slaves, until a thorough job had been done.

Because Polly was conventionally pious, her husband was a regular attendant at her church, although his daughter thought he inclined toward Unitarianism. After a disastrous theatre fire, he had served as chairman of a committee to collect money for a memorial, and Monumental Church on the site of the disaster was tribute to his fund-raising abilities. Here the Marshalls had a pew, and the Chief Justice was quite uncomfortable in the cramped space until he learned that he could open the pew door, and thrust his long legs out into the aisle during the sermon.

He was fond of children and frequently exchanged smiles with a little boy not far behind whose angelic face and long curls adorned John Allan's pew. This was Edgar Poe, adopted by the pew owner after the boy's actress-mother died during an engagement in Richmond.

Marshall's own children were rather strictly raised. First in their lives came the necessity for quiet because of their mother's health. But even if it had not been for that, Marshall was not the man to coddle his offspring. They remembered him as affectionate and just. But justice to a child is not the virtue which adults would have him believe. Nevertheless, the Chief Justice partook of the nature of fathers in that he bragged of his children's charms and intelligence frequently without noticeable justification. The one girl, Mary, was his very obvious favorite—no unusual circumstance and not resented by her five brothers.

[6]

For that age of slow motion, when most men spent all their days within a few miles of their homes, Marshall had comparatively little home life. His court duties sent him off almost as soon as they brought him home. For example, he had hardly returned from the sans-culotte session at Raleigh before he was on the road to Washington to attend the first session of the Supreme Court in fourteen months.

It was not going to be as light a term or as free from controversy as his previous ones, for the roar of politics could be heard from the bench.

During the debate and comment on the judicial reform, there had been much Republican fury at the impertinence of the Su-

preme Court in daring to issue an order to the Secretary of State
to show cause why a writ should not be launched against him.
This in the eyes of Representative William B. Giles, a bitter Jeffersonian leader, amounted to prying "into the Executive Cabinet
to examine its concerns." The shrill but dreaded voice of John
Randolph had been heard speaking of this "inquisitorial capacity."

Six Federalists, with the Republican Congress talking freely
about impeachment, would have to decide whether they should
issue a writ against the President's principal adviser, knowing that
if they did, it would be ignored, and if they did not, they would be
accused of a shameful retreat. The Chief Justice, who would have
to announce that decision, was engaged in some quiet thinking.

XII

☆ ☆ ☆

The First Offensive

I N THE WASHINGTON boarding house where the Supreme Court justices spent such of their evenings as were not devoted to dining out, the case of *Marbury* vs. *Madison* loomed large. But they considered it against a background of somewhat larger world events. The most important of these was the threat of renewed war in Europe, which was intimately involved in Jefferson's negotiations to buy New Orleans, since it was supposed Napoleon might sell it rather than see the port snatched by England, whose domination of the sea would make such a step easy.

The justices also considered their biggest case against the background of an incident which would more nearly affect their order. Five days before the Supreme Court opened its session, Jefferson had transmitted to Congress a message suggesting that "proceedings of redress" be instituted because of the conduct of John Pickering, Federal District Judge for New Hampshire. Pickering habitually appeared on the bench drunk and turned out to be insane. The specific misconduct alleged against him, however, was that in an important case he refused to hear witnesses or counsel for the government. It was plain that the precedent of his case might be applied to a higher court.

Despite the serious nature of the incident, the hearing of *Marbury* vs. *Madison* opened on a note of comedy. Former Attorney General Charles Lee, representing Marbury, had some difficulty proving that the commissions had ever been issued. The Secretary of State was ignoring the proceedings; the Senate was not inclined to co-operate by producing its records. Yet on the bench, presiding over the court, sat the man who had signed the commissions. Gravely, Marshall listened while their existence was proved by men who had seen them, including his brother James, to whom the Chief Justice had written nearly two years earlier:

"I fear some blame may be imputed to me . . . I should have sent out the commissions which had been signed & sealed except for the hurry of the time & the absence of Mr. Wagner [his clerk] who had been called on by the President to act as his private secretary."

Having surmounted the hurdle of proving that the commissions existed, Lee proceeded to argue the law for some time. He went all the way from the clause in the original Judiciary Act of 1789, which gave the Supreme Court power to issue writs of mandamus "in cases warranted by the principles and usages of law," to the thesis that the judicial officers of the Union could not be deprived of their jobs by the Executive. There was no argument on the other side.

Jefferson's life-long complaint that this was a "moot" case—one cooked up without any real issue at stake just to get the court to come to a decision—was justified by the brief deliberation which the court allowed itself after argument. The six Justices reached a speedy decision, much too speedy if they had not considered the problem in some detail in advance. Certainly they had been familiar with the arguments on both sides, because if the Republicans refused to be heard in court, they had been heard in Congress for a long time. Nothing that any lawyer might have put forward had not already been aired in great detail.

The bar was to hear these arguments once more, in fact several times more, as Marshall read the opinion. For an hour and a half, he rehearsed the question of whether Marbury was entitled to his commission. He answered that the man was rightfully a justice of the peace.

The question of who determines such rights was easy for Marshall. The courts are obviously created for that purpose. In a difference of opinion as to what Marbury was entitled to get, the law was involved and the courts interpreted the law.

Reaching the interesting point as to how far the courts could go in "interfering" with the Executive department, the reader took some time. Judges certainly could not pass upon political actions or the conduct of foreign affairs. But there were some things which executive officers were required to do by law, and if they violated the law, there must be some remedy. The Chief Justice here went into one of his favorite tricks of logic, the analogy. If an Act of Congress required an officer of the government to record the names of wounded veterans on the pension rolls or deliver patents for public lands to the purchasers, the same point of law would arise. Here Marshall used his other favorite trick, the rhetorical question, demanding:

"Would the wounded veteran be without remedy? Would the purchaser of land be deprived of his property? Is it to be contended that the heads of departments are not amenable to the laws of their country?"

If at this point Marshall had answered the last question, he would have surprised his audience even more than he did a half hour later. But there was a little prelude while he worked up to the point of where Marbury should look for his redress. The lanky figure of the Chief Justice was hidden in his robes of black; his lean face was bent toward the paper from which he read; from time to time he swept his right arm before him in a curious circular gesture which was the one physical embellishment of his oratory. He was working up to his climax, for he had found a way out of the dilemma which seemed to require him either to send Madison an order that the Secretary would not obey or bow to the Republican version of the court's impotence.

His way out was to say that the heads of departments ought to be amenable to the law, that Marbury ought to have a remedy in the courts, but that there was no valid law to cover the point at issue. Lawyer Lee had asked for the writ of mandamus under Section 13 of the Judiciary Act of 1789. That section, asserted the Chief Justice with the concurrence of his brethren, was unconstitutional and void, and therefore they would have to throw the whole case out of court and dismiss the application for a writ.

Marshall had achieved a most ingenious paradox. He had said that the laws of his country afforded Marbury a remedy, but then he added that the law on which Marbury relied was "repugnant to the Constitution." The reason was that the Constitution itself listed the limited class of lawsuits in which the Supreme Court could assume original jurisdiction; that is, could hear without their coming up on appeal from a lower court. Nowhere in the Constitution was power given to Congress to add to the original jurisdiction of the Supreme Court. Therefore, the clause in the Act of 1789 which presumed to give the court power to issue a mandamus was invalid. Marshall on this point was what came to be known as a strict constructionist.

As the Chief Justice's deep voice droned on through the complex and repetitious pages of his opinion, the listeners began to see that his ingenuity had elements of genius. For the first time, the Supreme Court was presuming to find an Act of Congress unconstitutional, but the ground was so carefully chosen that neither the President nor the legislature could do anything about it. Madison would only make himself and his chief ridiculous if he came storming into court demanding that a mandamus be issued against him. Congress could only force the six Justices to take jurisdiction of a case by impeaching them and getting new men in their places.

Marshall, therefore, had accomplished two great things by his decision. He had answered—and as it turned out, forever—the question of what agency of government has final decision in interpreting the Constitution. He had also asserted the complete independence of the Judiciary by lecturing the Executive on its duty without giving the Executive an opportunity to defy an order.

The only previous chance the Supreme Court had been vouchsafed to pass on an Act of Congress had been the trial of Hylton, when the government tested the right of Congress to levy a carriage tax. That decision had upheld an Act of Congress, and other Federal laws were to be upheld steadily. It would be more than fifty years before the Supreme Court voided another Act of Congress, and that would be the Dred Scott decision in which the law barring slaves from "free" territory was declared unconstitutional. It took a war to settle that dispute, but other Acts of Congress have been set aside with less trouble. The reasoning, accepted by everyone now, is based on Marshall's *Marbury* vs. *Madison* opinion:

"The question whether an act repugnant to the Constitution can become the law of the land is a question deeply interesting to the United States; but, happily, not of an intricacy proportioned to its interest. It is emphatically the province and duty of the judicial department to say what the law is. Those who apply the rule to particular cases must, of necessity, expound and interpret that rule. If two laws conflict with each other, the courts must decide on the operation of each. So, if a law be in opposition to the Constitution: if both the law and the Constitution apply to a particular case . . . the court must determine which of these conflicting rules governs the case. This is of the very essence of judicial duty."

It is curious that the most enthusiastic biographers of both Marshall and Jefferson—the late Senator Albert J. Beveridge for

Marshall and Ambassador Claude Bowers for Jefferson—thought that the press of the day virtually ignored this landmark in constitutional law. In point of fact, it was published in full in a good many papers all over the country such as the *National Intelligencer* in Washington, *Aurora* in Philadelphia, the *Spectator* in New York. But the importance of the decision in the year 1803 was based on different parts than were stressed by the biographers of the next century.

Despite Jefferson's theory that each branch of government and each State was its own interpreter of the Constitution, the principle of judicial supremacy in this field was quite generally held. The Republicans had been against it when the courts upheld laws they found intolerably oppressive. The Federalists were to be against it under the same circumstances. But men of all parties who were not passionately involved in the quarrels of party and policy—this meant almost all men—expected the courts to interpret the laws. Even Jefferson expected as much in the State courts dealing with a State constitution.

The real significance of Marshall's decision for the men of that day was the statement that Marbury was entitled to his commission. Republicans were furious that the Supreme Court had undertaken to pass judgment on a case over which in the next breath— or some breaths removed—it said it had no jurisdiction. This was a blow below the belt. There was no appropriate way to answer it. And of course Marbury never did get his commission.

The real significance of the decision for men of later generations was that it started the virtual deification of the Supreme Court, to which Marshall was to contribute a great deal.

[2]

Republicans saw in the Marbury opinion confirmation of their pet fear that the Supreme Court would proceed now to declare unconstitutional their own Judiciary Act abolishing courts and sending Supreme Court Justices back to circuit. A case positively inviting such an opinion was on the docket. It was an appeal from a decision by Marshall in the Richmond court four months earlier, and the lawyers argued that he should not under the Constitution have been sitting in an inferior court. He disqualified himself, of course, and it fell to Paterson to read the Court's decision.

No bit of legislation was quite so much hated by Federalists as this Republican Judiciary Act. Their Congressional orators had freely predicted that the Supreme Court would upset it. Their disappointment was matched only by Republican jubilation when Paterson upheld the law and pointed out that the fact that all Supreme Court Justices for twelve years performed circuit duty without question seemed a sufficient answer to the question. For a moment Marshall enjoyed a bit of popularity in the Republican press, which seems to have overlooked his abstention from the case. Said the *Aurora:*

"The weight of your authority then calmed the tumult of faction, and you stood, as you must continue to stand, a star of the first magnitude."

The constitutional issues were coming to the fore again in a new guise, as foreign policy became once more the dominant issue in domestic politics. Federalism was to desert the principles of its founders partly for the sake of sectional interest, partly for the joy of thwarting Republicans. The process by which Marshall was left a man without a party—an excellent thing for a Chief Justice—began in 1803.

As the European powers steered a determined course toward war, Napoleon decided to rid himself of such useless encumbrances as Louisiana. Instead of the pin point of New Orleans island at the toe of the Louisiana boot, he offered the whole body —an expanse of wilderness and plain and desert which funnelled upwards from the present State, widening as it went until at the top it covered Montana, North Dakota, and part of Minnesota. It would double the area of the United States. The deal was completed on April 30; for $15,000,000 the United States acquired a dozen states or more at the bargain price of little over a million each, with perhaps forty thousand Creole inhabitants and an unknown number of Indians.

While this treaty made its slow way across the Atlantic, there was a lull in the political activity in Washington. Congress had adjourned, and the Supreme Court was taking to the circuit, its Chief also immersing himself in the sea of George Washington's private and public papers. In Europe peace collapsed in May, and that same month the pugnacious Chase told a grand jury in Baltimore what he thought of government, State and Federal. The jury was meeting in a tavern dining room, and perhaps the Judge was stimulated by the atmosphere of good food and good drink, although there is no evidence that he was anything but strictly sober.

His charge, however, was intemperate. A considerable gathering of the curious had assembled in the back of the room because Chase's pronouncements were famous. One of the recognized divertisements of the day was attendance at public functions where a piquant speech might be heard. Chase was peppery at all times.

He began by charging the grand jury as to its duties, and then he wandered off into what was commonplace up to that time but would now be considered the most improper conduct. His comments on politics started with a prediction of ruin because the free state of Maryland had introduced universal male suffrage. He then moved on to the iniquities of Federal politics, saying:

"The independence of the national judiciary is already shaken to its foundations."

If that had been true, Chase would hardly have been regaling Baltimoreans in a tavern with his views on the national administration. But he assured his audience that the repeal of the Judiciary Act, so recently pronounced constitutional by his Supreme Court brethren, would put an end to "security of property and personal liberty."

At intervals in this charge, Chase pushed his spectacles up on his forehead and entertained the audience with bits of extemporaneous sarcasm directed against Jefferson and the Republican majority of Congress. But only his carefully prepared remarks were printed. They were quite enough to touch off a tremendous debate on how much partisanship should be permitted a judge.

[3]

The reverberations of Chase's charge were still resounding through the press when news of the renewed war in Europe and the sale of Louisiana arrived together. The actual treaty reached Jefferson on July 3, and gave him an excellent topic for his Fourth of July announcement to the people. The blessings of liberty were to be conferred upon an area larger than that which benefited by the original declaration.

Marshall, swamped with the volume of Washington's correspondence and nagged by his publisher for speed, observed the repercussions to the acquisition of Louisiana with some alarm. He had sympathy with the rejoicing of ordinary mortals, and he was dismayed by the indignation of those Federalist leaders in New England who were shrieking that secession was the only answer to this attempt to drag the wilderness into the Union. The men of the northeastern seaboard saw their influence in government permanently ended by admission of states brought up in the Jeffersonian tradition. They saw their lands in Ohio and Illinois depreciating in value as restless settlers pushed into the new territory beyond the Mississippi.

Marshall would have seen their objections with no less disgust if he had known that Jefferson shared their opinions to some extent. The President was bothered because only on the most advanced of Hamiltonian principles could he base the legality of this treaty. Nowhere in the Constitution was there any authority to add new territory; nowhere in his own principles was there any provision for taking people into any nation without their consent. Yet the purchase of Louisiana would not wait upon an amendment to the Constitution.

Jefferson decided that he and Congress, which would ratify the deed and appropriate the money, could only throw themselves upon the mercy of the country. Then he evolved the idea that he had been in the position of the guardian of a minor, investing the child's money until it should become of age. For a man who believed in the rule of the people, this was treading dangerous ground, the road to megalomania. His Congressional supporters, less wedded to principle, easily defeated the Federalists in vote after vote, and on December 20 the United States flag went up in New Orleans.

Marshall meanwhile was dashing off sheet after sheet of the Washington biography—Wayne was appalled by the mass of the first installment, which ran to 800 pages with very little mention of the hero. Some of it, Marshall conceded, might be placed in the second volume, and both were to come out the next summer, in time for campaign reading before the election of 1804.

The Chief Justice interrupted his interminable writing to move on to Washington for the February, 1804, term of court. In the intervals of the few cases on the docket, he and his colleagues visited the Senate, where they could hear their order roundly denounced and feebly defended in the impeachment trial of Pickering, which was in progress without the culprit's attendance. The defense was that an insane man could not plead and in impeachment proceedings could not be considered guilty of "high crimes and misdemeanors." The majority brushed this aside as an irrelevant technicality—after the passion of the day had cooled it seemed that there was no other recourse if an insane judge refused to resign—and on March 12, the Senate convicted Pickering by 19 to 7. As if they were only waiting for this signal, the House within an hour passed a resolution to impeach Chase, and the status of judges was thrown into the presidential campaign of 1804.

[4]

As was to be customary, almost everything else that anyone could think of was thrown into the campaign, too. But it was far less abusive than the contest of 1800. Perhaps that was because the result was so easy to predict. Jefferson, ousting Burr in favor of old Governor George Clinton of New York, was obviously an easy victor over Marshall's old colleague, Pinckney, and Rufus King, the Federalist standard bearers. King himself had gone into the campaign with no hope of success, writing to a friend that he had "no doubt that the Pr. will be re-elected."

The Federalists were dispensing with their brains in the campaign. Hamilton, Marshall, Cabot, and even King himself were outside the real party aims. The bigots who held with Fisher Ames that they were synonymous with the wise, the rich, and the good were more interested in an idea fathered by Timothy Pickering that New England should withdraw from the Union, and take New York along, perhaps New Jersey too, with the aid of Burr. Pickering had spoken to Burr and been much encouraged by the Vice President's manner.

It seems obvious that Burr was trying to enlist a few Federalist votes for the race he was making to be Governor of New York that spring. He easily fooled the rather slow Pickering into believing he could be had. Hamilton, with no such illusions, led the way in defeating Burr in New York, and on a July day at Weehawken all hope of enlisting either of these two brilliant men in the Federalist campaign died with Hamilton. The Vice President, indicted for murder after their duel, was no longer a man to whom any Federalist could offer public support.

Federalists were reduced to extremely petty issues that summer and autumn. The marriage of Jerome Bonaparte to Betsy Patterson was made the subject of an insinuation that Republicans were seeking an alliance with Napoleon, for the fair Betsy's relatives were Republican leaders. Jefferson's manners and the horrid attempt to intimidate the judiciary were rehashed, and Federalists made much of a bumptious young Irish snob and poet, Thomas Moore, who was directing fashionable sneers at American manners that year. At twenty-five, he fancied himself as an arbiter of both manners and morals, and came away from a White House dinner complaining loudly of the ignorance and bad taste of his host. Tom Moore's own idea of good manners was to publish this verse about the man whose hospitality he had just enjoyed:

> The weary statesman for repose hath fled
> From halls of council to his negro's shed;
> Where, blest, he woos some black Aspasia's grace
> And dreams of freedom in his slave's embrace.

On their side, the Republicans had the great advantage of pointing to constructive, popular achievements. Taxes were down, Louisiana acquired, prosperity returning with the European war, and the price of neutrality not yet apparent. Chase's conduct came in for its share of sarcasm, for it developed that the people had a partiality for a judicial demeanor on the bench, and one of the more reasonably stated Republican views ran:

"Whence and for what cause has originated this novel cry about the sanctity and impunity of Judges? It seems as if they had a charter from heaven to do as they pleased, and it was a sin against the elect to say, why do ye so?"

It was freely predicted by the more rabid partisans that Chase would be thrown out when the Senate met again, and that he would be followed by the rest of the Federalist judges. Meanwhile the first breach in the court had been made. Just after the end of the 1804 term, Moore resigned because of ill health and Jefferson had his first chance to appoint a Supreme Court Justice. It was generally believed he was saving his favorite jurist, Spencer Roane of Virginia, for Marshall's place and perhaps Roane, who was at the head of his State judiciary, would not accept a subordinate spot in the Federal system. With very little delay, therefore, Jefferson appointed William Johnson, who at thirty-two was the youngest man yet to serve on the high court.

Johnson was regarded as a disciple of Jefferson, and was rugged enough to handle the circuit duties of his new office. Although a young man, he had been a judge for several years and was accounted a prodigy in legal learning. Marshall must have been greatly relieved at the caliber of Jefferson's appointment, for he knew something of his new colleague's background. Johnson had studied law in the office of Charles Pinckney and was reputed to be as sound a constitutional man as he proved himself during many years of brilliant Court service.

The first two volumes of *The Life of George Washington* by John Marshall burst upon an apathetic public in midsummer of 1804. It disappointed nearly everybody concerned, and influenced no votes in the fall elections. There had been only about 4,000 subscribers, and a great many of these were clamoring for their money back—they had paid it as much as two years before—after they got the two volumes.

The first was devoted entirely to the history of the colonies; in fact, it was later published separately as such. But even when the patient reader labored into the second volume, he met an almost perfect example of how not to write biography. Scholars of the caliber of Beard were to express admiration of the work as history, for Marshall had an orderly mind and an even temper, but for an understanding of the man, Washington, even the scholar would have to look elsewhere. At the beginning of the second volume, it seemed that Marshall was about to make up in speed what he had lost in the previous hundred thousand words. A single page is all he needs to describe his hero's ancestors, infancy, boyhood, and youth. Washington seems to have been born nineteen years old, for at that age Marshall takes him into a leisurely account of the French and Indian wars. The chief political bias discernible in this section of the work is that the authorship of the Declaration of Independence is relegated to a footnote which explains that "the draft reported by the committee has been generally attributed to Mr. Jefferson." The political effect of the work was nullified because the second volume failed to get its subject past the War of Independence.

Marshall himself admitted that the two volumes were full of inaccuracies, careless writing, and verbosity. He had not wanted to sign his name to it, and yielded only to Wayne's anguished cries that he would be ruined.

Even Federalist reviews were lukewarm, although one or two indulged in what Marshall himself called "more of panegyric than was merited."

He was working hard on the third volume all through this summer and autumn, but he was not curbing his pen nor checking grammar and punctuation. He did authorize Wayne to cut the manuscript, and as the country streamed to the polls to give Jefferson a landslide vote over Pinckney, the Chief Justice plunged into his fourth volume. He was working hard now, although he realized that his grandiose dream of profits from the biography was groundless. The money he did get was welcome, however, and by no means inconsiderable. At the end of the year, he and Bushrod Washington had received $8,760 in royalties.

Much as he was interested in the money, Marshall was more interested in news from Washington about preparations for the impeachment trial of Samuel Chase. He knew as well as most of the newspaper readers of the country that Chase had been selected as the first target only because he seemed the most vulnerable. The rest were to follow. Republican leaders made no secret of that, and a month before the Chief Justice left his home to get ready for the February court, Giles, elevated now to the Senate, was speaking frankly to a member of the opposition as they sat before the fire in the cozy little Senate Chamber.

"We want your offices for the purpose of giving them to men who will fill them better," said the man who was to be one of Chase's judges to his Federalist colleague, John Quincy Adams.

XIII

☆ ☆ ☆

A Judge on Trial

THE BITTERNESS of party had extended even to the outward forms of social life when Marshall returned to the capital. Jefferson's New Year reception had been graced by only three Federalists, and two of them, Senators Adams and William Plumer, were soon to become Republicans. Washington was resounding with its usual tattle of faintly lewd political gossip—a specialty of the town from its birth—but the big treat was the rare combination of an impeachment and a fraud hearing at the same session.

Both were to be decided at the "lame duck" session. The 1804 election had reduced Federalist strength in the Senate to seven and in the House to twenty-five, but nine members of the party held their places in the upper house, which would be the judge of Chase, until March 4. However, before the impeachment trial would come the equally exciting spectacle of a full-dress airing of the biggest land scandal in American history.

It was called the Yazoo frauds, and it was already ten years old. Originating in the poverty of the State of Georgia, which had enormous territory but few people and almost no revenues, it had shaken the State to its political foundations and was now about to rock the nation.

Yazoo was a name given loosely to a big but empty expanse of Georgia's western territory, valueless until Eli Whitney's cotton gin sent Southern land values soaring. The Yazoo land was ideal for cotton, and in 1795 a syndicate of speculators appeared before the Georgia legislature to seek a concession. They did not come empty handed. Money, shares, and slaves were bid freely for votes. The bill to sell 35,000,000 acres for $500,000 passed with only one member of the majority not bribed.

The news spread through Georgia. The rage of the populace lost nothing from the facts that the purchasers were nearly all non-residents, and that a paltry 2,000,000 acres had been reserved for the settlement of native Georgians. The next Georgia legislature repealed the corrupt sale, but the original purchasers had already sold out, mostly in the Middle and New England States, and soon the price was up to fifteen and even twenty cents an acre, ten or fifteen times the sum paid to Georgia. A war of pamphlets broke out, with Georgians assailing and Northerners defending the deal. Hamilton, consulted as a legal expert by the speculators, gave his opinion that the contract for the sale was valid in spite of the corruption. The land companies which were profiting clung to this position. They insisted that no mere legislature could void a contract; if the State thought it had been wronged let it go to court, prove its case and seek a legal remedy.

Yazoo entered national politics because Congress passed an act to buy the territory from Georgia for $1,250,000 and to have the Federal government settle all claims against it. The commissioners to investigate what these claims might be were Madison, Gallatin, and Attorney General Lincoln. They recommended to the House that 5,000,000 acres be sold in part to pay off the claims of Yazoo purchasers. They admitted the whole transaction was based on fraud, but they added that a great many innocent purchasers—no one had yet thought of mentioning widows and orphans—would be hurt if no provision was made to settle the claims.

The Congressional session of 1804 had been enlivened by a stirring debate on the merits of sanctifying this fraud, and a resolution to compromise the Yazoo claims was put over until the next session. That was the issue which was rivalling the Chase impeachment in popular attention when Marshall met his brethren—and welcomed the new addition, young Johnson—at their Capitol Hill boardinghouse.

[2]

While Vice President Burr was carefully preparing the Senate Chamber for an impeachment trial, the elect of Washington, including Justices of the Supreme Court, dropped in on the House to hear the great Yazoo debate. That show owed its interest chiefly to the fervor of one man, John Randolph of Roanoke, who had settled his unpredictable genius on a determination to wipe this blot of iniquity from his country's name.

Randolph's zeal was that of the disinterested crusader, all the hotter for its impersonal tone. He had been visiting in Georgia at the time of the repeal campaign, and had retained a vivid memory of the citizenry's reaction to brazen corruption. He thought the spirit of Georgians deserved a better return than this compromise with thieves and the customers of thieves. Alone among the Jeffersonian leaders, he sought pure justice in this case; no other Republicans of prominence were willing to move against the President's commissioners since they included his two principal advisers. Federalists were willing to acquiesce; most of the beneficiaries were of their party, and their martyred Hamilton had pronounced their cause lawful if not just.

Randolph was not a good party man. On a raw winter's day he rose in the House and embarked upon a notable career of Congressional insurgency with a speech which even for him was a masterly piece of invective. The Chief Justice, listening to a debate which might affect his own enjoyment of the Fairfax estate, since Virginians sometimes talked of taking it back by act of the legislature, listened to the first split in the Jeffersonian ranks.

Generations of Congressmen learned to fear Randolph's venomed tongue and talented trigger finger. The gentleman from Roanoke was a duellist whether on the floor of the House or the glades of Bladensburg, where the capital's code of honor was settled with pistols. Randolph's dog crouched at his feet as he spoke; he usually wore his broad planter's hat at his desk, and nearly always he came to Congress with spurs on his heels and a riding whip twitching nervously in his hand. John Quincy Adams left this description of a first impression of Randolph:

"The voice, a throaty pipe, symbolized the arrival of a freakish apparition; very tall, very thin, scrawny of neck, the chin barely shadowed with fuzz like that of immature boyhood; a laughable homunculus but for the eyes, hollow and terrible, that burned below the square brow."

Marshall had two good reasons for observing him closely, for not only was Randolph the soul of the attack on the Yazoo frauds but he was chief manager for the impeachment of Chase. He had flung himself into both fights with the intensity he bestowed upon anything he deemed worthy of his notice.

This day his thesis was the simple one that honest governments did not compromise with corruption. Justice and the survival of pure liberty, he held, demanded that the vile creatures who had debauched the legislature of Georgia should not profit from their crimes. He had a target on the floor for his best shafts. One of the Yazoo bands, the New England Mississippi Company, had employed the Postmaster General, Gideon Granger, as its chief lobbyist for passage of the bill. The Postmaster General was not yet a member of the cabinet, but he was a good man to have in a Congressional fight, for he controlled the government's biggest slice of patronage even then. Granger had been and still was offensively active in the very chamber where the House met. He had been a speculator in Western lands, too, and Randolph pointed to him as he cried:

"His gigantic grasp embraces with one hand the shores of Lake Erie, and stretches with the other to the Bay of Mobile. Millions of acres are easily digested by such stomachs."

Granger was shamed, and Randolph almost achieved the impossible. A measure strongly backed by the administration which had just won an overwhelming vote of confidence at the polls, a measure which the official opposition supported, too, was passed by only 63 to 58. Furthermore, he was able to block a bill setting up the mechanics for carrying out the commissioner's recommendation.

Marshall returned to his lodgings from these debates to work alternately on his biography of Washington—he had brought the uncompleted manuscript of the fourth volume with him—and on the defense of Chase's impeachment. His recorded utterances show more concern with the biography, and one night Senator Adams fell into conversation with him over a dinner in Georgetown. Adams noted in his diary:

"He complained that, from having been forced to precipitate so much the publication, there were so many errors and imperfections in it that he was ashamed of it."

He talked freely about his book, but on the impeachment he was silent, although observers thought he seemed to be frightened. He might well be. He had small defense for Chase's conduct, but the removal of a Justice of the Supreme Court was not to his liking, for he was sure it would undermine the independence of all judges. He had actually suggested in a letter to Chase that perhaps it would be better to "yield to an appellate jurisdiction in the legislature." That sounds more like Jefferson than Marshall. It was the only time in the Chief Justice's career that he considered favorably the possibility of admitting a higher judicial power on this earth than his own court.

[3]

Aaron Burr had outdone himself in stage-managing the trial. The
Senate Chamber was tastefully arranged with benches and desks
covered in blue, green, and crimson cloth. A temporary gallery
had been built; boxes were provided for the fashionable; the presiding officer, Burr himself, was meticulously dressed in the latest
fashion as if his home had not just been sold for debt.

The Vice President, soon to retire from office, was almost as
keenly watched as the principals. It was his first public appearance
since his duel, and spectators looked for the brand of Cain. They
did not see it, although Senator Plumer had written:

"The high office of President is filled by an *infidel,* that of Vice-
President by a *murderer*."

Both sides had prepared carefully for the trial. Senator Beveridge, biographer of Marshall, was scandalized by the fact that the
House managers as prosecutors were conferring in advance with
Republican Senators who would be judges. Ambassador Bowers,
biographer of Jefferson, was outraged because counsel for the defense went into frequent huddles with Federalist Senators who
would be judges.

Randolph, who, everyone thought, had been completely exhausted by his effort to block the Yazoo frauds, was chief prosecutor. The panel of managers was completed by Representatives
Peter Early and George Campbell, good party men but dull speakers; Joseph Nicholson, who was believed by some to be slated for
Chase's place and who ended his career as a Federal district judge,
and Caesar Rodney, soon to be Attorney General.

Chase had employed more brilliant lawyers. His old friend,
Luther Martin, the shabby old toper who was generally believed
to be without a superior at the bar, drunk or sober, was supported
by a battery of younger orators. Hopkinson, the author of "Hail
Columbia," was one. Robert Goodloe Harper, a belligerent Federalist who had lost his seat in Congress in the Republican land-

slide two years before, was another. Former Attorney General Charles Lee and Philip Barton Key, whose brother was to make the name immortal with "The Star Spangled Banner," could be counted upon to do what lawyers might for their client, whose politics they warmly endorsed.

The impeachment had been started after Chase's charge to the Baltimore jury. But the House managers threw in seven other grounds for impeachment built around his conduct in the Callender and Fries trials and his attempt to start a Delaware grand jury on a witch hunt for alleged seditionists.

Randolph opened the case for the managers in his high voice and with an unusual restraint which impressed the audience. He was heard by the beauty and chivalry of Washington, packed into Burr's neat gallery and boxes, and by more interested spectators such as Chase's colleagues. Those "terrible" eyes sought the white-haired, red-faced defendant as he put the essence of the whole case:

"It appears to me that one great distinction remains yet to be taken—a distinction between a judge zealous to punish and repress crime generally, and a judge anxious only to enforce a particular law whereby he may recommend himself to power or to his party. It is this hideous feature of the respondent's judicial character on which I would fix your attention. We do not charge him with a general zeal in the discharge of his high office, but with an indecent zeal in particular cases for laws of doubtful and suspicious aspect. Through the whole tenor of his judicial conduct runs the spirit of party."

The managers called plenty of witnesses to prove their point. Unfortunately for them, they called witnesses who proved too much—that Chase had been sarcastic and discomfited lawyers by making the courtroom laugh at them, that his manners were bad, that he had lectured the Delaware grand jury tediously and kept members from their haying.

This sort of testimony weakened the proof that he had delivered a positively rabid partisan speech to the grand jury in Baltimore, that he had forced a prejudiced talesman to serve on Callender's jury, that he refused to admit the testimony of a witness who wanted to testify to the truth of part of Callender's defense only because the testimony did not relate to the whole of that defense, that he bullied witnesses and attorneys.

One of the first witnesses for the defense was the Chief Justice's brother, William, called to deny the story of a Richmond lawyer who had sworn that he heard Chase tell the United States Marshal to strike off the panel "any of those creatures or people called democrats." William made a good impression by saying that the lawyer had never been in Chase's chambers and that the judge had told him he wanted men of Callender's politics on the jury. The effect of this was reduced by Randolph's cross-examination. Were there, the shrill voice demanded, any Republicans on the jury? William was obliged to admit that there were none. On re-examination he was asked if there were none on the panel from which the jury had been drawn. William still said no, and Randolph, who had been present at the trial, disconcerted him by remembering the names of three—the one who was out of town, the one who had received no notice, and the one who had been excused on the plea of William's brother. It seemed that jury-packing had been proved, although perhaps not against Chase.

The next witness was more interesting, for it was the brother. Washington society in the boxes craned forward to get a better glimpse of the lanky figure, a worried look on the lean dark features, as the Chief Justice of the United States took the stand in defense of a colleague.

[4]

The brilliant defense counsel would have done better to leave him sitting among the spectators. Marshall made a better case for the managers than most of their own witnesses. His only point of consequence on direct testimony was that he had procured the dismissal of the lone Republican juror out of friendship for the man.

This clinched testimony that Chase had not ordered Republicans excluded from the jury. Marshall's direct testimony was the least of his ordeal. He had hardly finished before the figure of John Randolph uncoiled its length, and some very embarrassing questions were squeaked at the Chief Justice. Randolph was almost courtly as he asked Marshall to explain what the best practice might be in some of the circumstances which had arisen at the Callender trial, since he admitted having been present during part of it.

Marshall cautiously replied that the Richmond courtroom that day had witnessed scenes "which do not always appear at trials." Randolph pressed him politely about a Chase ruling that questions which the Callender lawyers wanted to ask one of their witnesses, John Taylor, be submitted in writing first.

"I have never known it requested," Marshall admitted, "that a question should be reduced to writing in the first instance in the whole course of my practice."

Driven further into a corner by insistence on hearing any precedent for excluding Taylor's testimony because it did not relate to every point in the indictment, he further admitted:

"I never did hear that objection made in court except in this particular case."

He testified to the fact that Chase stopped Callender's lawyers every time they tried to argue the validity of the Sedition Act, and he conceded that this was not usual practice. Marshall showed some talent at verbal fencing in avoiding comment on Chase's manner. In reply to one question, he said he should be asked what the Judge's conduct was, not what he thought of it. Pressed to say whether Chase had been "tyrannical, overbearing and oppressive," he replied that he would state only the facts and then went on to say how often Chase stopped the lawyers. He still managed to avoid describing his colleague's manner on the bench. The worst that Randolph could get him to admit was that it was considered "decorous" for a judge to hear counsel on such points as Callender's lawyers had wanted to raise.

As testimony, it was honest and damaging. There could be little doubt that Marshall disapproved of the way Chase had conducted the Callender trial. The effect of his words upon Chase's chances was shown by the reaction of two intense partisans. Randolph, in his closing speech, paid fulsome tribute to the Chief Justice's learning and experience, to the honest impartiality of this "able and excellent judge." That stressed the wickedness of Chase's conduct. But Senator Plumer, who was still a Federalist, could not forgive Marshall for failing to hurl thunderbolts of defiance at the prosecutors. "Too much caution—too much fear—too much cunning," mourned the Senator.

Men like Plumer were hardly appeased, although the Republicans found an additional cause for denouncing the Court, when in the midst of the trial Marshall composed an opinion which he knew would enrage Chase's prosecutors. It involved the bankruptcy act which he had helped to write, and under which his old friend, client, and partner, Robert Morris, had been released from debtor's prison.

Lawyers for the debtor, a man named Fisher, suggested that the bankruptcy act was unconstitutional since nowhere in the Constitution was there explicit authority to legislate on this subject. Specifically, they objected to the provision which made the United States a preferred creditor. Marshall in his opinion inserted a passage which foreshadowed a great deal of debate on the "implied powers" of which he was to be a notable exponent. It was contended on behalf of Fisher that only laws without which one of the specified powers of the Federal government could not be carried on were properly authorized. But Marshall made the Court's first bold assertion of broader scope in the Constitution when he said:

"It would produce endless difficulties if the opinion should be maintained that no law was authorized which was not indispensably necessary to give effect to a specified power. . . . Congress must possess the choice of means, and must be empowered to use any means which are in fact conducive to the exercise of a power granted by the Constitution."

This decision got a little less attention than it deserved, since the testimony in Chase's trial had now ended, and the final pleas by counsel were to be made. The arguments by orators on both sides consumed a solid week. The talents of the talking gladiators, especially defense counsel, were much admired, and their speeches widely reprinted. The interminable eloquence of the day, which gained applause from the number of different ways in which a speaker could say the same thing, held the listeners almost throughout. If he skimped on his words, he might be criticized even by his friends. Pickering, for example, wrote disapprovingly:

"Mr. Harper, I am told, will speak not more than three hours; but I much doubt the possibility of his compressing within that space all he will deem important on so copious a theme."

The real issue, however, could have been simply stated. The defense held that an impeachment could be logically maintained only if definite and indictable crimes and misdemeanors could be proved against the accused. The managers insisted that gross misconduct in office was amply sufficient, and demanded that the lives of citizens should not be entrusted to arbitrary judges.

The defense lawyers had the best of the oratory, for by the time he came to his final appearance, the most eloquent of the managers, Randolph, was sick and nervous and had lost his notes. (He reduced his remarks to two and a half hours.) The managers made better sense, although duller and if anything more verbose, but they clouded that sense in many contradictions and seemed to condemn Chase as much for his manners as for his misconduct. This had some effect on the voting, which finally began ceremoniously on March 1.

Each Senator was called upon in alphabetical order to rise and vote guilty or not guilty, the roll call being repeated for each article separately. Two-thirds of those voting were necessary to convict. Since there were thirty-four Senators, that meant that twenty-three must support the impeachment if it were to stand, and the Republicans had twenty-five. The suspense was almost exhausting, because the strongest article of impeachment, the one dealing with the Baltimore charge, had been left to the last. As the roll was called, it became evident that the decision was going to rest largely with three Republican Senators named Smith, one each from Vermont, New York, and Ohio. The managers needed every one of them to convict by the time the roll call got to "S." Every one of them said: "Not guilty," and the two-thirds vote failed; nineteen Senators had been for conviction, fifteen for acquittal.

The Supreme Court had come through the ordeal unscathed but thoroughly frightened. Never again would Chase bluster in the old manner on circuit. Justices of the Supreme Court thereafter refrained from open electioneering. The whole tone of the Federal judiciary became instantly more in keeping with popular ideals of an impartial bench. But something else had happened that was more apparent to future historians than to the men who then saw Thomas Jefferson and his party as the political victors on an ascending scale of popularity. Morison and Commager, in the cool light that a century and a quarter of retrospect gives to historical events, thought that Chase's conviction would have been followed by a clean sweep of the Court's majority.

"But," they added, "this trial proved to be the high-water mark of 'Jacobinism.' Federalism and conservatism rallied under the captaincy of Chief Justice Marshall, and from behind the Supreme Court barricade developed a subtle offensive of ideas—the supremacy of the nation and the sanctity of property—that in due time would leave little of Jeffersonian democracy but a memory and a tradition."

XIV

☆　☆　☆

Building the Barricade

T HE BARRICADE of the Supreme Court was not the only
obstacle to the progress of Jeffersonian democracy. It was
not even the chief obstacle. It served the best purpose of
most barricades, however, which is to close a gap between bigger
and more impassable barriers than itself. It was like a block thrown
across a city street between massive buildings, or across a pass
through rugged mountains.

The two great bulwarks flanking the Supreme Court barricade
were the repercussions of a world war on one side and on the other
those considerable masses of people for whom Jefferson's philosophy made no provision. War is not a diet on which democracy
can thrive, and the ever-widening circles of the Napoleonic conflict sucked the new American republic into the maelstrom. Jeffersonian democracy was not rooted widely enough or deeply
enough among all the people to resist the suction.

Jefferson held about the same opinion of city workers that
Hamilton held of farmers. The sage of Monticello regarded his
great rival as a conscienceless monarchist and aristocrat because he
could not see the civic virtues which were hidden behind the

rugged simplicity of tillers of the soil. Jefferson was one of those idealists who attached the adjective "honest" almost exclusively to the noun "husbandman." Therefore, in his triumphant party of the people, there was little place for the non-agricultural worker. Agrarianism, however, was to prove an insufficient basis for a genuine democracy. The simple organizational standards of rural communities, leading to ideas of local and State supremacy over national administration, were inadequate for a nation entering upon the industrial revolution.

Jefferson's opponents, men like Marshall, did not realize (or would not admit) that the sympathy which had once existed between the French revolutionists and American "Jacobins" had long since been dissipated by events. When Jeffersonian democracy reached its high-water mark during the Chase trial, a one-time French revolutionary general had been an emperor for nearly three months. The ideas which his troops and traders were spreading over a large part of Europe might seem radical to Hapsburgs in Austria, Hohenzollerns and Wittelsbachs in Germany, Bourbons in Spain, and even Tories in England, but they were intolerably imperialist and aggressive for a Jeffersonian.

The change in France and the sobering effects of power combined to eradicate the enthusiasm for the French cause which had plagued the administrations of Washington and Adams. The fine frenzy on behalf of a people fighting for freedom against despots could not be transferred to a despot—even a despot in a simple gray riding coat professing to rule in the name of the people. A real spirit of neutrality pervaded the ranks of the majority party, but Federalists in New England were less impartial, seeing in a British victory the possibility of an orderly and prosperous trade. Many of them were getting rich out of the war, and were inclined to the side whose purchases and command of the sea made prosperity possible. Impressment of seamen, interference with ships, even seizure of cargoes were the price to be paid for wealth.

With the optimism of partisanship, some of these renegade Hamiltonians supposed that they could carry the Chief Justice along with them. Their chief desire was to recover control of the government—save the country from the unfit hands of the people, they put it to themselves. They were encouraged to hope for Supreme Court approval partly because five members were Federalists, but also because the tribunal had handed down a decision which rash party members took as a sign that the Court would be willing to curb Jefferson's authority. The case had been this:

A merchant whose trade had been interfered with by a collector of the port during the days of XYZ excitement demanded damages, and the officer pleaded the instructions of President Adams. It was suggested that the orderly processes of administration would be impossible if every subordinate was held accountable for instructions from above. On the other hand, the notion that officials are mere machines who break or obey the law impartially on command was not tenable either.

"I confess," said Marshall in commenting on this dilemma, "the first bias of my mind was very strong in favor of the opinion that, though the instructions of the Executive could not give a right, they might yet excuse from damages."

The more he thought about the results, however, the less he liked the idea. Where did the citizen go for redress? So Marshall, deciding in the end for the merchant and setting a precedent for the trials of Hitler's agents 140 years later, used a sentence which is not heard very often from the Supreme Court.

"I have been convinced that I was mistaken," he said.

It was a pity he could not take the same objective view of his literary efforts. He had brought with him to Washington in 1805 the manuscript of the fourth volume of Washington's biography. In the midst of the Yazoo debate, the Chase impeachment, and Jefferson's second inauguration, he scribbled and corrected, and after the trial forwarded to Wayne through young Hopkinson a great bulky untidy document which carried his hero through the war and retirement from the army. He had left only a single volume for Washington's life at Mount Vernon after the war, his share in calling the Constitutional Convention, his presidency of

that body, his two terms as President, his acceptance of the command of the army in the crisis with France. Marshall also was allowing himself a year to write the section of the biography which
contemporaries would find most exciting. He would have to cover
a great deal of ground, and the fact that, in spite of experience with
the first four volumes, he thought the fifth could be done well in a
year was not a hopeful sign.

[2]

The session of 1805 had been an unusually busy one. The Chief
Justice was eager to get home where on January 13 his tenth and
last child, Edward Carrington Marshall, had been born. He was
much more concerned with his family, the prospect of finishing
the Washington biography and the duties of his farms and circuit
riding than with the state of the world in general or politics in
particular. But the combination of world and national politics was
preparing some work for him.

Nearest at hand was Aaron Burr, revolving in his handsome
head improbable but tenaciously held schemes for soaring from
the ashes of his defeats to new heights of glory and renown. He
was not yet fifty years old, and his health and ambition were as
keen as ever.

Like thousands of his compatriots, he looked west, and looked
beyond the confines of his own country to the vast Spanish provinces, temptingly weak, temptingly rich. Furthermore, Spaniards
were holding up the trade of Americans, and it was generally believed that war would result. Burr saw an opportunity there, and
it occurred to him that his future might be financed by the British
Government. He knew that the British Minister, Anthony Merry,
had as his chief diplomatic aim the division of the Union. Burr
knew that Merry had been consulted in secessionist plots by New
Englanders. On the basis of this knowledge, therefore, the retiring Vice President proposed that British gold be supplied to him
so that he could split dissatisfied Westerners off from the United
States and erect a new country in the Southwest.

Historians have been unable to agree as to just how serious Burr was when he indulged in this secessionist talk, or in a similar offer which he made later to the Spanish Minister. The bulk of the evidence points to the conclusion that he was seeking to get them to finance his schemes by a sheer swindle, but in any case his dealings with the envoys remained a profound secret to all his contemporaries. Nearly everything he did indicates that his real aim was to emulate Napoleon—an Emperor Aaron placing the crown of Mexico upon the head of his beloved daughter, Theodosia.

In the spring of 1805 he went West. He won a very motley crew of adherents. Perhaps the most interesting was an Irish intellectual and visionary named Harman Blennerhassett, who had settled on an island in the Ohio River. Blennerhassett was wealthy, and had built a tasteful mansion, well-furnished with the best European importations.

Senator John Smith of Ohio and Jonathan Dayton, former Federalist Speaker of the House and a big speculator in Western lands, were also sympathetic. In Kentucky both Senators, John Adair and John Brown, were friends from the days of Burr's Vice Presidency. In Tennessee the commander of the militia, Andrew Jackson, put on a big parade for the visitor. As a duellist of some renown, Jackson was angered by the misfortunes which the killing of Hamilton had brought upon his visitor.

But the key figure in Burr's plan was General James Wilkinson, highest ranking officer in the American Army, who was in command at New Orleans. A unique combination of treachery and incompetence, Wilkinson was distrusted by many of his contemporaries, but not until the Spanish archives were captured in Havana in 1898 was it known that the ranking General of the army had been a paid spy of Spain for nearly twenty years at the time he joined Burr.

That summer of 1805 followers of national and international events such as Marshall began to hear of Burr's doings in connection with a rather jingoistic campaign for war with Spain. The papers which Marshall read quoted orators who talked of "insults beyond human endurance" and hoped for "an occasion that may offer for conferring on our oppressed Spanish brethren in Mexico those inestimable blessings of freedom which we ourselves enjoy."

[3]

Arriving in Washington for the 1806 term of the Supreme Court, Marshall found the conversation turning constantly to the probability of war. Jefferson in his annual message had declared that unless Spanish soldiers stopped entering American territory, unless Spanish officials stopped interfering with American trade, the American people would fight. Randolph even had introduced a resolution to declare that a state of hostilities existed.

The Chief Justice was an interested spectator of the events of the session, but he was not yet involved. However, he was hearing rumors about Burr, for his brother-in-law Daviess, United States Attorney for Kentucky, was busily circulating some of them. Daviess wrote to Jefferson that the former Vice President was engaged in dangerous enterprises.

Of more concern to Marshall at the time was a shift from Spain to England as a target for hostile American remarks. During his stay in Washington for the 1806 term, he heard some of the Congressional debates on measures to combat the British action in barring neutral commerce from Europe. British rules were so vigorously enforced that British warships patrolled outside New York harbor, stopping American ships and seizing American seamen. The Chief Justice was relieved when in March, 1806, the retaliation decided upon proved to be no worse than a Non-Importation Act forbidding the admission of certain British goods.

This outburst of anger against Britain and Jefferson's peaceful negotiations with Spain behind the cloak of his belligerent message had ended the danger of war on the western frontier. But Burr did not know this when he set out for the West on a road infinitely more ruinous than that which had taken him to Weehawken two years earlier to meet Hamilton.

XV

☆　☆　☆

The Meaning of Treason

IF MARSHALL read the new paper which his brothers-in-law, Daviess and Humphrey Marshall, had established in Kentucky under the name of *Western World*, he saw in its columns the first public intimation that Burr might be a traitor. Daviess was tired of waiting for Jefferson to act on his reports that the "murderer" of Hamilton was plotting disunion. Burr's associate, Blennerhassett, had written some newspaper articles in favor of secession, and *Western World*'s editors put this and a few rumors together to make a sensational story.

Meanwhile Wilkinson had decided that he could be at once loyal to his government and his Spanish employers by betraying Burr. Early in October the General received from Samuel Swartwout of New York, a protégé of Burr, a glowing letter in which (after he had decoded it) Wilkinson could read that the "gods invite us to glory and fortune." Swartwout had brought the ciphered letter overland; soon a copy entrusted to Dr. Erich Bollman arrived by sea. Bollman was something of a hero to Americans, for he had led a remarkable adventure designed to free the Marquis de Lafayette from prison. The New World had rung with accounts of his daring and love of liberty.

Wilkinson brooded over his situation for two weeks, and then on October 21 sent what he said was a true summary of Burr's plans to Jefferson along with a highly colored version of the peril in which New Orleans stood and his own brave determination to defend it to the death. Slightly different information coupled with the same assurances of fidelity went by another messenger to the Spanish Viceroy in Mexico. Later Wilkinson actually billed the United States government for the expenses of this second courier's trip.

Jefferson could hardly have doubted the fidelity of the Western country to the Union. But he had good reason to fear that the hot-headed frontiersmen, who had been crying out against the iniquity of Spain, might start a war on their own initiative. With a man of Burr's superb organizing abilities to lead them, they might upset the whole precarious structure of peace between Spaniards and Americans.

The Cabinet was called into session promptly on receipt of Wilkinson's letter. Without being too greatly deceived by the protestations of the General, the Secretaries took a serious view of Burr's designs. On November 27, Jefferson issued a proclamation warning the country that unnamed individuals were engaged in a conspiracy against Spain. The President called upon them to desist and directed loyal persons to seize upon the plotters and their supplies.

A few days later the Proclamation reached Blennerhassett's neighbors. By this time a couple of dozen young men had gathered at the island, and the local militia decided that they were an army. Much was later made of the fact that these men were armed. It would have been far more surprising if they were not. The West was not the sort of country in which firearms were lightly put aside, and a few years later General Jackson remarked in one of his picturesque phrases that he never in his life had seen a Kentuckian without a rifle, a bottle of whisky, and a slab of tobacco.

Blennerhassett and his group were quite as badly frightened as the militia. They slipped down river in the night, leaving the mansion to be plundered next day by the militiamen, who meanwhile had been strengthened by a night of drinking and were further refreshed by the admirable contents of Blennerhassett's cellar.

In Washington, Jefferson's annual message to Congress contained a paragraph about the turmoil in the West. The President informed his audience, which seems to have included the Chief Justice, that a conspiracy to organize a military expedition against Spain had been discovered. There was no hint of suspicion that plots against the United States were involved.

In the West, however, a military expedition against Spain would seem no very heinous offense. Wilkinson knew this quite well, so he proceeded to conjure up a horrid plot against New Orleans. To give it color, he virtually established martial law, defied the courts, warned the citizens of the imminent arrival of a horde of banditti bent on capturing the city, and began to fling "dangerous" men into jail. Most of them were dangerous only to Wilkinson.

Among them were Swartwout, Bollman, and General Adair. The first two were carried aboard a warship to be delivered to the authorities in Washington; the third followed a little later. They were not taken before the courts, and when writs of habeas corpus were sworn out, the General retorted that he was acting as commander of the army, and anyway the men were on their way to justice. With them went what Wilkinson swore was an exact translation of Burr's cipher letter.

The object of all this hysteria meanwhile was floating serenely down the Mississippi. But in Mississippi Territory, the Acting Governor, Cowles Mead, called out the militia and stopped him. Mead later wrote that "this mighty alarm, with all its exaggeration, has eventuated in nine boats and one hundred men, and the major part of these boys or young men just from school."

That same week the shrill voice of John Randolph was heard

in the House of Representatives demanding to know details of the incidents which had inspired the President's message. Jefferson's answer was delivered on January 22, 1807. It was a complete denunciation of Aaron Burr as a traitor who had plotted to divide his country. The President stated flatly that there was no question of the culprit's guilt. He transmitted with this statement part of the Wilkinson correspondence, including the cipher letter from Burr.

While the country was digesting this sensation, Swartwout and Bollman were brought to the capital and confined in the marine barracks. Next day Jefferson's Senate leader, Giles of Virginia, introduced a resolution to suspend the writ of habeas corpus in this great emergency, the purpose obviously being to keep the two dangerous criminals in prison pending trial, and the measure was passed under suspension of the rules with one dissenting vote.

The reaction to this was sudden and explosive. Congressmen still remembered and perhaps exaggerated the part which the suspension of writs of habeas corpus had played in colonial complaints against England. The Senate had asked the House to consider the bill secretly and pass it promptly. By a vote of 123 to 3, the House repudiated the request for secrecy, and after a debate in which personal liberty was somewhat pointedly brought to the attention of Senators, the suspension of habeas corpus was beaten by the resounding vote of 113 to 19. The Burr conspiracy was, therefore, left to the courts.

[2]

The case first came before John Marshall and his colleagues early in February, 1807. There was a new member at this term, Brockholst Livingston of New York, a vigorous New Yorker of nearly fifty—vigorous in mind and body—who turned out to be no greater a prop for Jeffersonian views than Johnson. Justice Paterson had died in the previous September, and the Livingstons were one of the most powerful families in New York. They also produced a good many judges, and the new appointee was one of the most distinguished.

Almost his first case was an appeal by Swartwout and Bollman from a ruling of the District of Columbia court which had decided by two to one that the prisoners should be held without bail until their trial. At the same time Burr himself was facing the grand jury in Mississippi. That body, unwilling to inconvenience any gentleman because of violating a law forbidding filibustering against Spain, refused to indict Burr. In fact, the jurors went out of their way to declare that he had not given "just alarm or in-quietude to the good people of this Territory," that the militia should not have been called out, that Wilkinson's activities in far-away New Orleans were "destructive of personal liberty."

The Judge, however, was a more suspicious man than the jurors, and he refused to release the bonds given for Burr's appearance. At the same time news reached the Territory that Wilkinson was sending out men to seize Burr and deliver him to New Orleans. The little filibusterer's friends advised him to get away while he could. One of them provided his best horse, and with the vision of glory gone glimmering, Burr headed eastward into the forest. He was soon recognized, captured and brought under guard through wilderness trails and backwoods villages to stand his trial. His flight and march back to civilization took several weeks, and mean-while the details of his supposed conspiracy were spread from one end of the country to the other.

In Washington, Marshall and his colleagues had to take a more judicial look at the evidence than was necessary for the letter writers, the editors, the diarists and even the Congress. The first serious charge of treason levelled against a man of note had been made by the President of the United States. The Executive had declared solemnly that the state was in danger. Two of the chief culprit's confidential agents were in custody. An outlying territory of the country was under martial law.

In these circumstances, the Supreme Court would have its first chance to interpret what the drafters of the Constitution had meant when they so carefully defined treason. Danger to the state, fear of insurrection had been used against Englishmen for generations as an excuse to get rid of opponents of those in power. The loose interpretation which English judges in the past had given to the word "treason" had expanded it to include almost anything which a ruthless ruler or a ruthless judge did not like. So the Constitution made a singularly clear definition.

"Treason," it said in the third section of the article creating the judiciary, "against the United States shall consist only in levying war against them, or in adhering to their enemies, giving them aid and comfort. No person shall be convicted of treason unless on the testimony of two witnesses to the same overt act, or on confession in open court."

The country was now to learn whether this attempt to protect the citizen, even the unpopular and dangerous citizen, from mass hysteria and the enmity of the government could be made to stand up in practice. Interest in the case was so keen that in Washington it rivalled women's fashions in gossip and the newspapers. The empire gown had been introduced to society, supposedly by Mrs. Jerome Bonaparte, whose husband had been snatched from her by his angry brother and made King of Westphalia. The style, "nudity being all the rage," was called by some "astonishingly betwitching," but Mrs. Josiah Quincy of Boston exclaimed, "What a state of manners and morals!"

Some of these distractions were seen and admired in court that February day when Marshall read the opinion of the majority of the court—Johnson dissented and spoke for Chase as well, who was absent through illness—that Swartwout and Bollman should be discharged for lack of proof of treason within the meaning of the constitutional definition. The evidence was presented in a good deal less time than the arguments, for it was not very voluminous.

The chief item, besides the letters and affidavit from Wilkinson, was a sworn statement by General William Eaton, who for the last eighteen months had been memorializing the government for payments he had incurred in North Africa. Eaton had performed one of the most notable of military exploits—a march from Egypt along a coast to be made famous in a later war by Rommel and the British Eighth Army to the capture of Derna. It had been a remarkable military feat, and Eaton had been wildly greeted as a hero on his return. However, his claims had not been paid.

Suddenly one of his long letters detailing his expenses and his services inspired action. Early in February he had written again to Jefferson, who promptly saw to it that a bill to settle Eaton's claim was introduced into the House. Perhaps it was only a coincidence that three days later Eaton's detailed affidavit on Burr's perfidy was signed. His story was this:

Nearly a year before, he had seen Burr at the former Vice President's lodgings in Washington, and had been approached to accept a command in his expedition. Burr had outlined, besides the scheme for his Mexican venture, a plan to overthrow the government of the United States. With the aid of dissatisfied naval officers such as Commodores Truxtun and Stephen Decatur, father of a more famous naval man, he was sure that he could assassinate the President, seize the government and expel Congress. It was a wild plan, and Eaton was deeply shocked. He went to Jefferson and urged him to appoint Burr to some foreign mission to get him out of the way. Otherwise, Eaton warned, there would be trouble on the Mississippi.

Eaton never did explain to anyone's satisfaction why he merely tried to get Burr a job instead of telling the President of his real danger. This was all the stranger since he found Jefferson did not become in the least alarmed by the hint of trouble in the West. The General, failing to get a post for Burr, refrained from further disclosures and went back to his efforts to get paid—or so he said.

When Marshall came to this deposition in his opinion, he did not need to waste much time on it. Whatever it might prove about Burr, it was not specific as to Bollman and Swartwout. They could be connected with it only through Wilkinson's testimony that the whole Burr plan was treasonable. Therefore, the Supreme Court had to look at Wilkinson's own words and his version of Burr's letter.

But first, the Chief Justice pointed out, there was the plain statement of the Constitution that treason consisted in levying war. It did not consist in conspiring to levy war. If the country wanted to make this a crime, it would have to pass a special law to that effect. But it could not call the conspiracy treason. The Constitution took care of that because its framers thought it safer to define treason carefully and allow other crimes to be covered by laws, but not have other crimes twisted into treason "under the influence of those passions which the occasion seldom fails to excite."

All Wilkinson's correspondence seemed to prove, the Court held, that Mexico was the object of the expedition. This, too, might be a crime, but it was not treason. The same was true of the reference to coming to New Orleans. This sounded to the Court as if it might be a conspiracy to rob, if proved. If the government wished to prove treason, the Court would tell them what levying war meant.

"There must be," said Marshall, "an actual assemblage of men for the purpose of executing a treasonable design."

No evidence of any such gathering was before the court. Of course, the judges did not mean to infer that only men actually in arms at the place where war was to be levied could be guilty. A ring leader at a distance could be equally traitorous. Bollman and Swartwout, furthermore, had certainly not committed any crime in the District of Columbia. The Supreme Court was unanimous on this point, and lashed out at Wilkinson's high-handed action in sending civilians under military arrest in time of peace halfway across the country when there were perfectly competent courts in the same city to try them. "Extremely dangerous" was the way they described the theory, acted upon by Wilkinson, that a commanding general might send anyone anywhere to be tried for any offense he pleased.

[3]

Jefferson himself took the verdict calmly; he was gunning for Burr, and was not alarmed by the release of underlings. But as usual some of his friends were more fanatic. There was revival of impeachment talk, and only slightly more sober legislators suggested that the Supreme Court be deprived of jurisdiction over all criminal cases.

There was small chance of that, however, and if it could have been done, it would not have saved Marshall from continuing his association with the Burr trial. For as a circuit judge, he was to preside with District Judge Griffin over the legal battle to which the Bollman-Swartwout case had been a preliminary skirmish. Burr was being brought to Richmond and Jefferson was spending the public money, of which he was usually very careful, like water to gather evidence which would convict.

Critics have commented on the almost ferocious zeal with which the President pursued his fallen rival. It was not malice, however, which prompted Jefferson in the midst of constantly more dangerous international negotiations to spend hours directing the prosecution. He was convinced that Burr was guilty, and he had inherited Hamilton's fear of the dapper little genius's abilities. Both Hamilton and Jefferson were accustomed to trust their intuitions, and they had very little more than that to go on in reaching their conclusion that Burr was a menace to society.

Marshall, returning to Richmond at the end of March, found that the prisoner was waiting for him, still under military guard. Two mitigating circumstances cheered the judge as he faced what was plainly going to be a long and arduous trial—the hearings and arguments and cross-examinations lasted for seven months altogether. One was that he could live at home. The other was that the final volume of the Washington biography was off his mind and safely shipped to Wayne in Philadelphia. He had kept almost to his schedule, but the rush showed in the writing.

On March 30, the case opened calmly and quietly in a little

room at the Eagle Tavern without any spectators. George Hay, United States District Attorney, wanted an audience but yielded when he was promised that larger quarters would be sought if any argument arose. Actually the only business was a presentation of the record, a little testimony from Burr's captors and a motion that the prisoner be committed to prison to await trial for treason as well as on a misdemeanor charge. Marshall set bail at $5,000 until next day when this interesting proposition could be argued.

[4]

The trial was held in the big hall of the House of Delegates in order to accommodate the spectators. No other in the history of the country has produced so much contemporary and historical excitement, not even the impeachment of a President or the conviction of the goriest murderer. Even after more than a hundred years the biographers of Marshall and Jefferson were keeping green the bitterness of those legal wrangles of 1807.

Jefferson is still accused of a personal and mean persecution of a political rival. He wrote to Governor Claiborne in New Orleans that the opposition "will try to make something of the infringement of liberty by the military arrest and deportation of citizens, but if it does not go beyond such offenders as Swartwout, Bollman, Burr, Blennerhassett, Tyler [one of the men with Blennerhassett] etc., they will be supported by public approbation." This has been taken to mean that Jefferson for his own purposes was willing to condone tyranny if it had public approbation. That is reading a good deal into a single sentence.

On the other side, Marshall is accused of the most avid political partisanship. It is true that Federalists tended to side with the man Jefferson hated—it would have been a miracle of politics if they had not—and Burr's counsel consisted of eminent Federalist lawyers. The evidence against Marshall, however, is about like that against Jefferson.

The fact that his speech was mild and that he showed a monumental patience in listening to counsel and to witnesses month

after month was cited as evidence of fear and shame at the part he
was playing. When one side accused him of allowing the other to
say unkind things about the President, he refrained from argument, and because he refrained was said to cringe. When in response to demands of Burr's counsel, he issued a subpoena to the
President of the United States to appear in court with orders
which, Burr said, would show the government tried to murder
him, Marshall was charged with *lèse-majesté*. Jefferson very
properly refused to attend, but he did supply the papers, and they
did not prove Burr's point.

In the course of his first of many written opinions in the case,
Marshall quoted Blackstone on discharging prisoners for lack of
evidence before trial, and added that this was not enough to support an argument that "the hand of malignity may grasp any individual against whom its hate may be directed." Both Senator
Beveridge and Ambassador Bowers think Marshall meant Jefferson when he said "the hand of malignity." The Senator approves;
the Ambassador does not. The Chief Justice himself, during the
noon intermission that day, told reporters he did not mean to
reflect upon the government at all. And an impartial reading of
his words would seem to suggest that "Wilkinson" should be substituted for "hand of malignity" if a name must be put to them.

But the crowning proof of Marshall's partisanship is seen in an
incident which happened outside the courtroom. On that first
day, the government had no more evidence against Burr than it
had produced against Swartwout and Bollman, so Marshall refused to hold him without bail on a charge of treason. He agreed
to "high misdemeanor" and fixed the prisoner's bond at the then
large figure of $10,000. During the three weeks that Burr was at
liberty on this ruling, one of Marshall's old friends and legal
colleagues, John Wickham, who was one of the distinguished
battery of defense counsel, gave a dinner party. He invited his
client, too, and Richmond was treated to the horrid spectacle of a
judge and an accused man he was to try sitting at the same board.
A good deal of ingenuity has been wasted on this indiscretion (if

it was one) with much research going into the question of whether Marshall knew when he entered Wickham's home that Burr was to be there. Whether he did or not, a distinguished historian of Marshall's career, Edward S. Corwin, calls it the darkest blot on the Chief Justice's judicial record.

When posterity becomes as heated as that over the trial and its implications, one may perhaps imagine the excitement that gripped the little city of Richmond in 1807. Lawyers and the curious crowded the accommodations as much as on racing day or during the constitutional ratification convention. Theodosia came to comfort her father and charm his friends. Witnesses were objects of curiosity and interest. Among them was Eaton, swaggering about in Oriental garb and spending freely the money which a grateful government had awarded him within a month of his affidavit against Burr. Wilkinson turned up late, and earned some contempt by swallowing an insult from young Swartwout. Andrew Jackson walked the streets, tall and spare and assertive. The taverns did a tremendous business, and high stakes were wagered on the outcome of the trial—Eaton lost a good deal of his government money that way. Washington Irving, then twenty-four, had been sent as a reporter by Burr's New York friends, and his lively pen recorded a part of the colorful scene. As on every public occasion in the Virginia capital, the roughly clad men of the mountains and woods mingled with the be-ruffled gentlemen of the city and Tidewater, while tobacco juice was liberally sprinkled over the streets, the taverns, and the court-room itself.

[5]

When court convened on May 22 for the purpose of having a grand jury consider whether or not to indict Burr, a good many of the spectators were curious citizens come to Richmond from miles away as to a fair. They so overtaxed the little city's public and private accommodations that hundreds were living in tents and covered wagons on the outskirts. There was a tremendous press at the doors. Winfield Scott was one of the tallest, strongest young men in Virginia. But he had some difficulty forcing his way into the hall. He was especially struck, as he looked over the sea of heads, by the defendant and the judge. Burr was "as composed, as immovable as one of Canova's living marbles." Marshall seemed to be "the master spirit of the scene."

Scott and the rest of the audience were privileged to listen to one of the great legal and political trials of the century, with an immense array of talent on both sides—but most of it employed for Burr.

The little man's counsel was headed in popular esteem by Edmund Randolph, moving into old age now but still full of dignity and the ability to awe most Virginians. Luther Martin was on his way to take up the cudgels for a friend. Wickham, to whom Marshall had turned over his practice when he went to France, was joined by two younger lawyers, Benjamin Botts and John Baker, both rising legal lights of the State.

Hay, purposeful and industrious if not brilliant, something like his father-in-law, Monroe, was the chief prosecutor. The government had hired as his aides William Wirt, a great orator and legal luminary who was to set the country's record for tenure in the Attorney General's office with a twelve-year span, and Alexander MacRae, a man who reinforced much learning in the law with a bludgeon of invective in debate.

All of these men enjoyed the forum of a crowded courtroom. All of them were eager political partisans.

The first skirmish was an attempt by Burr to get rid of two inveterate political enemies on the grand jury—Giles and W. C. Nicholas, one of the leading Jeffersonians in the State. Both agreed to withdraw, and John Randolph and Dr. William Foushee, whom Marshall had defeated for a seat in the Virginia Constitutional Convention twenty years before, were chosen to fill the vacant places. Burr won another round when Marshall appointed Randolph as foreman, for by this time anyone who was an enemy of Jefferson could be a friend to Randolph.

The second skirmish was a plea by the prosecution that the court commit Burr to prison on a charge of treason before the grand jury acted. Wilkinson, the government's star witness, was on his way to Richmond, and the district attorney professed to be afraid that the defendant would run away before the General arrived. After a deal of argument designed more for public consumption than the enlightenment of the court, Marshall agreed, and Burr furnished more bail.

After the court and the grand jury had been waiting a couple of weeks for Wilkinson, Burr himself made a motion. He wanted a subpoena served on the President commanding him to produce the papers mentioned in the message to Congress. The ensuing argument provided a great deal of the pyrotechnical language which the public of that day found stimulating reading. Burr's lawyers, led by the long-winded and abusive Martin, hoped that the papers would show that Jefferson had ordered their client killed out of hand. They spent a great deal of time insisting that a President was as amenable to court orders as any other citizen. The prosecution reached heights of frenzy in repudiating the notion that the Chief Executive should be made to trot back and forth with papers for any court.

After days of this sort of thing, Marshall ruled quite sensibly that if the government had papers which a defendant believed essential to his defense, the court could not deny him the order that they be produced. The Executive must be the judge of whether public safety permitted compliance. Therefore he issued the subpoena to Thomas Jefferson. The President wrote an opinion far calmer than that of the prosecutors. He would not come to Richmond—he could not admit the right of a co-ordinate branch of the government to hale him there—but the papers were supplied. They did not prove the bloodthirsty spirit which Burr had hoped.

Meanwhile, on June 13, the tardy Wilkinson arrived. He had expected to find himself a hero. He protested quite indignantly that there were men who thought him a cheat and a liar. He confirmed their opinion after he had spent four days on the stand relating his story. The slim young officer of the Revolution had grown fat and now tried to retrieve his personal appearance through the gaudiness of his uniform. But he was sweating and ill at ease before the grand jury got through with him—it had so little belief in the honesty of the army's ranking General that he himself escaped an indictment by the narrow margin of two votes.

He was forced to admit that in sending Burr's cipher letter to Jefferson he had omitted the first sentence, which showed that it was in answer to a letter of his. He admitted, too, that he had erased certain words and had written in others. After listening to him for a couple of days, Andrew Jackson wrote to a friend that the affair seemed to him "a political persecution." The uncharitable John Randolph told a Congressional colleague:

"Wilkinson is the only man I ever saw who was from the bark to the very core a villain."

Eaton provided the next most picturesque evidence, holding to his story of the affidavit. A sergeant of the army who had joined the expedition swore that Burr had been sinking arms in the river after he learned of Wilkinson's betrayal. The soldier also said he had been asked to get some of his comrades to desert to join the expedition. Others testified to Burr's intimations that he had intended to divide the Union. Curiously enough these intimations seemed to have been given only to strangers; none of the men he had ever met before remembered such words. It was even more curious that during the intervals of the trial, gentlemen were arguing with each other quite openly as to the propriety of secession. The Chief Justice himself took part in at least one such friendly discussion, upholding the nationalist theory. But no one supposed from this conversation that his verbal antagonists were guilty of treason. A later generation and a war would be needed to reach that conclusion.

Other witnesses, who knew the accused man somewhat better than Eaton or the sergeant, testified that Burr had tried to get them to join him but had mentioned nothing except an expedition to Mexico or, failing that, the settlement of his lands on the Washita. Commodore Thomas Truxtun and Commodore Stephen Decatur both offered this testimony. Forty-three other witnesses told their versions of the expedition, and on June 24 the grand jury indicted Burr and Blennerhassett for both treason and misdemeanor.

Throughout the arguments, Marshall had been at some pains to keep the legal definition of treason before the grand jury. This body therefore selected as the actual act of war the gathering on December 13, 1806, at Blennerhassett's island in the Ohio (which was part of Wood County, Virginia). The occasion was that on which the militia had sought to capture the expedition and actually had plundered Blennerhassett's home. The misdemeanor charged was that at the same time and place, the two defendants had launched a military force against a country friendly to the United States, to wit Spain.

Aaron Burr slept in the Richmond jail that night, but two days later Marshall permitted him to be moved, when court was not in session, to Luther Martin's house where he was kept in a barred and guarded but comfortable room. However, Burr was not the sole center of attraction any longer. New exciting discussions were going the rounds of the taverns and the drawing rooms of Richmond.

[6]

On June 25, the day after the indictment, the little city heard that three days before, while everyone who could crowd into the House of Delegates was listening to Wilkinson, the frigate *Chesapeake*, Commodore James Barron in command, had been overhauled by a British warship, the *Leopard*, which was patrolling off Norfolk. The English captain demanded that the American submit to a search for British deserters. Barron indignantly refused, whereupon the *Leopard* opened fire without further warning. The *Chesapeake* was not fitted to resist, and after three men were killed and eighteen wounded, Barron surrendered. The Eng-

lish took off three men who were native Americans and one British deserter before they permitted the *Chesapeake* to make her
way back to Norfolk.

Richmond was not the only city in the United States that went
wild with fury. (That day Napoleon and Czar Alexander of Russia
signed the Peace of Tilsit which put the two Emperors in a very
uneasy alliance against England and stiffened London's determination to yield no advantage at sea.) As far north as New England the cry of rage against British insolence and brutality swept
the land. It was extremely faint beyond New York. The Federalists, pro-English through antipathy to France and clinging to their
trading interests, were in no mood to resent any insults which did
not come from Republicans or Frenchmen. Jefferson was writing
to all his friends abroad a sort of form letter in which this passage
to du Pont is typical:

"Never since the battle of Lexington have I seen this country
in such a state of exasperation as at present, and even that did not
produce such unanimity."

However, Jefferson would not let the *Chesapeake* incident distract him from directing a good deal of the strategy of the Burr
prosecution—he had an extra mail inaugurated between Richmond and Washington so he could keep in closer touch. In the
same letter to du Pont, he added:

"Burr's conspiracy has been one of the most flagitious of which
history will ever furnish an example."

Jefferson went into great detail with Hay as to how the case
should be conducted. He questioned whether the insulting Martin
should not be arrested "as *particeps criminis* with Burr" because
of a rumor from Baltimore that the lawyer, this "unprincipled &
impudent federal bull-dog," had known all about the conspiracy
for months. He wrote to the Governor of South Carolina asking
for the arrest of Alston, Burr's son-in-law, because he had heard
that a man named Horan had heard from one Span that a Mr.

Butler had been told that Alston knew of Burr's enterprise. The President advised the District Attorney on precedents, and went into an extensive harangue against *Marbury* vs. *Madison*, which had been cited in the course of argument.

"I think it material to stop at the threshold the citing that case as authority," he protested, "and to have it denied to be law."

While he was urging Hay to be belligerent in the Richmond courtroom, he was not tempted to transfer his anger to the field of diplomacy. Jefferson was determined to give England a chance to apologize, to make such restitution as was possible, to disavow the policy of impressment. Instructions to this effect were sent by one of the government's fastest ships to Monroe in London. The rage of citizens could be expended meanwhile in building harbor defenses and closing American ports to British vessels. Then Jefferson called Congress to meet in special session in October. He was blamed for the delay, but he wanted to give his negotiations a chance to show some progress.

He had higher hopes of this than he had of convicting Burr. The grand jury proceedings had not been encouraging. He kept hearing from Hay that the prisoner was popular with certain sections of society—one section was represented by Andrew Jackson, who made street corner speeches denouncing Wilkinson and Jefferson and in praise of Burr. The President also heard that the court was most unfriendly, and to du Pont he wrote:

"Although there is not a man in the United States who is not satisfied of the depth of his guilt, such are the jealous provisions of our laws in favor of the accused that I question if he can be convicted."

In Richmond at least, there were a good many men who by no means shared Jefferson's certainty of Burr's guilt. Jackson had won some converts. Burr's own calm dignity had won others. The not very convincing stories of the prosecution witnesses won still more, especially as in perspective the armed might of the prisoner had seemed ridiculously inadequate to the treasonable ambitions attributed to him. However, there were still plenty who agreed with Jefferson when Marshall set the trial for August 3, ordered Burr removed to a comfortable three-room suite on the airy top floor of the State penitentiary, and set off for the country for a few weeks of quiet family life.

He needed the rest, for Richmond had been a carnival all summer, with dinners and dances, gambling and drinking, even a little racing and fighting to supplement the entertainment of the trial. Marshall, a great man for dining out with friends, had been "in company" almost every evening that was not taken up with writing opinions for the next day's court session.

[7]

It was just at this time that Wayne put the last volume of the Washington biography on the market, and Marshall, already a target for political abuse because of his conduct of the Burr trial, became the object of some rather sharp attacks for "mistreating" the memory of a national hero. He deserved the unkind remarks, for the whole tone of this final section of the work was sharply slanted, although it was also a little better reading than some of the other volumes.

Inevitably, it was read as a partisan document. It would have been impossible to publish a life of Washington which would not be so regarded. But Marshall's writing cannot be considered objective today, although his worst faults were those of omission. For instance, he dismissed the Constitutional Convention, over which Washington had presided with such skill for five weary months, in two paragraphs.

What exasperated the Republicans most was a series of little partisan digs which were not sufficiently keen to achieve popularity nor sufficiently impressive to be convincing. The author gave a little more space to Hamilton than to Jefferson in describing their careers up to the time they entered the Cabinet, and he neglected to mention that Jefferson was the author of the Declaration of Independence. He minimized the early enthusiasm for the French Revolution. He editorialized on his belief that a "continuance of the close connexion" with France at the time of the Neutrality Proclamation might have proved dangerous to the United States. This constituted a stern warning to the country in 1807, and was meant as a rebuke to the supposed pro-French policy of the Administration. That Marshall so recognized it was evident from the fact that he eliminated the paragraph from the second edition many years later. He also editorialized on the folly of what his readers knew was a reference to Jeffersonian dogma, when he wrote:

"There seems to be something infectious in the example of a powerful and enlightened nation verging towards democracy, which imposes on the human mind, and leads human reason in fetters."

In his use of Washington's letters to Jefferson and Hamilton urging unity, he showed that both Secretaries were at fault, but since Hamilton was dead and Jefferson in power, the net effect was to exhibit the sage of Monticello as a quarrelsome, stubborn man. But what most enraged the Republicans was the truthful description of Washington as a Federalist. One example of the way in which this political bias was shown came in Marshall's reference to Washington's position after the XYZ hysteria had died down a little. Said the biographer:

"Those who had embraced the cause of France . . . were visibly recovering both strength and confidence. It is not therefore wonderful that general Washington should have expressed himself more freely than had been his custom, respecting American parties, and that he should have exerted an influence which he had not been in the habit of employing, to induce men whose talents he respected, but who had declined political life, to enter into the national and state legislatures."

This was a pat on the back for himself, for he had been "in-duced" to run for Congress. It was also a slap at the Republicans. They did not forgive him. Nor did they neglect to point out that his work gave the British a handle to attack the American Admin-istration. This criticism had some validity. Jefferson might be expected to call the work a "five volumed libel," but even John Adams, mellowing in his old age although scattering his barbed remarks impartially over all the public men of his lifetime, thought it was "fashioned to sell high in the London market." The British did use the Marshall opus a little to justify themselves, but in gen-eral it was too dull for effective propaganda. A typical comment, that of the *Edinburgh Review*, one of the most respected journals in the language at that time, included this sentence:

"But mere bulk, we suspect, gives no durable quality to works made of words, and it is not by the space they cover that they are likely to attract the notice of mankind."

And *Blackwood's Magazine*, in an article on American writers of the period, commented:

" 'Washington's Life,' so called, is a great, heavy book that should have been called by some other name. As a lawyer, as a judge whose decisions, year after year, in the Supreme Court of the United States would have done credit and honor to West-minster Hall in the proud season of English law, we must, we do, revere Chief Justice Marshall. But we cannot—will not—forgive such a man for having made such a book about such another man as George Washington. Full of power, full of truth as the work undoubtedly is one gets sick and tired of the very name of Wash-ington before he gets half through . . . and all this without find-ing out who Washington was or what he has done."

These are harsh words. Marshall himself never denied that they were deserved. He spent a good deal of his time apologizing for the biography. Hardly was it finished than he began to attempt

revisions which would improve it—they did very little good—
and all his life he remained pitifully grateful for any crumbs of
praise which his ponderous writings drew from reviewers or
friends.

But in the summer of 1807, he came back to Richmond to take
up the burden of the Burr trial, and to keep the house quiet for
Polly.

[8]

The evidence in the Burr trial was relatively simple. But the
arguments about that testimony were long and tedious. Marshall
spent a good many hot summer nights writing up opinions to deliver after listening to counsel all day.

First he listened to a long procession of prospective jurymen
announce their certainty that Burr was guilty. Loudly or softly,
belligerently or mildly, bitter or composed, they filed through
the court in endless variety as to everything except one point—
all of them had made up their minds about the case. Not until August 15 was the jury filled, and most of the twelve had expressed
the opinion that the prisoner was a traitor. They were accepted
only for lack of more impartial citizens.

Eaton was the first witness the government put on the stand,
and his presence was promptly challenged. The defense said the
act of levying war must be proved before there could be testimony
as to Burr's motives and character. All the rest of the day Marshall
listened to argument on this point, adorned with the citation of
precedents both good and bad, which showed the erudition of
counsel but did not much enlighten anyone as to the law. Marshall
came into court next day with a long opinion. (Most of his rulings
were of tedious length in this trial, but it was the only way he
could pay back the verbose gentlemen of the bar who contended
quite as energetically for oratorical honors as they did for Burr's
life.) Marshall's opinion was that neither side had proved anything specific by their debate and precedents. It would certainly
seem to be more orderly procedure to prove what happened be-

fore going into the why of it, he said, but the government lawyers might suit themselves. However, the witness should confine himself to intentions as to the crime charged in the indictment—levying war at Blennerhassett's island—and not go wandering off into other intentions until the main point had been proved.

Eaton's testimony was not so easily curbed. Put on the stand after the Chief Justice's ruling, he talked at great length about himself and his grievances against the government, and finally got around to Burr. Two sentences in his testimony summed up what he had to say pertinent to the case before the court:

"Concerning any overt act which goes to prove Aaron Burr guilty of treason I know nothing. But concerning Colonel Burr's expressions of treasonable intentions, I know much."

He insisted that Burr had told him an army would be ready to separate the Western States from the Union, and that Burr planned to draw the line at the Allegheny Mountains. Eaton was unshaken by the cross-examination, but Truxtun, a man with as many grievances against the government as Eaton and better known to Burr, testified that when he was approached by the prisoner to join the expedition, nothing was said about secession, but only about Mexico. The government then proceeded to their attempt to prove an actual act of war.

Two of Blennerhassett's workmen came first. One was the messenger who had taken Mrs. Blennerhassett's warning to Burr not to return to the island. He said that his employer told him they were going to Mexico where Burr would be Emperor and his daughter Queen. He quoted Blennerhassett as saying also that it would be a good thing if the Union were divided. While it did not come into the testimony, the Irishman had written some newspaper articles on secession, but so had a great many other people, especially New Englanders, who were not accused of treason. The witness on the stand testified further that on another occasion, Blennerhassett had sent him to buy some arms belonging to the government. The messenger was told that if the man who had them in charge would not sell, it was to be suggested that he might connive in allowing Blennerhassett to steal them.

The other workman testified that on the night before the Blennerhassett party fled from the island, a General Tupper of Ohio had come across the river and tried to arrest the master of the house. The witness quoted him as saying:

"Your body is in my hands in the name of the commonwealth."

At that, he said, several of the men aimed their muskets at the General, one of them saying he would just as soon shoot as not, and Tupper permitted them all to depart. Tupper himself was not called as a witness.

The most damaging testimony because it was not inspired by hope of gain or fear of punishment was given by Colonel George Morgan and two of his sons who had entertained Burr at their Ohio home when he was on his way to Blennerhasset's island. They swore that Burr had talked much about the inevitability of disunion, and wondered why the West submitted to its grievances. He did not think the Union could last five years at the most, and he wished he had a thousand husky young fellows. At dinner, repeating the same sort of talk, Burr said that with two hundred men he could drive Jefferson and Congress into the Potomac— this was the best corroboration of Eaton's story ever given—and with five hundred he could take New York. In the hall after dinner, Burr invited one of the sons to join a military expedition. When the youth replied that it would depend upon the purpose of the expedition, he got no reply.

The other five witnesses heard were counted rather in Burr's favor than against him. One said he had watched Blennerhassett's island from the shore and saw people moving around a fire. He thought they were armed but he was too far away to be sure, and some of them acted like sentries but perhaps they were only loitering near the blaze. Another witness said he visited the island on the night of this gathering and saw several men cleaning their rifles. He saw no other arms. A third man who had come to the island with a couple of friends thinking to join the expedition saw a man running bullets, but no other evidences of war. Another of Blennerhasset's household said he had been asked to join the expedition but knew of it only as a project to settle on the Washita where he had been promised a piece of land. Blennerhassett's former business partner told of selling Burr food and boats, of Blennerhasset's complete incompetency for military adventure, of seeing the assemblage on the island and thinking it orderly, of the statement of one of the leaders that he would not resist authority but would not let a mob stop him.

More than 120 government witnesses remained to be heard, but the prosecution said that none of them could add anything to the testimony proving that Burr and Blennerhassett had levied war against the United States on December 13. The 120-odd were there to testify to what Pooh-Bah would have called "corroborative detail." Burr's counsel objected. There had been no proof of the act of levying war against the United States at Blennerhassett's island on December 13, they insisted, and therefore it was improper to receive evidence which was only collateral to something which had not happened.

On this point the lawyers talked for ten days, Marshall's old friend Wickham alone consuming two in his opening remarks. The courtroom was like a furnace most of the time, and a very badly ventilated furnace at that. Through all the waves of heat and eloquence, the Chief Justice sat patiently with Judge Griffin beside him—posterity ignores Griffin almost as completely as the spectators did—and tirelessly took notes. There were long passages when no notes were needed, for hours on end were devoted to pure rhetoric. The best remembered specimen—school children have been learning it ever since—was Wirt's answer to his own question, "Who is Blennerhassett?" The gallant Virginian excelled himself in describing the delights of the island, the beauties of nature, and of Mrs. Blennerhassett, and then burst forth:

"In the midst of all this peace, this innocent simplicity and this tranquility, this feast of the mind, this pure banquet of the heart, the destroyer comes; he comes to change this paradise into a hell. Yet the flowers do not wither at his approach. No monitory shuddering through the bosom of their unfortunate possessor warns him of the ruin that is coming upon him."

This flight of fancy was much admired, and was one of the best things Marshall heard during those ten days of debate. He also enjoyed, for he was seen to grin, the ridicule which Botts poured over some of his rival's eloquence. The court reporter had missed a really purple passage by Wirt which survives only because Botts pretended to mourn his own inability to rise to "the introduction of a sleeping Venus with all the luxury of voluptuous and wanton nakedness to charm the reason through the refined medium of sensuality."

[9]

The important questions which the lawyers adorned with figures of speech were by no means as complicated as the language. They were in essence these:

1. Can a man who was not present when the act of treason was committed be convicted as a principal?

2. Can a man accused of having inspired the treasonable act of others be convicted on different evidence than would justify the conviction of those who took part in the act?

3. Can testimony against the man not present when the treasonable act was committed be admitted before the act itself has been sufficiently proved, in the opinion of the court?

4. Could testimony be admitted as to other possible offenses not included in the indictment?

The importance of these questions lay in the meaning they would give to treason. The answers would decide whether, in the future, government prosecutors would be able to get around the plain constitutional provision that they must produce at least two witnesses to an act of levying war against the United States.

Marshall took the week end for his opinion, and on a sweltering Monday, August 31, he read it to a breathlessly packed audience in the steaming House of Delegates. It runs to nearly fifty closely printed pages, and it has led the government in time of crisis to rely upon special laws of espionage and riot rather than on the formerly vague concept of treason. For Marshall's opinion, long and rambling and in some minor passages mistaken, established a bulwark of defense for the citizen. To prove treason, the government would have to prove the act of war and then prove the individual's part in that act.

Only six months before, the Supreme Court through its Chief Justice had explained that a man who took even a remote part in a treasonable assembly was a traitor. In Richmond the same Chief Justice seems to have taken a slightly different view of the matter. He said that the only treason charged was the incident at the island, "and the whole question to which the inquiry of the court is now directed is whether the prisoner was legally present at that fact." Marshall decided that he was not, which disposed of question number one. But he went on to point out that there was the accusation that Burr had induced others to commit treason, and that brought him to question number two.

The Chief Justice explained that Burr was not indicted on this count, but that if he had been, then the inducement to others to levy war on the United States would have been the overt act which the government must prove by two witnesses. He admitted that the fact of such inducement was difficult to prove, but difficulty was no reason for violating the Constitution.

"To advise or procure a treason is in the nature of conspiring or plotting treason, which is not treason in itself," he explained.

Therefore, if the country wanted to punish such offenses, it would have to make a law to that effect, he declared, and suspects would have to be indicted under that law and not for treason.

The other two questions seemed to Marshall to be answered in the very asking. No further testimony could be heard until the court was satisfied there had been evidence of a gathering "in a condition to make war" and not just "a secret furtive assemblage." Obviously evidence of other crimes could be admitted only after the main point had been shown.

The government admitted that it had only corroborative evidence to offer with its 120-odd remaining witnesses. All of it was irrelevant because the real fact for the jury to decide was whether Burr and Blennerhassett had been guilty of levying war on the United States. The jurors had before them all the evidence on that point, and it was up to them to decide.

In closing, Marshall took notice of some rhetoric by Hay and Wirt which seemed to imply that he would be impeached if he ruled against them. Before the trial started Jefferson had confided to Giles his hope that if the prosecution failed, the Constitution would be amended to eliminate "the error . . . which makes any branch [by this Jefferson meant the courts] independent of the nation." Looking back at the failure to remove Chase, the President was sure amendment to provide an easier method of dismissing judges was essential because, he wrote, "impeachment is a farce which will not be tried again." However, Marshall, sitting in Richmond and listening to the thinly veiled threats of the prosecutors, could not know Jefferson would not try the "farce" again.

"That this court dares not usurp power is most true," he announced. "That this court dares not shrink from its duty is not less true."

This statement had nothing to do with Burr, but it seems to have had as much effect upon the jury as some of the evidence, and more than most of the speeches. The Chief Justice had made a remarkable impression upon the jurymen as he sat, calm and judicial, above the wrangling lawyers and the swashbuckling witnesses. Besides, the foreman of the jury was Polly's brother-in-law, Edward Carrington. The whole family had learned to heed Marshall's opinions, and assuredly he had conveyed his belief that no

overt act of war had been proved. The jury was out only a little
while Tuesday morning before it came back with a verdict, "not
proved to be guilty under this indictment by any evidence submitted to us." Burr's counsel raved at this as a reflection on the
presiding judges, and no doubt it was meant to be, but Marshall
quieted the storm by ruling that the jury's words should be left
on the bill of indictment, while the more customary and simpler
"not guilty" should appear on the record.

[10]

There was still to be six weeks of Burr trial for Marshall. The
prosecution moved from the indictment for treason to the indictment for a misdemeanor—the attempt against Spanish territory—
and here a great many of the witnesses had a chance to be heard.
Jefferson, furious at the acquittal for treason, continued to send
Hay instructions on prosecuting the additional charge, and he
never forgave Marshall. To the end of his life he believed the
Chief Justice had conspired to free Burr and prevent the real evidence from getting before the public.

The weight of the evidence tended to clear the prisoner even
on the misdemeanor count. At the end, Hay wanted to quash the
indictment, but Marshall let the case go to the jury, which brought
in a verdict of "not guilty" after half an hour's deliberation. There
followed a motion to commit the defendants on charges of treason
and misdemeanor committed in Ohio, referring to the activities of
the little band after Blennerhassett and Burr joined forces. This
argument lasted until October 20, when the Chief Justice succeeded in infuriating Burr by granting the government's request.
Marshall said the preponderance of evidence was in favor of the
prisoner, but that the final decision might well be left to a grand
jury. He fixed bail at $5,000, and as soon as he had adjourned court,
he set out for a rest in the mountains.

Behind him there were gigantic popular demonstrations. He
and Burr were hanged in effigy in Baltimore along with Blennerhassett and Luther Martin. The Chief Justice in some papers was

assured that he would forever "blot the fair page of American history." Jefferson informed his Attorney General that he would have two main preoccupations in the coming session of Congress, first the Burr case and second the conduct of Great Britain. In his message to the special session, the President transmitted a copy of the Burr proceedings with the suggestion that the legislators determine whether the prosecution had failed because of the law, defective testimony or the manner in which the law was administered. Some read into the message a request for impeachment, a sentiment which would have been strengthened if Jefferson had left in a passage in his original draft which compared the trial to that of Fries. In the section which he crossed out on second thought, he also criticized withholding evidence from the jury and suggested that the laws had been twisted to save the criminals.

Popular opinion was so strong that John Quincy Adams called on the Senate to expel Senator Smith for his share in the Burr affair, and the motion lost by only a single vote. Burr himself slipped away, bankrupt but hopeful, to tread cheerfully a road of exile and poverty, tragedy in the drowning of Theodosia at sea, an old age of unexciting obscurity, a final marriage to and divorce from a rich widow and death at last with a few faithful friends around him.

XVI

☆ ☆ ☆

Measures Short of War

EXCITEMENT over the Burr trial might have lasted longer if the international situation had not been so interesting. By the time Marshall had come down from the mountains, driven his gig to Raleigh and back, held his regular court in Virginia and set out for the winter term of the Supreme Court in Washington, the country's attention had been quite thoroughly diverted from trials for treason. The New England Federalists who were toying with the idea of disunion and secession in a serious way were perhaps the most concerned, and they were not airing the matter publicly but saving the decision in the back of their minds in case of an emergency. The Chief Justice himself wrote cheerfully, referring to public reaction to his part in the Burr trial:

"I have sufficient bodily employment to prevent my mind from perplexing itself about the attentions paid me in Baltimore and elsewhere."

Marshall was more interested in meeting a new addition to the Supreme Court. While the country was being agitated by stories of Burr's conspiracy, Congress increased the membership of the highest tribunal to seven. They were less concerned with getting a third Republican on the bench than with creating a new circuit in the West. It was becoming intolerable for litigants in far off Kentucky, Tennessee, and Ohio to journey East. In filling the new post, Jefferson sought the advice of the Congressional Caucus, and their choice was Campbell, one of the managers of the Chase impeachment. Since a member of Congress may not fill a job which he has helped create, Jefferson took as second choice Thomas Todd, Chief Justice of the Kentucky Court of Appeals.

When Marshall met him at the opening of Court in 1808, he saw an almost perfect example of the American success story. Todd had celebrated his forty-third birthday only a few days before, and a magazine writer described him as a "model of beauty and intelligence." Born in Virginia, he had emigrated to Kentucky in '86, earned his keep by teaching a judge's daughter, studied law by firelight and started practice with even less cash than Marshall —37½ cents. He needed all his strength and patience because his circuit of Kentucky, Tennessee, and Ohio was the most rugged in the country.

The travels of a circuit judge constituted an athletic life. Joseph Story of Boston, lawyer son of one of the "Indians" who had dumped British tea in the harbor in '73, was only twenty-eight in this year of 1808, but he wrote of a journey to the capital:

"If you have . . . learned to commiserate the wretch who is soused into a horsepond or bespattered with mud, I pray you reserve that compassion for me. Between Philadelphia and Baltimore, one hundred miles, and between Baltimore and Washington, forty miles, are as execrable roads as can be found in Christendom. You could hardly believe yourself in a Christian country, unless every now and then in the intervals of a tremendous jolt you should indulge your fancy. Take my word for it, I am reduced to a mere jelly. No unfortunate wight pounded in a mortar has a less *bony* claim to consistency."

The Chief Justice was tougher and more accustomed to the rigors of the road. He had learned to roll with the punches, although he had not fitted up his carriage, as his colleague Cushing had, with built-in contrivances for holding food and books and clothing.

The Justices of the Supreme Court, however, were more than usually interested in the political scene that winter. Their own cases were of no great note or complexity. Yet Story, back after another harrowing journey, remarked that one of them had been argued for nine days, with Luther Martin, who was among the eight lawyers employed, taking up a third of that time.

"I heard as much as I could, but I was fatigued almost to death," said Story.

He was lucky compared to the Justices. He could get away when he could bear no more. They had to sit and listen. (Their successors have learned to curb the eloquence of counsel, and the modern pleader before the high court is sometimes allowed as much as an hour and a printed brief to say what the lawyers of Marshall's day strung out into days.) Despite his boredom in the nine days hearing, however, Story was much impressed.

"I have witnessed the profession in all its glory," he wrote to a friend at home.

By this he meant the bar, not the bench. During this visit, he took his meals with the judges frequently, and on the whole preferred them to legislators. In the midst of tense days in foreign policy, when the question of retaliation against England was being rivalled for popular attention by proposals for rearmament and governmental reorganizations, the Bostonian said of Congress:

"You cannot form any correct opinion of the good-humored complacency with which it consents to do nothing." (Jefferson once said this was because there were so many lawyers "whose trade is talking.")

The Chief Justice was the leader of the lighter conversation in which the court indulged during leisure hours at the boardinghouse. Story was privileged to hear some of it, and remarked of Marshall:

"I love his laugh—it is too hearty for an intriguer—and his good temper and unwearied patience are equally agreeable on the bench and in the study."

[2]

The political sensation of that session of Congress and term of court was a substitute for fighting which Jefferson had decided to try. He was wise not to engage the British fleet in action. At that time England had a thousand or more ships of war; the United States exactly twelve. But Americans operated a great many merchant vessels, and Jefferson supposed that their cargoes were essential to the life of the British Isles. Therefore, he proposed a complete embargo on American shipping, and Congress passed his measure promptly over the futile protests of the handful of Federalists, aided in the House by the insurgent Randolph.

Merchants and shipowners of New England saw their property threatened, and by a man they hated. Furthermore, they believed he was acting at the behest of France rather than for the protection of Americans. The Cabots and the Pickerings were not much worried about sailors who manned their ships and were being forcibly impressed into British naval service. The seamen were expendable. But 800,000 tons of shipping were laid up, rotting in idleness. If a few were smuggled out and managed to reach the Continent, the French happily confiscated vessel and cargo on the pious plea that they were helping Jefferson enforce the law. Bitterly, the New England men of means chanted a popular song:

> Our ships all in motion
> Once whitened the ocean,
> They sailed and returned with a cargo;
> Now doomed to decay
> They have fallen a prey
> To Jefferson, worms and embargo.

The singers saw that England was fighting the battle of Americans, and of all free men. If the bulwark of the British Isles fell, there would be no barrier to Napoleon's domination of the whole Western world. The United States would have that conquering and restless spirit as a neighbor in Canada, in the Floridas and all along the Western frontier. That same spirit would inherit England's control of the oceans.

The Chief Justice of the United States partook of the feelings of his party. His own experience on his one trip to Europe had left him with no friendship for France. He did not believe in Jefferson's neutrality. He was convinced that virtually all Republicans were concealed Francophiles working for the triumph of Napoleonic arms even at the expense of their own country. Before Jefferson's substitute for war had been in effect a year, Marshall was writing to the secessionist Pickering:

"Nothing can be more completely demonstrated than the inefficacy of the embargo, yet that demonstration seems to be of no avail. I fear most seriously that the same spirit which so tenaciously maintains this measure will impel us to a war with the only power which protects any part of the civilized world from the despotism of that tyrant with whom we shall then be ravaged."

This comment was made in the course of congratulating Pickering on speeches in the Senate which painted a fearful picture of French armies transported on captured British fleets to the sack of American cities. It was a prospect which all good Federalists except clear-sighted old John Adams thought imminent.

Like Pickering and his friends, Marshall was ready to put up with a great deal more British arrogance than he had been willing to accept when he was Secretary of State. Jefferson's desire to get rid of British tyranny at sea, and then deal with Napoleon later if necessary, struck Marshall as a prime example of his kinsman's myopia and folly, not to say dangerous sympathy with the wrong side. On the other hand, the Chief Justice did not like the growing talk of secession among his New England friends. They were snarling against the Administration more openly than ever, although some of them were taking advantage of the embargo to establish mills. Factory development gained such impetus that Jefferson could write to Lafayette:

"Our Embargo has produced one very happy permanent effect. It has set us all on domestic manufactures and will, I verily believe, reduce our future demands on England fully one half."

[3]

No one was forgetting that this was a Presidential year. Madison was Jefferson's candidate. Randolph was active on behalf of a Republican nomination for Monroe, and there was a lively contest which strained relations between the two Virginians whom Jefferson regarded as his closest political friends. The Federalists settled on Marshall's old XYZ colleague, Pinckney, and indulged in some very foolish optimism. Actually Pinckney received 47 electoral votes to 122 for Madison.

The results were not known, but could be easily predicted, when the Tenth Congress met in November. The embargo was not moderating England's tone in the slightest, but exports had fallen from 108 million to 22 million dollars, and imports from 138 million to not quite 57 million dollars. Jefferson, nevertheless, was determined to push his pet measure. Evasion, he thought, was the only fault. So instead of relaxing the embargo, he called for stronger enforcement machinery.

In Massachusetts, juries were refusing to convict violators. In South Carolina, Jefferson's own appointee, Justice Johnson, held that the collector of the port was "not justified by the instructions of the Executive in increasing restraints upon commerce" over and above those already created by the law. Administration leaders were as angry as if Marshall had written the opinion, and Attorney General Rodney wrote:

"You can scarcely elevate a man to a seat in a Court of Justice before he catches the leprosy of the Bench."

To correct these flaws, Jefferson had his majority leader in the Senate introduce a piece of legislation which struck Federalists very much as the Alien and Sedition Laws had impressed Republicans. Gallatin, usually not a man for extreme measures and one of the bitterest critics of Federalist attempts to enforce the Sedition Act, declared:

"Congress must either invest the Executive with the most arbitrary powers and sufficient force to carry the Embargo into effect or give it up altogether."

His party preferred arbitrary measures, and the resulting legislation empowered government officials to keep coasting vessels from sailing if the ships "apparently" were on their way to forbidden territory. Shipowners were required to give bond for six times the value of their cargoes before sailing on permitted voyages. Quotas were set for each State's importation of food. Finally, government inspectors were authorized to refuse clearance without any avowed reason, even if all of the provisions of the law were met.

This "Force Act" coupled with Jefferson's proposal to use the government's surplus for internal improvements—roads and waterways in the West mostly—set New England off into paroxysms of rage. Timothy Dwight, President of Yale and one of many Federalist ministers who included politics in their sermons, preached on the text: "Come out therefore from among them be ye separate, saith the Lord."

"It is better to suffer the AMPUTATION of a Limb than to lose the WHOLE BODY," said the *Boston Gazette*. "We must prepare for the operation."

Younger Republicans such as Henry Clay were becoming eager partisans of war, and they were as acrimonious as the Federalists. State legislators took up the embargo issue, and in Kentucky, Humphrey Marshall called Clay a liar. The two men slipped across the Ohio River at Louisville on a nippy morning in January and

eased their temperaments by exchanging three shots. The Chief
Justice's belligerent brother-in-law was grazed by a bullet passing
across his slightly protuberant stomach. Clay was hit in the fleshy
part of the thigh. The merits of the argument generally remained
unaltered.

The Chief Justice, driving into Washington for the gay social
season which coincided with the February term of court and Jefferson's last weeks in office, found the capital seething with excitement over a break in the Republican ranks. The President was
unable to hold the Northern members of his party in line—Presidential authority always weakens with the certainty of retirement
—and a Non-Intercourse Act was being passed to take the place
of the Embargo in March. It forbade the importation of British
goods from any country, but it contained a provision that if either
Britain or France gave up its policy of harrying Americans, the
President might by proclamation lift all commercial restrictions
against the country which first accepted American overtures.

This did not satisfy the Federalists. They were sure that Non-
Intercourse was as bad as the Embargo for their trade and for England's fight against dictatorship. Marshall found the extremists
talking about State rights and separation from the Union just as
the Republicans had done in '98. He was seeing an early example
of the historical axiom that men who are disappointed at getting or
keeping control of the Federal government, become ardent champions of State rights—if they have control in their own States.
Staunch Federalist though he was, this line of reasoning did not
appeal to Marshall. He was pleased to find on the docket for the
1809 term a case which would permit him to say so publicly.

[4]

The case, known in the language of the courts as *U.S.* vs. *Peters*,
should have been called "The Siege of Rittenhouse Castle." It had
originated in one of the deeds of daring during the War of Independence, and had been in the courts since before the adoption
of the Constitution. Of course it involved prize money.

The persistent litigant, Gideon Olmstead, had been a middle-aged sea captain when he and three of his men captured the British sloop *Active*. They were near Egg Harbor, New Jersey, when two armed American vessels, one a Continental ship and the other sailing with papers issued by the sovereign State of Pennsylvania, took the *Active* to Philadelphia. The State courts conducted the first hearing and awarded one-quarter of the proceeds of his prize to Olmstead. He carried the case to the Court of Appeals of the Confederation, which ruled that he and his men were entitled to the whole thing. Pennsylvania protested, and the money was invested in United States securities while the case was re-argued.

The custodian of the securities was David Rittenhouse, then State Treasurer. He died before the case was settled, but at last, in 1803, Olmstead won his suit again—this time in the Federal District Court. The State of Pennsylvania still refused to comply with the verdict and passed a law to prevent State officials from obeying the Federal judge. So after some fruitless negotiation, Olmstead, now eighty-two, went to the Supreme Court for an order to compel Federal Judge Richard Peters to execute his own ruling. The Judge was reluctant to do so, he wrote, "to avoid embroiling the government of the United States and that of Pennsylvania."

The Supreme Court was not so timid. After hearing the evidence, Marshall handed down the decision which in effect commanded Judge Peters to go in and fight. Pennsylvania could not intimidate the Justices in Washington. This ruling required no more than a simple order to the Judge, but the Chief Justice saw an opportunity to dissociate himself from the State rights position of his Federalist friends. So he delivered his favorite maxims concerning the supremacy of the National government—it was by no means so obvious then as it has since become, thanks largely to such decisions as this—and said:

"If the legislatures of the several states may, at will, annul the judgments of the courts of the United States, and destroy the rights acquired under those judgments, the constitution itself becomes a solemn mockery."

The decision was a complete rebuke to the position taken by the authors of the Kentucky and Virginia Resolutions in '98. But those authors, for once, applauded a Marshall ruling. In '98 they had been firm in their belief that each state should interpret Federal law for itself. Now that New England Federalists wished to apply that doctrine to laws passed by the State rights men of ten years before, Republicans became great defenders of the Supreme Court.

"Here is a point at which the independence of the Judiciary, in its strict and constitutional sense, exists and demands to be supported and maintained," said the *Aurora*, usually so bitterly critical of Federal court authority.

When Pennsylvania called out the militia to prevent the United States Marshal from serving the writs which Peters issued in accordance with the Supreme Court order, Republicans spoke of treason. They talked of hanging State righters to gibbets. They were as stern as Marshall, and like him were talking at New England quite as much as at Pennsylvania.

Meanwhile, the "Siege of Rittenhouse Castle" had begun. The occupants of the former Treasurer's mansion were his two elderly daughters. They were the custodians of the bonds which Peters had awarded to Olmstead. Under the command of General Michael Bright, the militia barred the way to their home. The Marshal replied by calling for a posse of 2,000 men to force his way in, and the Federal grand jury indicted Bright. The Republican administration in Washington stood firm in support of the Federal courts, and State troops finally gave way. The Rittenhouse daughters were more recalcitrant, and had to be put under arrest in their own home. Finally the State appropriated the money to pay old Olmstead, and the case was closed when General Bright, sentenced to jail by Bushrod Washington, was released by the new President, Madison, in a month.

For a brief period, the Supreme Court actually was popular. Republicans recognized the support given to their international policy. Federalists forgave the little lecture. The New Englanders even forgot its moral, too, in the fervor of their enthusiasm for England and resentment over restrictions on their commerce. This last they contrasted bitterly with the prosperity which prevailed elsewhere in the country, as evidenced by the government surplus.

The improved status of the Court was reflected most immediately in additional discomfort for the Justices. Their inadequate quarters were to be replaced at last, and space in the basement of the Capitol under the Senate Chamber was being prepared for them. But until the new courtroom could be completed, they had to meet wherever they could find space. At least once during this term, that turned out to be a tavern.

Adding to the physical discomfort was the arrival of the Yazoo swindle at the bar of their august tribunal. The Justices were uneasily conscious of being used for no good purpose. The case obviously was a put-up job. When the Eleventh Amendment barred citizens from suing a State, the New England speculators in Yazoo lands were blocked from demanding satisfaction from Georgia. So they devised a way to get around the Constitutional amendment.

Robert Fletcher of New Hampshire sued John Peck of Boston, demanding the return of $3,000 which he had paid for 15,000 acres of Yazoo lands. The papers in the case recited every single point on which any Yazoo dealer possibly could want a judicial ruling. It was obvious, too, that both parties to the litigation hoped that Peck would win. Under these circumstances, the Court was reluctant to hear it, but finally consented. It is not likely that Marshall was swayed by the fact that a decision for Peck might strengthen his own position if Virginia opponents of the Fairfax grant ever succeeded in having title to that property re-examined. Nevertheless, there was that coincidence.

The argument lasted for several days, a fact which may be ex-

plained in part by the appearance of Luther Martin for the plain-
tiff, Fletcher. Finally on March 4, the case for Peck, and therefore
for all the Yazoo speculators, was presented by John Quincy
Adams. Marshall had to interrupt his eloquence for a few hours
while the whole Court attended the inauguration. Towering over
little Madison, the Chief Justice administered the oath. He was
delighted to get rid of Jefferson, but his regard for his colleague
in the Virginia Constitutional Convention fight was no longer as
high as it had been. The ceremony over, he went back to listen to
the rest of Adams's plea on behalf of the Yazoo speculation.

That night the Justices gave up their boardinghouse session for
the inaugural ball, which was expected to be very splendid since
Dolly Madison had arranged it. But there were disappointed
guests. Adams, recently a convert to Republicanism, or more ac-
curately perhaps a refugee from Federalism, was pained to hear at
the ball that the Court was very reluctant to give any opinion in
his case since it "appeared manifestly made up." Of the ball itself,
Adams wrote:

"The crowd was excessive—the heat oppressive, and the entertainment bad."

Alarmed by the attitude which the Justices displayed toward
the suit of *Fletcher* vs. *Peck*, the lawyers told the Court they had
found errors in their pleadings. The Court graciously gave permission to remedy these defects, and said it would hear the case
again at the next term. Meanwhile, the angry invective of John
Randolph was turned tentatively toward what he conceived to be
a new plot to confirm the Yazoo swindlers in their loot.

Marshall did not linger much longer in Washington that year.
He was always glad to get away, but this time he was leaving behind a situation of which he disapproved but about which he could
do nothing. He was content to watch from afar while "Jemmy"
Madison looked for a way out of his foreign embroglio without
being caught in a world war which was moving rapidly and blood-
ily to its climax.

XVII

☆ ☆ ☆

Obligation of a Contract

MARSHALL, along with all Federalists, was delighted to hear that "Jemmy's" administration had opened with what seemed to be a diplomatic triumph. Only a little more than a month after the inauguration, he signed an agreement with the British Minister for simultaneous withdrawal of London's naval orders and repeal of the Non-Intercourse Act. The agreement made an exceptionally fast passage to London, arriving there on May 22. It also got exceptionally fast consideration. Within two days, George Canning, the Foreign Secretary, repudiated it coldly and recalled the Minister. As a successor he sent Francis James Jackson, a diplomat chiefly distinguished as the envoy who had been selected in 1807 to carry to Denmark a ruthless British ultimatum which led to the bombardment of Copenhagen.

Jackson carried out his instructions in such a characteristically arrogant manner that Madison told him the United States government would receive no more communications from him. Whereupon the Minister entered into close and friendly communication with Pickering, recently retired from the Senate by a Republican majority in the Massachusetts legislature.

Marshall had shared his party's rejoicing over the agreement and sorrow over its repudiation. But he could not approve of Pickering's eager pursuit of purely sectional interests. The Chief Justice remained a Federalist of what was rapidly becoming the old school—attached to a nationalist point of view regardless of the composition of the national Cabinet. Although still on friendly terms with the New England friends of his Congressional days, he no longer shared their politics. They supported the government in Washington only if they could control it; he supported it because of a genuine preference for strength in a central administration.

At this time, Marshall was immersed in a case which reaffirmed in the strongest possible manner his views on the supremacy of the Federal government. Every time he felt called upon to state this philosophy, it removed him a little further from his old political ties. This particular case did more than give him an opportunity to re-state his position. It bolstered Federal authority to the full extent of the judiciary's influence.

Perhaps, however, it was even more important in helping to fix in the practice of the American way of life one of the most rigorous safeguards on the sanctity of property which has ever been devised by the ingenuity of man. The basis for this safeguard was the clause in the Constitution which provides: "No state shall . . . pass any law impairing the obligation of contracts." The occasion was the Yazoo swindle, which in accordance with the order of the previous term was to be reargued in 1810. There was nothing new in this proceeding except that Joseph Story of Boston replaced John Quincy Adams as a pleader, for Adams had been appointed Minister to Russia.

Martin made a very loose and rambling oration on the iniquity of the original Yazoo grant. The great lawyer had been hired to lose his case—at least his client hoped to lose—and the State of Georgia had shifted the whole responsibility along with the land concerned to the United States. The State, therefore, was not represented, but neither was the Federal government.

Story took the cynical but realistic ground that if legislative land grants were to be upset in the courts just because of fraud, there would never be any end to litigation in the United States. Since, in the course of the next century, the government would dispose of 657,000,000 acres of the best land in America for less than it had cost in purchase price and surveyor's fees, there was perhaps some practical value to Story's warning. But the young lawyer grounded his argument for Peck on the rock of the Constitutional provision against impairing the obligation of a contract. The State of Georgia, he said, had made a contract; it could not be repealed.

The Supreme Court was unanimous in agreeing with him. Marshall's carefully written opinion put the seal on the obligation to live up to property agreements, no matter how they might have been reached. One legislature repealing the contract entered into by its predecessor, he maintained, was in much the same position as a private party to a contract repudiating it on his own initiative without the consent of the other.

"The framers of the constitution viewed with some apprehension the violent acts which might grow out of the feelings of the moment," said the Chief Justice, referring to the popular excitement which had preceded the repealing act.

It was not the business of the courts to consider whether this excitement had been justified, he insisted. It was their business to uphold the Constitution which the Fathers had designed "to shield themselves and their property from the effects of those sudden and strong passions to which men are exposed." The judicial robes would not be sullied by so much as thinking of graft, he indicated, saying:

"It would be indecent in the extreme, upon a private contract between two individuals, to enter into an inquiry respecting the corruption of the sovereign power of a State."

Whether this lofty indifference to a swindle would have been maintained in the face of corruption on the other side of a case it would be difficult to tell. Marshall was an astute collector of supporting principles for any cause he expounded, and it may be doubted that he would have regarded it as "indecent" to examine corruption if it had been used to perpetrate one of the anti-nationalist acts upon which he frowned.

The decision in *Fletcher* vs. *Peck* did a great deal more than confirm generations of grafters in undisturbed possession of their spoils. It gave to property rights the same protection which men hoped had been achieved by the first ten amendments for personal liberties. It put upon solid ground the Hamiltonian theory that government should be in the interest of property first and people second—or rather that, if the government served property, that very service was best for the people.

The inclusion of State laws within the definition of the word "contract" was the chief objection of Marshall's saner critics. They said that if the men who wrote the Constitution had wanted the interpretation which Marshall gave, they would have declared specifically that no State may repeal its own laws if the repeal would affect property adversely. The critics also pointed out that with any such clause in it, the Constitution could not have been ratified.

Marshall's decision was of great importance, therefore, in the development of judicial interpretation of property rights in the United States. It had no discernible effect upon the settlement of the Yazoo land cases themselves. The decision to accept the report of Jefferson's commissioners had been made by Congress years before, but Randolph had been able to block bills designed to pay off the speculators and their customers. The Supreme Court decision did nothing to hasten passage of the necessary appropriation. Randolph roused such a storm against the Court's acquiescence in corruption that he missed by only five votes passing a resolution which in effect condemned the decision. Not until four years afterwards, in an interval when Randolph had been defeated for re-election, did Congress finally vote the $5,000,000 appropriation to pay Yazoo claims.

[2]

The decision in *Fletcher* vs. *Peck* was a plea for the preservation of the national government's supremacy as well as a protection for property, but Marshall's friends in New England paid no heed. They were busy preparing to show their defiance of Madison's administration by giving Jackson a rousing reception. The British Minister made a triumphal tour of Federalist strongholds, reminding Story of the imprudent Genêt, and issuing appeals which the young lawyer thought "infamous." Boston staged a tremendous pro-British demonstration. The aristocratic members of the Ancient and Honorable Artillery Company of that city entertained the British Minister at dinner, and cheered happily when he proposed this toast:

"Perpetual harmony between Great Britain and the United States"—an unexceptionable sentiment until he added: "May the swords of this Ancient and Honorable Artillery Company be drawn against those who would interrupt it."

If the gentlemen who applauded had been cool enough to remember Citizen Genêt and his effect upon popular sentiment when he defied Washington, they might have been less surprised by the Republican victories in the elections that year. The intervention of foreigners, especially of Englishmen, in the politics of the United States has always provoked a violent reaction. The voters of New England were no exceptions, and soon Marshall was writing sorrowfully to Josiah Quincy, one of the bitterest of his party:

"The Federalists of the South participate with their brethren of the North in the gloomy anticipations which your late elections must inspire."

The new Congress was being invaded by a band of ardent, belligerent spirits who would soon be proud to be called "war hawks." One was Henry Clay, already briefly known to Washington society through two visits as a Senator to fill out unexpired terms. He had been returned to the House in his own right, and achieved the unique distinction of being elected Speaker on the day he took his seat. Clay was supported by an iron-faced young statesman from South Carolina, John Caldwell Calhoun, the beau ideal of Southern planters, and the equally young and ardent Richard M. Johnson, who was among those rare legislators who vote for a war and get hurt fighting in it.

Forced forward by these determined spirits, and pressed on the other side by the intolerantly pro-British views of the Federalists, Madison found diplomacy almost impossible. The causes for war were sufficient, but the gains to be anticipated were visible only to such optimistic souls as thought Canada would fall to American arms with hardly a struggle. Federalists saw clearly enough—as did Madison—that war would only intensify the difficulties under which American commerce labored. But the Federalists were not content to rest their case on its American merits. They preferred to becloud the issue because in their fanatical hatred of French revolutionaries and French dictatorship they had lost national perspective. The quality of the debate was indicated in a popular Federalist charge that the whole anti-British campaign was part of a Napoleonic plot to make Mrs. Jerome Bonaparte's infant son King of America, while the Sons of St. Patrick, Republicans to a man, downed their March 17 liquor to angry toasts against England. There were very few men in the country who could speak of foreign affairs without indulging in invective, few as gentle as the Vermonter who wrote antiwar verses to Madison, including the lines:

> Can War with all its hideous train
> Our reconcilement prove?
> Can ships destroy'd upon the main,

> Or desolation on the Plain,
> Or flaming roof, or bleeding vein,
> Or thousands of our brethren slain,
> Our injuries remove?

Young Washington Irving, in the capital after a journey which he described as "terrible and sublime—as full of adventurous matter and direful peril as one of Walter Scott's pantomimic, melodramatic, romantic tales," was able to preserve some balance, and wrote to his friend Brevoort:

"You would be amused were you to arrive here just now—to see the odd & heterogeneous circle of acquaintance I have formed. One day I am dining with a knot of honest, furious Federalists, who are damning all their opponents as a set of consummate scoundrels, panders of Bonaparte &c, &c. The next day I dine perhaps with some of the very men I have heard thus anathematized, and find them equally honest, warm & indignant—and if I take their word for it, I had been dining the day before with some of the greatest knaves in the nation, men absolutely paid & suborned by the British government."

There was some improvement to be noted in the manners of the House when Marshall and his colleagues rested from their court labors to hear a little legislative debate. Clay had inaugurated a new system of majority organization, converting the Speakership into a post of real power instead of confining his activities to mere presiding, as the Vice President did over the Senate. He also imposed greater decorum. Boldly, he required the much-feared Randolph to leave his dog outside. With infinite patience he sent messengers to waken dozing Congressmen, urging them to stay awake or go home to bed. Politely he insisted that even when awake they keep their feet off the desks.

The prestige which this sort of leadership gave to the young Speaker added to the authority of his position, his driving force, his charm over the card table or the bottle. When Harry Clay talked of exchanging the pale quill of peaceful diplomacy for the bright steel of the sword, his mastery of the House gave added strength to his arguments. Marshall, who was to learn to respect the leader of the war hawks as a lawyer, deplored his politics at this time. But the Chief Justice was concerned with a political issue which more nearly affected him. Ten years after the popular repudiation of Hamiltonian principles, the Supreme Court was about to lose its Federalist majority.

[3]

The Court was reduced to an equality of parties—three and three —when Cushing died on September 13, 1810. While Johnson, Livingston, and Todd had as sound a theory of judicial independence as Washington, Chase, or even Marshall himself, they were inclined toward Republican philosophy, and Cushing's successor might easily give them a lead which would disrupt the harmony of the supreme bench. Furthermore, Chase was becoming increasingly feeble. At sixty-nine, he was no longer the robust blusterer of the Alien and Sedition days. He was frequently absent because of illness, and his passing would leave Bushrod and the Chief Justice alone of the Old Guard.

The choice of Cushing's successor, therefore, was of immense concern to Marshall. He was to be kept in suspense for more than a year. Madison had a very real difficulty. He had to select a judge from New England, preferably Massachusetts, to hold the circuit in that region. He was not willing to select a mere party nonentity. At the same time, he was being urged by Jefferson to be exceedingly circumspect.

The sage of Monticello, who had expressed such joy over Cushing's death, had a real and personal interest in the make-up of the Supreme Court, transcending his concern as a party leader. He expected to have a case in which he was the defendant referred to that tribunal. If the verdict went against him he would be ruined, he himself declared, and he believed the Federal judiciary to be so utterly unscrupulous and so inimical to himself that it would stop at nothing to destroy him. The controversy which so alarmed Jefferson had originated in a freak of the Mississippi River. At one point near New Orleans, the stream had deposited a great deal of rich alluvial soil between its old bank and a new channel. One of the men whose land had been river-front property before this process was completed set up a claim to the new deposits. He employed Edward Livingston as his attorney, and won the case in the circuit court. As fee, he deeded to the lawyer half of the reclaimed land.

There was substantial popular outcry against the decision. The simple folk of Louisiana thought that they should get the good as well as the bad from the vagaries of their river. They suffered when floods washed them out of their homes. Why should they not benefit when the Mississippi chose to be generous? They disputed by force Livingston's attempts to improve his property. The Governor refused to stop them. Jefferson, then President, declaring that the land was national property (although the courts had awarded it to Livingston), upheld the local authorities. A court order forbade the United States Marshal to interfere with the lawyer, but that official preferred to obey Jefferson.

Livingston tried to get Congress to intervene, but failed, and finally in the Spring of 1810 brought suit against Jefferson for $100,000 in the Federal courts of Virginia. It was this suit which alarmed Jefferson, and he agitated privately for a more friendly bench to hear it. He hoped that Federal Judge Griffin, who was an old man, could be replaced. John Tyler, a good Jeffersonian, not to be confused with the later President of that name, was beseeching the former President to put in a good word for him for the job, seeing in it "a bed of roses in my latter days." This is not an unknown attitude toward the Federal judiciary, and Jefferson had not always approved of it. But he pushed Tyler's cause, writing in May to Madison:

"From what I can learn Griffin cannot stand it long, and really the state has suffered long enough by having such a cypher in so important an office, and infinitely the more from the want of any counterpoint to the rancorous hatred which Marshall bears to the government of his country, & from the cunning & sophistry within which he is able to enshroud himself. It will be difficult to find a character of firmness enough to preserve his independence on the same bench with Marshall. Tyler, I am certain, would do it."

This was a reference to the fact that in circuit court, Tyler, who won the appointment, would share the bench with Marshall as Griffin had done. Two weeks later, Jefferson was blaming the Chief Justice for Livingston's suit.

"It is a little doubted that his knowledge of Marshall's character has induced him to bring this action," Jefferson wrote to Madison. "His twistifications of the law in the case of Marbury, in that of Burr, & the late Yazoo case shew how dexterously he can reconcile law to his personal biasses."

In the same letter, Jefferson declared that in Marshall's hands "the law is nothing more than an ambiguous text, to be explained by his sophistry into any meaning which may subserve his personal malice." So when Cushing died, Jefferson was eager to get a good opponent for Marshall named to the high court, which would hear the case on appeal if necessary. Again he wrote, this time to Gallatin, mentioning that in connection with his own case, Marshall's "inveteracy is profound, and his mind of that gloomy malignity which will never let him forego the opportunity of satiating it on a victim." This was the letter in which he called Cushing's death a godsend to him, and he ended by recommending his former Attorney General, Levi Lincoln. In a later letter to Madison, he urged Lincoln again, with Granger of the Yazoo lobby as his second choice, and Story the only possible alternative, although Jefferson disapproved of that gentleman as much for his youth as for his Tory principles.

Marshall, of course, was quite as much interested in the man who was to succeed Cushing. But he was not able to press his views upon the President, and he could only wait and hope. He was not much concerned with Jefferson's case (when it came to trial, he concurred with Tyler in a verdict for the former President) but he was going to have to live with the Supreme Court nominee, work with him, and break him into the ways of a national court.

Lincoln had the opportunity to refuse the post twice. Madison then appointed Alexander Wolcott, Republican boss of Connecticut, so flagrant a political hack that the Senate, in which there were only seven Federalists to twenty-seven of the nominee's party, rejected him by a vote of nine to twenty-four. The next name sent up was that of John Quincy Adams, with whom Marshall would have rejoiced to sit, and the Minister to Russia was confirmed unanimously, for he was a former Senator and the Upper House is tender of the feelings of its own. Months later the mail got to and from St. Petersburg with Adams's refusal. He was, he said, "conscious of too little law . . . too much of a political politician."

Meanwhile, the term of February, 1811, came with illness cutting the Supreme Court in half. Livingston and Washington were the only two who joined the Chief in their new quarters under the Senate. The three waited for ten days, then under the law as it stood at that time, adjourned until the next year. Four months later Marshall heard that Chase had died, and there were two vacancies on the Court. Madison found "Old Bacon Face" easier to replace than the New Englander. He nominated Gabriel Duval, a mild, capable man who was serving as Comptroller of the Treasury, then the second office in that Department, and resumed the search for a seventh Justice. He finally settled on Story, and presented Marshall with the ideal colleague.

Story had aroused Republican animosity by voting against the embargo during his one term in Congress, and since then had been courted assiduously by Federalists. Jefferson denounced him, but Madison was not the mere rubber stamp for his great predecessor which his enemies thought him. He recognized Story's quality, and besides the Bostonian was not averse to the war which was drawing nearer every day. So on November 15, Story and Duval were confirmed together; the Supreme Court once more was complete.

[4]

Marshall did not greet his new colleagues when the 1812 term convened. He had fallen a victim to the rigors of travel at last, and had broken a collar bone when the stage in which he was travelling from Richmond to Washington upset on the road. However, he was able to mount the bench, his arm strapped to his side, on February 14.

It took him only a short time to realize that in losing two old colleagues, he had gained at least one young ally. Duval, three years older than the Chief Justice and a confirmed Republican, became almost as uncompromising an upholder of Supreme Court authority as Johnson. But Story was the great acquisition for Marshall. He was only thirty-two, eager, bald, and spectacled, and had already displayed his freedom from party ties. Marshall had liked him when they met two years earlier. He grew to love his disciple, for Story was nothing less. The new Justice was a glutton for work and already prodigiously learned in his profession.

Story speedily fell under the spell of those qualities in Marshall which he himself lacked. Story was eager and bubbling over with energy. He was almost awed by the tremendous gravity with which the tall Chief Justice could preside over the most tedious arguments. The unwearied patience, the kindness with which Marshall administered even the slightest rebuke were in themselves admirable, Story thought, but he was reduced to almost worshipful prose when he contemplated the speed with which the great man could cut through the heart of argument to a decision, and the humor with which he flavored its application. Story was very solemn about the Court and basked uncritically in flattery. But Marshall could crack jokes about his own position, and Story was much impressed by this ability. When a lawyer somewhat fulsomely remarked that the Chief Justice had attained the acme of judicial distinction, Marshall replied:

"Let me tell you what that means, young man. The acme of judicial distinction means the ability to look a lawyer straight in the eyes for two hours and not hear a damned word he says."

Marshall never grew accustomed to the fact that he was a man to be sought after. He was firm in his beliefs, but he did not appreciate at all the heights on which some of his countrymen were beginning to place him, and this modesty was appealing. His surprise when, after an accident, he was besieged by callers and ladies bringing jelly and soup, was unaffected. Story marvelled at this trait, and within a few years it had become a custom for him to marvel at his Chief for any reason. Like many young men who embrace liberalism ardently but emotionally, without any reasoned basis for their beliefs, Story grew more and more conservative as he grew older, and more and more one with Marshall, who had always been conservative. The younger judge's zeal, industry, and deference made him a powerful aide in the work of the court—and gave rise to the legend that the relatively unschooled Chief Justice customarily closed discussions of difficult cases with:

"There, Brother Story, that's the law. Now you find the precedents."

However, the discussions were not quite so simple. The Court formed a very close little corporation, socially as well as judicially. Living in the same boardinghouse, taking their meals at the same table, meeting in each other's rooms to argue out the cases until a decision was reached, the seven Justices were kept in harmony, even when they dissented, by the tactful authority and gentle patience of the Chief. He dominated them by firmness, but they all commented on the mildness of his manner. Perhaps the quantities of food they ate, aided by sound digestions, helped, for the Washington boardinghouse table had to be sturdily built to accommodate the viands. The ordinary dinner at the popular Indian Queen (75 cents) included roast mutton, goose, a chicken pie, vegetables, puddings, and breads. Decanters of whisky and brandy stood at convenient intervals. There was no charge for these beverages, but more exotic potations could be obtained, such as the famous Daniel Webster punch, for which the ingredients were Milford rum, brandy, champagne, arrack, maraschino, green tea, lemon juice, and sugar.

While it would be years before the wife of a Justice graced Washington, the seven did not lead monastic lives. They were such social lions that the season was said to begin with the opening of court, and strait-laced observers were shocked to see the Justices cutting open and sorting out their dinner and reception invitations on the bench before they opened court. Marshall was a very different social being from the awkward young Captain who had captivated little Mary Ambler in Yorktown. He dined at the White House occasionally, and with foreign diplomats frequently. He became sufficiently familiar with the great in Washington to be patronizing, and to refer to a rather aristocratic Minister's wife as "among the most simple and domestic women I ever saw."

But of course it was in the courtroom itself that Marshall and his colleagues attracted the most attention and contributed the most to the contemporary scene. The apartment in which they met at this time was under the Senate, the ceiling being formed by the arches which supported the Senate floor. Raised above the rest of the court, which had room for a double row of spectators' seats, the Justices looked down upon legal battles which were regarded by contemporaries as dramas worthy of the criticism and attention bestowed upon the theatre. Some of the lawyers entered into the spirit of the play, and were as highly applauded as actors. William Pinkney especially was the darling of the crowds, as well as a favorite of the bench. He was the most successful lawyer of his day with a practice which netted him $20,000 a year. The effect of his oratory was tremendous, and today is difficult to understand. Like his figure, his speech was florid but corseted; he painted both his face and his metaphors. Women especially flocked to hear him, and once he started an oration all over again because Mrs. Madison and some of her friends entered the courtroom just as he was finishing.

However impressive the lawyers might be, the Chief Justice held his own in the eyes of the audience. He could turn a pretty compliment to the eloquence of counsel as easily as he could look a lawyer in the eye for two hours and not hear a word he said. "He was born to be the Chief Justice of any country into which Providence should have cast him," Pinkney once remarked. He liked to derive as much of a decision as possible from the arguments of the side against which he ruled, and he usually started off by saying, "It is admitted." Webster once remarked that when Marshall used those words, he was prepared to be crushed. He could also use irony, as when he copied Pinkney's fulsome phrases to extol that orator to the skies, only to conclude:

"So exquisite was the skill of the artist, so dazzling the garb in which the figure was presented, that it required the exercise of that cold investigating faculty which ought always to belong to those who sit on this bench to discover its only imperfection—its want of resemblance."

The dominance of the Chief Justice was chiefly resented by his brethren in the matter of delivering opinions. Johnson had remonstrated against Marshall's assumption of the authority to read all the opinions he wanted, and was told that it was a mark of respect.

"I soon, however, found out the real cause," he wrote to Jefferson. "Cushing was incompetent, Chase could not be got to think or write, Paterson was a slow man and willingly declined the trouble, and the other two judges [Marshall and Washington] you know are commonly estimated as one Judge."

Johnson yielded, as did all the others throughout Marshall's years of service.

XVIII

☆ ☆ ☆

Death of a Party

THE WHOLE NATION was watching the Administration muddle its way into war. In Europe the great struggle was moving toward its dramatic climax, for that winter Napoleon was preparing his invasion of Russia. The world war was in its final phase, but the United States remained on the brink.

There still was almost as much reason to fight France as England, and extreme Federalists certainly would have preferred that alternative. Marshall so far agreed with them that he hoped Pickering would be sent back to the Senate and wrote to Josiah Quincy that the latest French outrage on American commerce "exhausted to the dregs our cup of servility and degradation." But at the same time, he maintained his judicial calm on the bench and enraged some of his friends by delivering what they considered a pro-French opinion.

The case involved a ship, originally American, which had been confiscated by France and converted into a vessel of war. She was driven by a storm into Philadelphia, where her former owners demanded that she be turned over to them. In the hearing, the whole of the nation's grievances against Napoleon were rehearsed, and no man was more sympathetic to the recital than the Chief Justice. But he ruled that the public ships of a friendly power must always be exempt from the operation of our laws. The United States contended for this principle as regarded its own ships; it must recognize the same law for others.

At this time Napoleon had complicated the international situation by saying that he had withdrawn his anti-American decrees. There was no evidence of any relaxation of the practice of seizing American ships and cargoes wherever found, but communications were slow and Madison wished to believe that the French were telling the truth. Supposing that Napoleon had yielded while the British remained stubborn, he drafted a war message. Actually, it was the British who were preparing to yield. The Cabinet was drafting a peaceful abrogation of the hated orders. Washington and London worked with about equal speed and at complete cross-purposes. On June 16, England repealed the orders; on June 18, the United States declared war. Wholly out of sympathy with war hawks in the West and South, with unhappy seekers after peace in the White House and with rabid secessionists in New England, Marshall maintained a discreet silence except for two private letters. One of them could only give the Administration the impression that he stood for the unity of the country in time of war. The other could only give the Opposition the impression that he hoped political divisions would be drawn solely on the issue of peace or war.

The first of these letters was written to Monroe, who had recently succeeded Robert Smith as Secretary of State. Monroe had sent to the Chief Justice a collection of documents on the reasons for war, including the President's message, the report of the Committee on Foreign Relations and the declaration itself. In reply, Marshall wrote:

"Permit me to subjoin to my thanks for this mark of your attention my fervent wish that this momentous measure may, in its

operation on the interest & honor of our country, disappoint only
its enemies."

A month later, however, Marshall wrote a much longer letter
to Monroe's predecessor, who had been expelled from the Cabinet
for disloyalty to the Administration and had issued a public defense of his own conduct. The Chief Justice expressed approval.
He went into a long analysis of all American grievances against
France, making no mention of any cause of complaint against
England. He agreed with Smith that everyone ought to try to
rescue the country from the ruin which the war would bring, a
war which he blamed in part on Madison's folly in allowing himself to be duped if not dominated by Napoleon.

"All minor considerations should be waived," Marshall wrote;
"the lines of subdivision between parties, if not absolutely effaced,
should at least be convened for a time; and the great division between the friends of peace & the advocates of war ought alone to
remain. It is an object of such magnitude as to give to almost every
other comparative insignificance, and all who wish peace ought
to unite in the means which may facilitate its attainment, whatever may have been their differences of opinion on other points."

Dislike of war and distrust of the Republicans had led Marshall
thus far on the path to encouragement of secession. He went no
further, and he took no part in Federalist demonstrations although
the extremists were considering the possibility of drawing him
from the comparative security of the bench into the middle of
their schemes for defeating Madison for re-election on the peace
issue. Some of them, those who were not involved in secession
plots, reached the conclusion that the Chief Justice, or even perhaps Justice Washington, might carry Virginia against little
Jemmy and would unite Federalist and neutral votes everywhere.

The idea was advanced first by Benjamin Stoddert, who had
been the first Secretary of the Navy when the post was created
in Adams's administration and whose home in Georgetown was a
center of Federalist gayety and strategy during Congressional

sessions. The boom spread, and in July Rufus King in New York was noting:

"Mr. Coleman showed me two letters from Benj. Stoddert of Maryland urging Marshall as fed. Candidate for President, and King or Clinton as V.P., Marshall alone being able to take Virginia from Madison."

A little later King was approached again, asked whether he would serve under either Marshall or Washington. He refused, apparently not so much because he objected to second place as because he wanted to be free to oppose the pretension of the Clinton mentioned. This was De Witt, brilliant nephew of old George Clinton. Federalists were flirting with this Republican to lead a peace ticket, and King did not approve. But King kept noting strong recommendations for a ticket headed by Marshall.

That discreet gentleman was not talking about the Presidency even as much as he talked about the war. He had been asked just before the declaration of war to head an exploring expedition into the wilds of Virginia. The purpose was to investigate the possibilities of water transportation across the mountains. The State legislature wanted to know whether it would be possible and feasible to use Mr. Fulton's new invention to tap the trade of Kentucky and Ohio. The Chief Justice of the United States seemed an odd choice, but he was keenly interested in such internal improvements and was sufficiently rugged to stand the trip.

So Marshall missed the beginnings of the war and the heat of the Presidential campaign. Instead he tramped through forests, canoed on rivers, recaptured something of the spirit of his frontier childhood and made notes which added up to the fact that the proposed waterway was possible but too expensive.

[2]

An American who could escape news of the war that year was lucky. The war hawks and the Administration alike were completely unaware of the implications of their declaration. Both thought it would mean a pleasant parade of the militia through Canada to annex that British province, and some profitable raiding of British commerce. Frontiersmen were also eager to settle a few scores with the Indians.

It did not occur to Madison and Monroe, Clay and Calhoun that wars are expensive and that governmental machinery designed for a minimum of interference in the lives of people is not very well geared to raising armies, let alone supplying those armies. Congress adjourned without making any provisions for taxes or loans or recruiting—and without being asked for these things.

The country was as unfortunate in its military leaders as in the civilians. The Generals were remarkable, even in a non-military country, for their incompetence. The United States at this time had about fifteen times the population of Canada, but never put any overwhelming force of men on the frontier, and the armies that did get there were lucky (with the aid of some naval brilliance on the lakes) to end the war in possession of their own borders. At no time were they any serious threat to Canada. At sea, however, the tiny American Navy made up for the disgrace of the Army.

Marshall was spared a public campaign on the issue of the war. De Witt Clinton wangled a nomination by a group of peace Republicans, and after a great deal of bickering, the Federalists decided to support him. They had been drawn by the isolation of . their position into the political folly of seeking to elect a man they did not like in order to defeat someone they liked less. There can be little enthusiasm for a party whose leaders are in this unhappy frame of mind, and the Federalists were a bitter, demoralized lot throughout the campaign. Even so, Clinton carried nine States, but the South and West were loyal to Madison, and they were enough.

Whether or not Marshall could have done any better than Clinton, he was well out of the contest. From his seat on the bench he had an excellent view of the incompetence which was the chief characteristic of the war administration. Perhaps the low point in the American government's opinion of itself—and of the people's opinion of it—came when the British captured Washington so speedily that the British commander, General Ross, sat down in the White House to a dinner which had been cooked for the Madisons. A single skirmish had been the only military defense of the capital. The President was a fugitive across the Potomac, and his official dwelling was being set ablaze along with the Capitol and other public buildings.

However, as Marshall had written to his friend Pickering months before, "peace or war will be determined by the events in Europe." He meant the decision rested with the fighting there rather than in the inconclusive skirmishes on this side of the Atlantic. He regarded it as some consolation that the United States had entered the war too late to do Napoleon much good. The Emperor was on the march toward Russia when Congress declared war. In the month that the last feeble American thrust of 1812 was made at Canada, the Grand Army was trailing in heroic retreat back toward Poland, a tattered, starving, freezing remnant of Napoleonic glory. A year later, Federalists were celebrating openly the triumphs of their country's enemy as France itself was invaded. Another celebration just before the capture of Washington was held when news arrived that Napoleon had abdicated in April, 1814. The fact that the full weight of British arms could now be turned against the United States did not dim the rejoicing of Pickering and his colleagues.

A convention of New England Federalism was held in Hartford in December, 1814, amid a profound secrecy of debate, but the meeting did not plump for secession after all, for more moderate counsels prevailed. Its report, adopted after the advocates of separation had been talked down, was published on January 6, 1815, and news of it started on its slow way toward the rest of the country. It eventually met and was overwhelmed by the electrifying word of Jackson's incredible victory over Wellington's veterans at New Orleans on the eighth. Hard on the heels of both came the information that peace had been signed at Ghent on Christmas Eve. The Federalists had won their point—they had peace at last—and if they had had a better record of leadership they might have capitalized on the fact that the peace terms changed nothing. The United States had gained not one single point for which war had been declared in 1812. But the Federalist party, saddled with its pro-British and unpatriotic war stand, could no longer survive. There was a faint flash of activity in 1816 when Rufus King collected 34 electoral votes to 183 for Monroe, but it was a last flicker and it left the Chief Justice of the United States definitely and completely a man without a party.

[3]

The business of the Supreme Court during the war seemed to young Story to be heavy—"I have been steeped to the very chin in business, and we are now almost overwhelmed with it," he wrote during the 1814 term—but the cases were chiefly of interest to the litigants, the lawyers, and the judges. The principal exception was one in which the Chief Justice did not participate because it directly concerned his brother James and indirectly himself and his Fairfax land. The case had been in litigation for a great many years; in fact Marshall himself had been one of the lawyers in its early stages. It came up on appeal, after a long and stormy history, during the term of 1813.

Some twenty years earlier, David Hunter, a prosperous farmer, had obtained from the State of Virginia nearly 800 acres of Fairfax land. The whole Fairfax estate had been confiscated during the War of Independence, but under the peace treaty any of it which had not been divided among actual settlers was supposed to be returned to the owners. Lord Fairfax's heir, Denny Martin Fairfax, sued Hunter and won in the Virginia court in 1794. Hunter appealed, but before the appeal was heard, the Jay Treaty was ratified. It confirmed all such titles as that of Fairfax, and was an additional blow to Hunter's title.

John Marshall's syndicate purchased their land later, but James Marshall meanwhile had bought for himself alone additional tracts from Fairfax, and among them was the land Hunter still claimed. Hunter allowed his claim to rest until 1809 when he revived it, and threw into jeopardy not only all of the various Fairfax purchases but most of the land which in the course of years had been acquired by Americans from former British owners. This time Hunter won in the Virginia courts, and the losers promptly appealed to the Supreme Court on the ground that the case involved the construction of a treaty.

With Marshall disqualifying himself and Todd absent because of illness, the other five judges heard the case. Four of them decided in an opinion written by Story that the Jay Treaty had protected the Fairfax title, and that to allow the Virginia court's ruling to stand "would be selling suits and controversies through the whole country." Justice Johnson dissented, but the case was not finished. The Virginia Court of Appeals unanimously informed the world that they were not bound by any decisions of any other tribunal and refused to accept orders from Washington. So the case came back to the Supreme Court again, and Story had a chance to write another opinion asserting the supremacy of the body of which he was a member. It was chiefly remarkable as completing his alienation from his old party friends, but it was also a solid statement of what has since become a truism, that the Supreme Court is supreme over State courts in matters affecting Federal laws or treaties.

The decision also cost the Justices an increase in salary. At the time Story was reading his words in Court, there was a bill pending to raise the pay of government officials to meet the high postwar cost of living, for beef was nearly 10 cents a pound, butter a quarter, and a woman servant could not be had for less than $30 a year plus food and clothing. But Congressional anger over the Hunter case was so hot that the Supreme Court was eliminated from the bill. Associate Justices were left at $3,500 a year and their Chief at $4,000.

For the rest, the Court's work during and just after the war was concerned with problems arising from the embargo and the actual hostilities. Although he had disliked the economic measures with which Jefferson sought to avert an armed conflict, Marshall did not attempt to controvert their legality.

In some of the other cases, involving captured ships and lost cargoes, he had opportunities to avow his fundamental concern for the rights of property. In one of them, he attempted to regain for the harassed neutral in war some of the privileges which in days of sober peace seem so reasonable but which excited belligerents will not tolerate when it comes to the point. Marshall tried to set up the rule that a neutral's property must be respected by belligerents even if found on an enemy ship. Posterity has refused to accept the judgment.

[4]

However, the troubles of neutrals were not to confront the judges of Marshall's day to any great extent because the war had diverted the course of American history as sharply as if the country had won it. Ever since the foundation of the republic, foreign affairs had been the rival and frequently the superior of all domestic issues in the popular mind. It was their fatally wrong stand on foreign policy, not the fact that they took a stand, which was killing the Federalist party at the very moment when a great many of its principles were winning the support of staunch but nationally-minded Republicans.

For all their anguished screams, the men of New England had come out of the war quite well financially. Daniel Webster, a fierce man in debate and a jovial one over the bottle, had entered Congress in 1813 as a red-hot antiwar Federalist. He was to remain as the faithful representative of New England mill and counting house, but he did not call himself a Federalist for very long. He was joined in fundamental policy to and parted by deep personal rivalry from Henry Clay. On the other hand, Clay's war hawk colleague, Calhoun, would soon be assuming a State rights position which he had not expounded before or during the war.

The years of interruption in trade had given an invincible stimulus to manufacturing. The wave of a postwar prosperity was carrying immigrants and comforts into the West. Some of the amenities of civilization were penetrating as far as Tennessee and Michigan. All the world seemed to have gone land mad, and the first big American boom was working up to the first serious national depression.

In the spring of 1816 the Federalist ticket had been soundly beaten in the New York State elections, and the man who was to be the party's last standard bearer later in the year was ready to admit defeat long before November. Rufus King went into a Presidential campaign, leaving this letter on record:

"I presume that the failure [in New York] will, as I think it should, discourage the Federalists from maintaining a fruitless struggle. It has probably become the real interest & policy of the Country that the Democracy should pursue its natural Course. Federalists of our age must be content with the past."

That same year, however, the old Hamiltonian principles were asserting their natural strength in a country which was not concerned with theory. A new tariff act, including some interestingly protective duties for the new textile mills, was passed. A new Bank of the United States was chartered, and it was not surrounded with even as many safeguards for the public as that of Hamilton had been.

With all these preoccupations, the country turned its back on the Atlantic Ocean and all that might lie on the other side. For another hundred years, the quarrels and turmoils and ambitions of Europe would affect the United States only indirectly. Political parties would divide on other issues than sympathy with or fear of European policies.

Chief Justice Marshall, entering upon his vigorous sixties, was fitting well into this new world. His decisions had marked him as the defender of property against the supposed onslaughts of radicals, and the disappearance of his old political party was an asset to a judge who did not have to change his principles. He would soon see the new problems of the country giving rise to another pair of parties, and one of them would adopt his philosophy. Meanwhile he was glad to officiate at the inauguration of his old schoolmate Monroe. For the first time, a President was to take the oath of office out of doors, and this year began the custom of inaugural ceremonies on a platform in front of the Capitol. The reason was that Speaker Clay had refused the use of the Representatives' Hall. He said the crowd would be too great for the new floor, but unkind gossips said he was only being spiteful because he was not appointed Secretary of State.

Washington was making a speedy comeback from the devastation of the war, although cows grazed along Sixteenth Street opposite St. John's Church, and Commodore Decatur's new home and the Dolly Madison house were the only buildings on Lafayette Square except the White House and the Church. The square itself was an untidy, treeless lot. But the city was booming. Harrison Gray Otis was impressed by the number of houses going up and by the fact that lots on Pennsylvania Avenue cost as much as a dollar a square foot, although some could be obtained for as little as fifteen cents. The Supreme Court, however, was still beset by housing difficulties. It was back in the Capitol for the terms of 1817 and 1818, but hidden in a smallish room in the North Wing "little better than a dungeon."

For most of the statesmen of Washington, it was a distressing period because of the uncertainty in policies, in actions, and in appointments. Because it was so uncertain, and therefore developed no important conflicts, it was to be called by some historians "The Era of Good Feeling," but John Quincy Adams, who had become Secretary of State, was more realistic.

"This Government," he wrote, "is indeed assuming daily more and more a character of cabal, and preparation, not for the next Presidential election, but for the one after—that is, working and counter-working, with many of the worst features of elective monarchies."

This was the penalty for not having an effective organized opposition. "The Era of Good Feeling" was apparent only in politics. Various sectional and economic issues were coming to the fore in no uncertain terms, with the protagonists clamoring for attention and bidding for support. Political attention might be riveted on the problem of the Presidential succession, but the expanding needs of the country could not wait for that. Some of those needs were to be brought before the bar of the Supreme Court before Congress or the Executive could get around to them.

XIX

☆ ☆ ☆

A Day in Court

WHEN THE Supreme Court met in its inadequate "dungeon" for the term of 1818, it took a more discerning eye than existed in Washington to see that there were troubled times ahead. The postwar boom had reached its peak and was on the brink of a plunge into black depression, but this was not visible from the Capitol. Complete lack of control over the economic forces of the country left the government both helpless and uninformed. There was little popular demand for government to do any more than pass out deeds to the public domain.

The West was being settled so fast that Indiana, Mississippi, and Illinois had followed Louisiana into the Union as full-fledged States, and Alabama was knocking on the door. Cotton, which had reached the high price of 16 cents at the close of the war, had shot up within three years to 34 cents, and land was selling for as much as $150 an acre. Money—or at least the bank notes of the State-chartered institutions which required little more than an address and access to a printer to issue negotiable paper—was apparently plentiful. Few men of affairs could resist the temptation of easy credit.

Society in the cities became grander than before. The paper fortunes which were being amassed in speculation and trade were being spent on gowns and entertainment and horses and parade. The New Englanders who, as a hangover from their State rights stand during the war, had voted against the tariff of 1816, were discovering the benefits of protection. They were becoming its most ardent advocates, while the Southerners who had pushed it through were cooling noticeably.

The real animosities of life in the capital were being supplied this year by the ladies in a revolt against the high tone taken by Eliza Hay, Monroe's daughter, who had set the town by the ears because she had refused to pay the first call on the wives of diplomats. Outside the drawing rooms of the ladies who followed or opposed Mrs. Hay was a purely bachelor society. Here men could gather with Clay in his favorite game of brag, a sort of illegitimate father to poker, and listen to his stories while large stakes were gambled across the table. Or they might hear Webster's rich voice rolling out his song:

> Solid men of Boston
> Drink no strong potations;
> Solid men of Boston
> Make no long orations.

Or perhaps they would laugh with the Bostonian who so greatly belied his favorite verse as he mimicked the bibulous gentleman— it was Webster's most famous story for years:

" 'S funny thing abou' me, drink never affec's me excep' in legs. *Think* perf'ly straight. *Talk* perf'ly straight. Only trouble with me is my wees get neek."

Physically Washington was improving but slowly. Mud was still the chief feature of travel. The enormous meals of the day were necessary perhaps to provide the physical energy to get about the city. An afternoon call sometimes turned into a major expedition—or so it would be regarded now—and men missed a convivial evening only a few miles away if the weather was bad just because it was physically impossible to cover the distance in time to get there and home again the same night.

The Supreme Court did not offer its usual quota of oratorical entertainment during this year's session. The docket did not seem to contemporaries to be very interesting. Toward the end of the term, a case involving Dartmouth College was scheduled, but when it was called up at eleven o'clock on the morning of March 10, only a few lawyers and officials were present. Even Story, that garrulous and gossipy Justice, did not consider it of sufficient note to mention in his letters home.

[2]

The Dartmouth College controversy up to this time had created a good deal more excitement in New England than among the habitués of the Supreme Court. All the darkest passions which can be attracted to differences over education, religion, and politics had become involved.

Dartmouth had been established by a royal charter which provided that a self-perpetuating board of trustees of twelve was to manage the affairs of the College forever. This worked well enough until Congregationalist and Presbyterian factions developed on the board. The Congregationalists won and dismissed the Presbyterian President of the College, who promptly appealed to the legislature. That body passed a law to convert the College into a State University. The College refused to recognize the new trustees, and for a time two institutions were in operation simultaneously.

The issue on which the controversy got into the courts was the refusal of the secretary and treasurer, who had gone over to the University, to surrender the records to the old trustees. They sued him in the State courts and lost. Then, on the plea that the legislature's change in the College charter violated the Constitution—

"obligation of a contract"—the College appealed to the Supreme Court.

The issue was so hot in New Hampshire that both sides had employed expensive counsel, but the University had been a little more careless in its selection than the College. The winners in the State courts had John Holmes, a witty politician, to charm the Court, and Wirt for solid achievement. But Wirt had just been appointed Attorney General and was so busy between his new work and the private cases which the government's chief law officer still was allowed to take that he admitted the session "will find me unprepared." On the other side were Webster and Hopkinson. Webster had appeared for the College in the State courts and while he was not especially profound as a lawyer, he had the advantage of all the arguments which his associates in the previous trial had prepared.

Perhaps because of the absence of spectators, the speeches of counsel were relatively brief. The four of them talked for less than three days. Webster furnished the most blatant excursion into subjects not involved, a long harangue on the natural right of private charities to be free from State interference. He was afraid all institutions of learning—he mentioned Harvard and Yale—would find themselves in danger. At last he got around to the contract clause of the Constitution and cited *Fletcher* vs. *Peck* and the other cases in which the Supreme Court already had asserted the inviolability of contracts.

The real question was whether a corporate charter was a contract. The State court had held that it was not, that the corporate franchise was a public device for the public benefit, and that the State was as thoroughly justified in changing it as in changing the duties of public officials. Wirt and Holmes took this line for the University. They were answered by Hopkinson, who undertook to justify the contention that a corporate charter was a contract, explaining that there was no distinction in the Constitution. He also pointed out that if charters were left to State caprice, there would be nothing to prevent corrupt and foolish men from undoing the good of their wise predecessors. He did not mention that the wise would also be barred from undoing the evil of the corrupt and foolish.

When the Justices gathered at their boardinghouse on March 12, after these arguments had ended, they found their Court was divided three ways. Marshall, Washington, and Story were willing to hand down an immediate decision in favor of the College. Duval and Todd were convinced that the New Hampshire court should be sustained on the ground that Dartmouth had a charter, not a contract. Johnson and Livingston could not make up their minds. The term was nearly over; the issue involved did not seem to require speed—the Supreme Court is more interested in the quality of its decisions than the rapidity with which they are reached. So on March 13, Marshall announced that the judges had as yet been unable to reach a decision, and the case would go over to next year. Court soon after adjourned, leaving Webster to fret and worry about the decision for the next eleven months.

[3]

There was a good deal of eager canvassing for the opinions of the two doubtful judges in the meantime. Webster always thought that the conversion of Johnson and Livingston was largely due to Chancellor Kent, who saw both of them and discussed the case. But during the summer and fall, Marshall was quietly working on his opinion without the benefit of his colleagues. He knew what he wanted to say, and on a constitutional issue, he had yet to need the assistance of Kent in winning a court majority.

He took the finished product to the 1819 term of court, which saw the Justices returned to their old quarters under the Senate, redecorated and a little enlarged. The *National Intelligencer* thought the room was an improvement on its previous state, although it proved from the beginning to be too small for both the spectators and the bar. There was a loss of dignity, one commentator thought, in the fact that the Justices had to don their robes in the presence of the audience before court opened. They sat on a raised platform at the east end of the room looking across at a bas-relief of Fame crowned with a rising sun and pointing significantly to the Constitution and to Justice, who was holding her scales. The space for the bar was set about three feet below the bench, furnished with a long table and cushioned armchairs on rollers. Two brown jugs and a few glasses for water completed the arrangements for comfort. Spectators crowded into the limited seats behind the bar or stood among the profusion of arches which upheld the Senate floor and which led a Senator to suggest that the Supreme Court room was "modelled after the prison of Constance in Marmion."

The first day of the session was taken up with formalities and with admiring the new apartment, which seemed luxurious after the hole and corner existence of the last four years. By the next morning, Marshall had obtained the concurrence of all his brethren except Duval—Todd was absent—to the Dartmouth Case opinion on which he had been working. It was well known that the University, much distressed by the mediocre appearance of its lawyers, had retained the redoubtable Pinkney, just back from two years as Minister to Russia, and Pinkney wanted a re-hearing. Eager to get back into his favorite arena, he had worked up what he considered a sound case on behalf of his clients.

In the close intimacy of the bar and bench Marshall must have known that Pinkney was prepared to seek a new argument. In the leisurely practice of that day, he normally would have been prepared to listen. But he had a good deal of respect for Pinkney's persuasive powers. He could well regard it as a triumph that he would be able to present a five-to-one decision on so delicate a point, and the Maryland advocate might manage to sway some of the weaker brethren if they heard him. Therefore, on the morning of February 2, as soon as the Justices had taken their places, Marshall pulled an eighteen-page document out of the sleeve of his robe and began to read. He had to ignore Pinkney rather pointedly, because the alert lawyer had leaped to his feet even before the Chief Justice could clear his throat.

The decision, of course, was a reversal of the State court, and helped protect all private non-profit corporations (as well as not a few less philanthropically organized) from that time forward. As was customary with the Chief Justice, he devoted most of his opinion to proving points which had general agreement, and stated the really controversial elements as a simple fact. In this case, the only new point he was deciding was whether such a charter as Dartmouth possessed was a contract. He said:

"It can require no argument to prove that the circumstances of this case constitute a contract."

If a governmental body wished to control a corporation, he said, the terms of that control must be written into the charter at the beginning, not thought up afterwards. And the Chief Justice gave a definition of a corporation which has been used by a great many legal lights since. It was:

"A corporation is an artificial being, invisible, intangible, and existing only in contemplation of law."

Story also had arrived in Washington with a written opinion on the case. It was to the same general effect, and a good deal easier to follow. Livingston, for one, thought it superior to that of the Chief Justice, but in Marshall's court, he himself read the opinions.

Under this one, the power of corporations, both profit and non-profit, expanded like flowers in the April sun. All sorts of enterprises relied upon the protection of this decision. The spread of banks and land companies and, before very much longer, railroads was rooted in stronger economic ground, but it took the form it did partly because of the inviolability of corporate franchises which Marshall had described. At the time there was not so much interest in it as later developed, but Story foresaw its importance, and wrote to Kent:

"Unless I am very much mistaken the principles on which that decision rests will be found to apply with an extensive reach to all

the great concerns of the people, and will check any undue encroachments upon civil rights, which the passions or the popular
doctrines of the day may stimulate our State Legislatures to
adopt."

If Story had written "property rights" instead of "civil rights,"
he would have been correct. It took the Supreme Court of later
days a long time to get rid of that "extensive reach." The notion
that the government is powerless to control the creatures it creates
was implicit in the Marshall decision. It was eliminated from our
jurisprudence partly by discovering the broader application of a
weapon known as the "police power." It is no longer safe for a
corporation to behave as if it were entitled to all the immunities
and privileges which the Dartmouth opinion seems to confer.

[4]

The angry remarks of the disappointed Pinkney and the triumphant shouts of Webster—both uttered decently out of court—
had hardly ceased when the Court took up a case which aroused a
good deal more popular excitement. It was of much more immediate concern to business directly and all the people indirectly.
Sturges vs. *Crowninshield* got the attention it merited partly because the country was in the throes of the worst depression in its
history up to that time.

In large measure, the hard times, which had been growing
worse for nearly a year, were the fruit of uncontrolled, unsuper-
vised and completely unscrupulous banking. A common method
adopted by banks to finance new enterprises was to print up paper
money which was not secured by anything except the name of the
bank. If the new enterprise was successful, everyone concerned
shared, including the bank. If the new enterprise failed, the
banker frequently extricated himself by refusing to honor the
printed money which had financed the venture.

Paper, therefore, became of uncertain value, whereupon the
banks in their own interest found it necessary to foreclose on

tangible property. They executed the foreclosures at the same time that they repudiated their own notes, so that a man might have bank notes to the face value of thousands of dollars but would lose valuable property because he could not pay a mortgage of a few hundreds in currency acceptable to the creditor. Soon values fell to ridiculous levels and bankruptcies began. The great commercial house of Smith and Buchanan had closed in Baltimore in the spring of 1818. By the end of summer, the new Bank of the United States was refusing to take any other bank paper than its own, which was ruinous to its debtors. Many of them, and State bankers too, retaliated by seeking to drive the Bank of the United States out of existence. Laws for taxing it were passed in several states, and in others a new requirement for doing business was a State charter, which of course the national institution could not get.

Intensified competition for the assets of the unwary actually increased the amount of paper as the depression wore on. Shortly before the Supreme Court met in February, 1819, Hezekiah Niles estimated in his usually reliable *Weekly Register* that there were 400 banks in the country, almost twice as many as there had been two years before. Nearly all of them were trying to restore faith in their paper money by printing more of it, and in the public mind "banks" and "speculation" were synonyms. The public did not know how accurate this sentiment was, because there were no regulations requiring banks to issue statements. These, and all other business institutions, insisted that the record of their assets and liabilities was as private as their consciences. But the system did not make for prosperity, even of banks, much as they contended that if they were let alone everything would be all right.

As a refuge from the economic storm which these practices had raised, some of the self-styled financiers had bought from accommodating State legislatures new bankruptcy statutes which enabled them to conceal their assets and defy their creditors. They saved themselves, but did not check the downward economic spiral. The *Weekly Register*, which carried on a journalistic crusade against the bankrupts, reported incident after incident of men continuing to live in luxury after they had "satisfied" their creditors with a few dollars on debts totalling thousands.

In various parts of the country, where the hard fate of honest debtors was being contrasted with the luxury of swindlers, there was considerable popular demand for two measures of relief. One was to place all debtors on the easy footing of the swindlers (rather than make the swindlers pay up) so that poor men could get free from debt. The other was to recover some of the losses from the hated Bank of the United States. It was partly in response to the second that some legislatures levied taxes on the Bank. But they were not quite so ready to relieve the poor of debts, for the rich who paid for bank charters and favorable legislation would not like the idea of extending the benefits of insolvency to all.

Of course, the issue was not altogether one between two bands of cheats. There was an equally intense and more honest struggle between the advocates of "hard" money and those who still believed that plenty of paper would get them out of the depression.

Under these circumstances, a great many business interests were affected by the case of Sturges vs. Crowninshield as a test of the validity of State bankruptcy laws and set for a hearing in 1819. Crowninshield had passed through the friendly New York bankruptcy law, owing Sturges the principal on two promissory notes which together amounted to less than $800. Sturges, a Massachusetts man, brought suit in the Federal court.

On appeal the Supreme Court listened to the usual long and learned argument. The case was re-argued in the evening gathering at the boardinghouse. As usual, Washington, Johnson, and Story did most of the talking and, with Marshall, thrashed out most of the knotty points. They were all agreed this time, and on February 17 Marshall delivered the unanimous opinion. No State, the Court held, could enact a bankruptcy law so long as the Federal government had one on its statute books, because authority in this field was given to Congress.

The decision was based on the constitutional provision empowering Congress "to establish . . . uniform laws on the subject of bankruptcies throughout the United States." If Congress exercised that option, Marshall held, the States could not enter the field because then the laws would not be uniform. The lawyers for Crowninshield had said that they could find no express prohibition in the Constitution. If the Fathers had meant to exclude States from this field, they should have said so. Marshall disposed of this argument in a passage which has been of value in expanding the powers of the Federal government. In effect, the Chief Justice read into the minds of the Fathers the intention to apply their rules to general subjects, leaving specific application to common sense, because, if they had attempted to list every individual instance, they might not have foreseen every contingency. In the case of the State law before the court, he went on, it would have been unconstitutional even if the Federal Congress had not legislated on the subject. A bankruptcy law in its very nature impairs the obligation of contracts, and therefore would not be legal if enacted by States.

By this time in his life, followers of Marshall's decisions—if they disagreed with his philosophy—were becoming weary of "obligation of a contract." In this case, there was a good deal of bitter criticism, both from the swindlers who would have to find other methods of evading their debts and from those who sought relief from real hardships. The Court was blamed for forbidding the States in the midst of a depression from coming to the aid of their people with moratoriums or similar devices for throwing the burden of hard times on those better able to bear it.

The storm over *Sturges* vs. *Crowninshield* was great, but nothing to that which went out over the country within a very few weeks more. This term of 1819 was proving a busy one for the Court, and five days after Marshall read his decision on bankruptcy, Webster rose as the first in a galaxy of legal talent to fight for the life of the Bank of the United States.

[5]

Mr. Webster's client was being attacked from two sides. While it was trying to repel the assault of the States in the basement of the Capitol, it was defending itself from the national legislature on the main floor. Four days before the Court fight opened, a Representative from Virginia had introduced a resolution to repeal the Bank's charter. That institution was well supported by a corps of agents, official and unofficial, who sat in Congress at this time, and the discussion was still droning along when Webster began his argument on February 22.

It was not yet the custom to celebrate George Washington's birthday, but the Supreme Court was crowded as though for a holiday. There was no lack of popular interest, as there had been when the Dartmouth case was heard. The belles and beaux of Washington could expect the best the country had to offer in courtroom debate.

"We have had a crowded audience of ladies and gentlemen," Story wrote; "the hall was full almost to suffocation, and many went away for want of room."

More than brilliant counsel attracted the spectators. A great many capital figures, both in and out of politics, were holders of bank stock. Congress itself was full of them. But that was not yet regarded as reprehensible. Story, for example, was a most circumspect man in these matters, but he did not regard it as conflicting with his public duty to serve as director and then president of the Merchants Bank of Salem, whose act of incorporation he had helped obtain while he was a member of the State legislature. So the fashionable crowd, while personally interested, was not necessarily made up of shady characters.

The case before the Court would determine whether the sudden rash of State laws against the Bank of the United States should stand. Maryland, which was first to enact such legislation, had provided that any bank not licensed by State authority must pay a tax of $15,000 a year or issue its notes on a State-stamped paper, for which it would have to pay. While theoretically this might apply to many banks, in practice it meant the Bank of the United States because that was the only banking institution in the country which had branches in more than one State. James McCulloch, the cashier of the Baltimore branch, refused to pay the tax, was sued and with considerable rapidity brought the appeal before the Supreme Court. If Maryland won, the Bank of the United States could (and with the State laws already adopted would) be taxed out of existence.

Fifteen years earlier the Court had asserted the supremacy of a Federal law in a somewhat similar case. It had held that States could not take away the Federal government's right to assert priority in the assets of a bankrupt. But the bench then had been solidly Federalist, and Marshall and Washington were the only two survivors of that decision. Besides, the popular outcry against the Bank of the United States was so bitter that the clamor had reached even to this basement room in the Capitol. Judges are not immune to public opinion, and enemies of the Bank hoped for a new deal.

Webster was at his best, and he had excellent source material for his speech. With his powerful chest and massive head held so that he gave the illusion of being a foot taller than his real height, he paraphrased for several hours all the reasons which Alexander Hamilton had written nearly thirty years before as to the necessity and constitutionality of a national bank. Then he offered the observation that the Maryland tax must be invalid because the power to tax is the power to destroy. In effect, he added, Maryland was taxing the Federal government when it taxed that government's agent.

Joseph Hopkinson, the opponent of his recent colleague in the Dartmouth case, and Walter Jones, once called by Marshall a great constitutional lawyer, spoke up for Maryland. They defied the Bank to find in the Constitution any provision which would forbid the States to levy taxes on commercial organizations. They were answered by Wirt, who had caught up with his work and, although still Attorney General, was employed by the Bank. Wirt took the dare, and cited what he insisted was the fact that the Constitution established the supremacy of all the United States over any part.

The Court by this time had listened to three days of argument, but now the two principal champions were to be heard. First came Luther Martin, seventy-five years old and reddened by brandy but with voice and legal acumen undimmed. All day Thursday, all day Friday he poured out a stream of rambling eloquence, mixed with shrewd hits. He rehearsed the debates which resulted in the ratification of the Constitution. He recalled how the advocates of that fundamental charter had denied that Federal authority would ever annul State laws and had agreed later with their opponents to the Tenth Amendment to make this clearer. The Tenth Amendment put the case as plainly as human language could: "The powers not delegated to the United States by the Constitution or prohibited by it to the States, are reserved to the States respectively, or to the people." If this meant what it said, Martin insisted, the power to lay a tax on a bank chartered by the Federal government was reserved to the States.

Martin had reserved his best hit, however, for the third day of his speech. The case was taking longer than had been expected, and was now in its sixth day of argument. It was a Saturday, but the hall was crowded as ever, and Martin did not seem to be tired. He talked like an angel, one of his admirers thought, and he ended his three-day plea by announcing that he had one final authority which he believed the Court would find conclusive. Without glancing at the Chief Justice he began to read from a speech which John Marshall had delivered in the Virginia ratification convention.

As he began to recite the assurances given in 1788 by the young delegate that the government was to be one of limited powers, Story noticed that his chief seemed a little nervous. Marshall's uneasiness increased when Martin quoted: "Can they go beyond the delegated powers?" The lawyer droned on through that long-forgotten speech, and at last he concluded both his quotation and his oration. As he sat down, Marshall drew a deep breath, and Court adjourned.

Over the week end, Story inquired what had prompted the manifest uneasiness and the sigh of relief.

"Why, to tell you the truth," replied Marshall, "I was afraid I had said some foolish things in the debate; but it was not so bad as I expected."

The consensus of opinion was that the best had been reserved for the last in this exciting case. Pinkney, groomed within an inch of his life, made the closing argument for the Bank, and Story was still filled with the wonder of as much of it as had been delivered when he wrote on Wednesday:

"Mr. Pinkney rose on Monday to conclude the argument; he spoke all that day and yesterday, and will probably conclude today. I never, in my whole life, heard a greater speech; it was worth a journey from Salem to hear it; his elocution was excessively vehement, but his eloquence was overwhelming. His language, his style, his figures, his arguments, were most brilliant and sparkling. He spoke like a great statesman and patriot, and a sound constitutional lawyer. All the cobwebs of sophistry and metaphysics about State rights and State sovereignty he brushed away with a mighty besom."

It was plain that Story agreed with the speaker. So did the rest of the Court. Pinkney had finished the nine days of argument on March 3. The Justices took a third of that time to read and draft their decision, and Marshall read it in Court on March 6. That the crowds had come to hear the oratorical display was evident from the fact that the Chief Justice's audience consisted entirely of lawyers and was not very large.

The Court did not confine itself to saying that the Maryland law was unconstitutional and therefore the Bank could not be taxed. As usual, Marshall ranged far afield, and threw in some sound blows for extending the boundaries of government to permit functions and regulations which would have appalled the men who ratified the Constitution. Like Webster, he delved into the constitutionality of the Bank itself and repeated his doctrine that Congress was entitled to use what it regarded as appropriate means to carry out the powers entrusted to it. In 1788 he had been cautious, but in 1819 he was willing to cut the States right out of any share of constitutional interpretation, saying:

"The government of the Union, then, is emphatically and truly a government of the people. In form and substance it emanates from them. Its powers are granted by them, and are to be exercised directly on them, and for their benefit."

He, too, repeated Hamilton's argument and delivered himself of the classic explanation of the power implied but not stated in the Constitution.

"Let the end be legitimate," he said, "let it be within the scope of the Constitution, and all means which are appropriate, which are plainly adapted to that end, which are not prohibited but consist with the letter and spirit of the Constitution, are constitutional."

Marshall then adopted Webster's phrase that the power to tax is the power to destroy—a phrase which was dragged out of its context to defend a great many curious theories in later years— and said Maryland had no more power to tax a United States Bank than to tax the United States mails.

All of these things Marshall said several times in the course of his opinion, for he was a great believer in the emphasis of repetition. The attacks upon it were featured by the same device. The whole country was so aroused by the debates over the Bank and arguments as to its responsibility for the depression that these attacks upon the Supreme Court were unusually prompt and vigorous.

"Our opinion in the Bank case has aroused the sleeping spirit of Virginia, if indeed it ever sleeps," the Chief Justice wrote to Story less than three weeks after the decision had been read.

All over the country, the long opinion was reprinted, and almost always reprinted to be denounced. Niles returned to the attack in successive numbers of his *Weekly Register*, sprinkling through the columns of his anger such remarks as:

"A deadly blow has been struck at the sovereignty of the states, and from a quarter so far removed from the people as to be hardly accessible to public opinion."

Marshall would have agreed with the first phrase, except that he would have regarded it as a tribute. He thought that the sovereignty of states was dangerous. Everything that had happened in his lifetime, everything that was to happen confirmed him in this belief.

The battle raged in the press for months. In New York the *General Advertiser* said of the judges that "their reason and their judgment had forsaken them," and that their decision was "in defiance of human rights, human joys and divine commandments." Spencer Roane, head of the Virginia high court, wrote a long series of articles in the Virginia papers attacking the decision in *McCulloch* vs. *Maryland*. Some of his remarks stung so severely that Marshall actually composed and sent off to Bushrod Washington a series of five essays in answer. Washington got them published anonymously, condensed into two, in a Philadelphia paper.

XX

☆ ☆ ☆

Era of Good Feeling

THERE WAS TO be a lull in the courts before Marshall took up the challenge of the growing agitation for State rights. It was a lull during which the opposition to the doctrines he had been enunciating gathered strength and prepared public opinion for the fray.

In the first place, Roane was continuing his attacks upon the Bank decision, but the Chief Justice was silent. He thought his decision was right, yet he was not at all satisfied with his written defense of it, nor could he find time to devise a better one. He might have been a little more bitter than he was if he had known that Virginia's Chief Justice had been buying Bank stock (for his son) while Marshall was selling his. Marshall had disposed of his holdings when he first heard of *McCulloch* vs. *Maryland* because he did not think it proper for a judge to rule in a case which would involve his personal profit. Roane, who had a shrewd notion of how the Supreme Court would jump, saw no reason to avoid a good investment for his son just because he disapproved of the legal decision.

In the second place, the depression was slow to dissipate, for deflation had succeeded inflation without noticeable improvement in the general economy.

And finally, the Supreme Court was becoming involved in the most dangerous contemporary political crisis, the struggle over admission of Missouri as a State with a constitution permitting slavery. Sectional lines had been drawn on the issue, and the bitterness which would one day lead to war was animating the debate. When Marshall returned to Washington for the 1820 term of court, he listened to a good deal of it. He told Story he was disturbed both by the sectional nature of the dispute and by the frequency with which Southerners dragged into their speeches attacks on his decision in *McCulloch* vs. *Maryland*. The advocates of admission of Missouri as a Slave State were declaring that if the principle proclaimed by the Supreme Court prevailed, it meant Congress had the authority to interfere with slavery in the South. This was a very strained argument, but slavery had taken a firm economic grip on the cotton States, so firm that it weakened logic.

The South was greatly changed since young lawyer Marshall opened his office in Richmond. There had always been big planters, but the independent small farmers had been able to make headway against them, at least in Virginia. During the War of Independence, these farmers seemed to have seized control of the State. Now, throughout the South, the plantation economy was driving general farmers out of their market. As they became poorer in relation to the planters, they became prouder. All that many of them had left to be proud about was their white skins, and they were beginning that fanatical concentration on this asset which was to ally them to the wealthy members of their own race in an odd sort of loyalty which sacrificed material interests to the cause of white supremacy.

The change was reflected in the political leadership of the South. Jefferson and Marshall, Madison and C. C. Pinckney had their philosophical differences, but all of them had two things in common. They all owned slaves and they all hated slavery. Each

of them recognized the essential evil in one man's outright owner-
ship of another. They recognized that the evil was greater in the
long run for the master than for the slave. They were advocates
of gradual emancipation, and studied ways and means of achieving it.

But the new leaders of their section had been moulded by King
Cotton. As the crop then was grown, slave hands were needed to
make it profitable—emancipation did not materially improve the
lot of most cotton hands—and profit as usual began to be confused
with morality. The grave and learned Calhoun was a man as honest in his convictions as Jefferson or Marshall. He regarded slavery
as a positive good, both to master and man. He represented his
people so well in this as in other matters that it was said when
Calhoun took snuff, South Carolina sneezed. Such men were prepared to carry the slavery argument farther than any of Marshall's
generation.

The Supreme Court had adjourned by the time this first national crisis over slavery was disposed of through the famous compromise. (Missouri was admitted with its pro-slave constitution
and Maine as a Free State, but the rest of the Louisiana Purchase
north of Missouri's southern boundary—latitude 36° 30'—should
be forever free.) It was a compromise which would stand until
Marshall's successor took a good look at the whole question and
decided that Southerners were correct in saying that Congress
had no power to forbid slavery in the territories. That decision—
a quarter of a century after Marshall's death—would also be the
first since *Marbury* vs. *Madison* to invalidate an Act of Congress.

With public opinion roused over Negro slavery as a result of
the Missouri debate, Marshall had the misfortune to preside in this
year's session of Richmond circuit court over a case which involved this delicate subject. A brig named the *Wilson* had been
seized by Federal officials as a smuggler, and the government
sought to confiscate the craft on the ground that she had been
carrying Negroes into the State. A Federal law forbade such
traffic into any State which had its own laws on the subject, and

Virginia had adopted such a statute. The owners of the *Wilson*
set up the claim that the Federal law was unconstitutional because
there was no authority in the Constitution permitting Federal enforcement of State laws, and nothing specific on the sort of transportation of Negroes involved in this case. (The Constitution
permitted Federal laws against the "migration or importation" of
slaves after 1808, but that was generally considered to mean those
from Africa, while the Negroes concerned in the *Wilson* case
were from another State.)

Marshall might have chosen to consider the question from the
standpoint of Congressional authority over the slave trade. But he
thought he had a better answer to the shipowners, and one which
would create less excitement. This was the convenient commerce
clause.

It seemed to the Chief Justice obvious that if Congress had
power "to regulate commerce," that meant all phases of navigation as well as what cargoes ships carried and how and where and
on what terms. It was a decision which might have been produc-
tive of a great deal of public debate if the slavery angle had been
elaborately developed. Marshall admitted as much in a letter to
Story, saying that he could have chosen the more controversial
solution. But he added that he was glad to have been able to find a
less sensational way of settling the dispute. He upheld the Federal
authority without mentioning the possibility of Federal power to
regulate the slave trade on the basis of the word "migration."

Lucky as he felt himself in this case, Marshall received a severe
jolt from another quarter at this time. The scholarly and astute
John Taylor came out with a remarkably powerful if rambling
book which is the classic of those who would curb the power of
the judiciary, give a strict construction to the Constitution, and
leave the States to deal with all of the problems of mankind except
those which are specifically mentioned by the Fathers. He called
it *Constructions Construed, and Constitutions Vindicated.* He
pointed out that the principles which the Supreme Court had
evolved were linked by an inexorable logic to the conclusion that

property rights came before human rights. Taylor foresaw quite
clearly that the first beneficiaries of a powerful centralized government would be the commercial and financial interests of the
country. He did not see that if the people regained control of their
government, they would be able to use those centralized powers
for their own benefit.

Jefferson was delighted with the work. Although on its first
appearance he refused to let the publisher use his praise, he expressed his own agreement with the sentiments about the judiciary, which he called "the subtle corps of sappers and miners constantly working underground to undermine the foundations of
our confederated fabric." The former President had a more personal object of distrust, however, for he added:

"An opinion is huddled up in conclave, perhaps by a majority
of one, delivered as if unanimous, and with the silent acquiescence
of lazy and timid associates, by a crafty chief judge, who sophisti-
cates the law to his mind, by the turn of his own reasoning."

This was not an error into which Taylor had fallen. Marshall
did dominate the Court, but there had never been any attempt to
impose a majority decision as a unanimous one. Marshall himself
had explained the process by which every opinion was submitted
to all the Justices.

"If any part of the reasoning be disapproved," he wrote, "it
must be so modified as to receive the approbation of all before it
can be delivered as the opinion of all."

Perhaps it was well that Virginians had the Supreme Court to
argue about, for in national politics there was an unprecedented
and an unrepeated vacuum. Monroe was unopposed for the Presidency, less for his own popularity than for lack of any organized
opposition. All the likely candidates except Clay were in his Cabinet, and each of them preferred to take his chances on the succession than on the doubtful prospect of insubordination. The Federalist candidate in the previous elections, now United States
Senator Rufus King of New York, was a visitor at the White

House instead of an opponent on the hustings. He observed that Monroe was "in fine temper" at the prospect of a unanimous vote in the electoral college—he missed it by one—but there were ominous rumblings of dissension.

Some of them were judicial, although the Chief Justice for once was not anticipating as formidable ructions as actually developed. He only knew that when he came riding back to Washington in 1821 it was horribly cold. For several days the thermometer had hit five degrees below zero or colder. For a brief time it seemed that the main preoccupation of the Court, along with the rest of the capital, would be the weather.

XXI

Lottery and Monopoly

NO PREMONITORY suspicions troubled Marshall when he first looked at the title *Cohens* vs. *Virginia* on the 1821 docket. But he realized that it was a proceeding of consequence as soon as he saw the counsel who had been retained to argue the case. David B. Ogden, one of the leaders of the New York bar, and William Pinkney, the highest-priced lawyer in America, represented the Cohens—very distinguished gladiators for a pair who so seldom appear in the history books that sometimes they are mentioned as only one man.

Actually they were obscure peddlers of lottery tickets and had been fined $100 by a Norfolk court for selling chances in a drawing authorized by Congress to raise funds for civic works in the City of Washington. Lotteries were so highly regarded as a method of getting money for institutions of learning and piety that the States were usually jealous of how they allowed outsiders to siphon off the spare cash of their speculative citizens. The Cohens in selling tickets for the National Lottery, Virginia held, violated her law against peddling chances in such alien gambles.

Ogden and Pinkney were not in court because they thought the
civil rights of the Cohens had been infringed. They were employed by men who saw that if they could take shelter under a
District of Columbia lottery authorized by Congress, they might
reap a harvest by invading any and every State.

Virginia, represented by her popular Senator, James Barbour,
offered the Justices all the reasons why the Federal courts should
not review State legislation. He added a new wrinkle by saying
that the Eleventh Amendment, which had been adopted to prevent
Federal court suits against States by citizens of other States, surely
ought to protect a State from such suits brought by her own citizens. Barbour's argument, in general, was a simplification of the
thesis of Taylor of Caroline. Ogden retorted that really there
were no sovereign States any more, that the United States were a
nation and no one of the parts existed independently of the others.

At this time threats of secession from the Missouri debate still
resounded; Ohio officials were defying Federal courts in a Bank
quarrel; the legislature of Marshall's own State was adopting what
amounted to nullification resolutions. With these incidents in
mind, Marshall saw an opportunity to assert the supremacy of the
Federal judiciary, not just of Congress, in no uncertain terms. To
do it, he lifted *Cohens* vs. *Virginia* out of the category of a contest
for the profits of the lottery business into a constitutional precedent which is still cited. It would have been enough for the case at
hand to assert that the Constitution gave his Court power to hear
appeals developing out of laws of the Union. This was a case involving the lottery law which Congress had passed. Therefore,
the Supreme Court was the proper tribunal to consider an appeal
questioning the validity of the Virginia statute in so far as it re-
lated to the Federal law.

Marshall said that, and in itself this part of his decision angered
most Virginians. But he went a good deal further. He found that
in forming the Constitution, the States had turned "large por-
tions" of their sovereignty over to the new national government.
In so doing, he decided, they also must have implied that the new

national government was supreme in those areas of sovereignty because the Constitution said that Federal laws should be binding on all States regardless of their own statutes or constitutions.

Then, stepping beyond any previous limits set in his decisions, he announced that there was also "a conservative power to maintain the principles established in the constitution." There was more than a power. This conservative principle was "among the great duties of government." On the basis of this reasoning, Marshall asserted that the Supreme Court was supreme not only by the Constitution but by the very nature of government itself. This was a statement of "implied powers" broader than that given in *McCulloch* vs. *Maryland*. It aroused the same diatribes from the same sources.

As for the Cohens, they were not so lucky. Having decided that the Supreme Court had jurisdiction, the Justices listened to the actual case before them and decided that the ticket peddlers had been convicted properly. Congress in setting up the lottery had confined it to the District of Columbia. Therefore, the laws of Virginia were not in conflict with the Federal statute, and the fine should stand. The rosy dreams of the lottery syndicate remained dreams.

In the midst of this case, the Supreme Court was called upon to rule on another matter of greater contemporary significance than posterity is likely to accord it. For the first time, inauguration day fell on a Sunday and Monroe consulted the Justices as to whether he should postpone the event until Monday. After conference, the Justices decided that he could, and an outraged Heaven took revenge by pouring sleet and snow upon the capital so that Pennsylvania Avenue was an impassable morass of mud and slush. Monroe's innovation of an outdoor ceremony was hastily abandoned, and Marshall administered the oath indoors.

A few weeks later Marshall was back in Richmond, and a little while after that the critics burst into print with an acrimony which had become almost a pattern for discussion of Supreme Court opinions. Wrapping themselves in the mantle of an English

Whiggery, which was as far behind them in time as we are ahead of them, the writers signed such pen names as "Somers" and "Fletcher of Saltoun" and "Algernon Sidney." The last was Roane, who got under Marshall's skin with a series of brilliant, vitriolic attacks on *Cohens* vs. *Virginia*. The Virginia judge was indignant over the manner in which, he supposed, the Chief Justice had inveigled the majority of his colleagues to abandon their own party's principles for his. Roane did not recognize that the first party of Supreme Court Justices is their own order; they are naturally inclined toward the exercise of their authority, just as Jefferson had been irresistibly drawn to exercise executive powers which he did not believe that a President really ought to possess. For the rest, Roane defended all over again the position that the States are independent and sovereign and fully equal to the Federal government.

Marshall thought that he had been "assaulted with a degree of virulence transcending what has appeared on any former occasion." Writing as much to Story, he added:

"There are other minor gentry who seek to curry favor & get into office by adding their mite of abuse, but I think for coarseness and malignity of invention Algernon Sidney surpasses all party writers who have ever made pretensions to any decency of character. There is on this subject no such thing as a free press in Virginia, and of consequence the calumnies and misrepresentations of this gentleman will remain uncontradicted & will by many be believed to be true. He will be supposed to be the champion of state rights instead of being what he really is, the champion of dismemberment."

Marshall exaggerated. The Algernon Sidney articles were well within the decencies of contemporary political debate, and there was no special reason why Justices of the Supreme Court should be exempt from the criticism. As for freedom of the press, Marshall himself kept Roane's articles from appearing in the country's leading law journal. The editor had planned to publish them and told Story, who informed his Chief. Marshall urged Story to discourage the idea on the ground of the coarseness of the language, its personal abuse, and its tediousness, but if the editor insisted, Story was to demand that a lengthy reply be included in the same issue. The editor was left in no doubt as to the attitude of the Chief Justice toward publication of his critic's article, and left the controversy alone although it was the most interesting legal decision of the year.

Jefferson was as pugnacious on the other side. The Supreme Court's latest outrage, as he regarded it, prompted him to bestow his formal but belated public endorsement upon Taylor's book. He also permitted publication of a letter in which he outlined his theory of the equality of State and Federal courts and governments in interpreting the Constitution.

This, too, aroused Marshall's ire. Referring to Jefferson as "the great Lama of the mountains," he told Story he was sure that Roane's articles had been inspired from Monticello. He also learned that it was Jefferson who had suggested publication in the law journal.

"He is among the most ambitious, & I suspect among the most unforgiving of men," Marshall wrote to Story. "His great power is over the mass of the people, & this power is chiefly acquired by professions of democracy. Every check on the wild impulse of the moment is a check on his own power, & he is unfriendly to the source from which it flows. He looks of course with ill will at an independent judiciary."

Neither of the two Virginians changed his mind about the other. Two years later Jefferson was still complaining about the Lottery case, and informed Justice Johnson that he believed Roane had "pulverized" Marshall's opinion. He gave vent to a favorite complaint when he added:

"This practice of Judge Marshall of travelling out of his case to prescribe what the law would be in a moot case not before the court is very irregular and censurable."

Marshall managed to regain a lofty sort of indignant composure, and once wrote to his old comrade "Light Horse Harry" Lee:

"I have never allowed myself to be irritated by Mr. Jefferson's unprovoked and unjustified aspersions on my conduct and principles, nor have I ever noticed them except on one occasion [in the XYZ affair] when I thought myself called on to do so, and when I thought that declining to enter upon my justification might have the appearance of crouching under the lash, and admitting the justice of its infliction."

[2]

Instead of dying out, as most wars of words do, this one grew and spread. For it was inflamed by deeds, as the attacks on the Court took tangible shape in the session of Congress which convened toward the end of 1821. One of Kentucky's Senators, Richard M. Johnson, represented both the mortgage-burdened, debt-ridden farmers of the West and the extreme State rights school. He offered an amendment to the Constitution which would have made the Senate the highest court in all cases of Constitutional interpretation. He did not know it, but Madison had placed this very idea before the Constitutional Convention. Johnson thought that those who were dissatisfied with any decision of the Supreme Court ought to be able to appeal to the Senate. His suggestion created a considerable stir, but the shrewd Webster—even shrewder at analyzing a political situation than a law suit—referred to it a little contemptuously as "all this smoke." He did not think there was much fire beneath it.

Webster was right, but his opinion did not make the Justices rest easier. Actually they continued to be subjected to assaults in Congress for nearly a decade. At one time it would be Jefferson's plan that each Justice be required to state his individual opinion on a Constitutional issue rather than let Marshall read for the Court. If Congress did not like the consensus of these views, said

the sage of Monticello, let a resolution be passed; if the Court refused to yield, let the Justices be removed by impeachment.

At another session, the attack would take the form of a move
to repeal that section of the law setting up the Court which gave
litigants the right to appeal from State courts. This proposal was
made repeatedly, and in 1831 the House Judiciary Committee actually reported it out favorably in the form of a bill. Marshall was
quite certain that it would be passed, and was profoundly depressed at the prospect of a serious defeat for a Federal principle
which he considered essential to good government. However, a
more than usually potent minority report had been filed. It was
signed by James Buchanan, a future President; by William W.
Ellsworth of Connecticut, son of a former Chief Justice, and Edward D. White of Louisiana, father of a future Chief Justice.
When it came to a vote, this most serious legislative threat to the
authority of the Supreme Court was beaten in the House by 158
to 51. The tribunal was held in higher esteem than Marshall had
supposed.

On still another occasion, the effort to curb unpopular decisions
was put in the form of a bill to require at least seven of the nine
Justices to concur in any decision which involved the validity of
State or Federal legislation. This attempt to upset the majority
rule in the Court has been a recurring phenomenon ever since, and
has never obtained.

The unpopularity of the Chief Justice and his brethren might
have been mitigated if an unusual and secret opinion which they
gave at this time could have been made public. Monroe had scruples about using Federal funds to make rivers navigable and roads
usable. An internal improvements measure had been forced
through Congress by Clay, darling of Kentucky and gladiator for
Eastern property interests, and the President asked the private
opinion of the Supreme Court on the constitutionality of the
measure. Justice Johnson collected separate opinions and reported
that all the Justices thought that the decision in *McCulloch* vs.
Maryland "completely commits them" to the view that the Fed-

eral government could use some of its money for the type of national benefit the bill contemplated. This bill was the favorite
measure of all those who were most annoyed by the strictness
with which the Supreme Court talked about "the obligation of a
contract."

Marshall himself was taking a gloomy view of the country
partly because of the unpopularity which was an aftermath of the
lottery case, partly because the authority of the Federal courts
was being flouted in various parts of the country, partly because
he feared he could not maintain his control of his own tribunal.
The Monroe Doctrine closing the Americas to any further European colonization had been enunciated, and the Chief Justice welcomed it as strengthening the national spirit. But he saw that such
a challenge as Monroe had flung to the world cannot be backed
up by a weak confederation of states. (Actually, then and for
many years later, the Doctrine was upheld by the strong arm of
the British Navy.)

However, the signs of weakness which troubled the Chief Justice were intimately connected with his own work. One was refusal of a State to accept a Federal court ruling; the other was a
well-founded apprehension that his brethren would not accept a
ruling of his own.

The first disquieting example had taken place in South Carolina,
and Marshall commented to Story:

"Our brother Johnson, I perceive, has hung himself on a democratic snag in a hedge composed entirely of thorny State-Rights
in South Carolina, and will find some difficulty, I fear, in getting
off into smooth, open ground."

Johnson, who was getting less fond of South Carolina and
slavery every term—he finally moved to Pennsylvania in disgust
—had made a bold attempt to interfere with a cherished Southern
law which provided that any free Negro entering port as part of
a ship's crew should be held in jail until the vessel sailed. In pur-
suance of this law, the authorities in Charleston had boarded a

British ship, taken off a British West Indian sailor named Henry Elkison and clapped him into prison. Johnson took the position that States could not interfere with the Federal government's regulation of commerce, and navigation was part of commerce. He ordered Elkison freed, but the whole of South Carolina went into as great a paroxysm as if Calhoun had taken snuff. The Court's decision was completely nullified for a short time, and threats of secession and forcible resistance were freely uttered.

The Marshall ruling which its propounder expected to meet the same fate had been made in circuit court. The Chief Justice had held that a corporation's agents must be able to show a written record and vote of the stockholders to validate every action taken. If this had been allowed to stand, it would have prevented the development of corporations in their present form, by which stockholders delegate all authority to their agents in the broadest manner possible. Marshall knew that corporations even then could not operate under any such ruling. He told Story he expected to be reversed, explaining:

"I suppose so, because I conjecture that the practice of banks has not conformed to my construction of the law. The Judge, however, who draws the opinion must have more ingenuity than I have if he draws a good one." (Nearly four years later Story himself displayed "more ingenuity" in one of his rare differences with his Chief, who took a philosophical view of the matter and in his dissent admitted that the majority had acted "perhaps to the advancement of public convenience.")

[3]

Justices of the Supreme Court entering Washington in the last year of Monroe's administration found that the great issues of economics had taken the place of liberty and morality and the distribution of power. This was true in politics. It was also true of the most interesting cases on their docket.

Congress was preoccupied with the practical advantages to be derived from Federal aid to roads and canals, and also with the potentialities of tariff protection. The Supreme Court was confronted with a case which would decide whether states could give monopolies to transportation companies. At least that was the immediate issue; as usual, far deeper ones were affected.

The case, listed as *Gibbons* vs. *Ogden,* was reached early in the term. In spite of the names of the principals, it was known that the transportation monopoly directly concerned was the Livingston-Fulton steamboat combine. The weakness of abstract theory in attracting supporters was shown by the fact that a great many politicians who had been denouncing the supposed credit monopoly of the Bank of the United States were eager partisans of the steamboat monopoly.

In fact, the transportation monopoly was a stronger threat to the survival of the Union than slavery or the tariff or Federal aid to roads and canals. If each State could exercise complete authority over the transportation within its borders and entering its territory, the same rivalry which had wrecked the Confederation would be inevitable. It was actually in existence. New York and New Jersey had enacted mutually retaliatory legislation which permitted confiscation of steam vessels violating their mutually contradictory laws. Connecticut barred Livingston-Fulton licensees from her waters. Ohio demanded freedom for the boats of her citizens in return for permission for vessels of other States to ply her rivers and lakes. Such commercial wars had led to the abandonment of the Confederation. The Union would be equally vulnerable if these fights were to be continued.

It was fortunate that the fundamental attack upon the system had been directed at the basic monopoly of Fulton and Robert Livingston. Just after the inventor and his partner made their demonstration in 1807 by running a steamboat from New York to Albany, the State legislature granted them a thirty-year monopoly on steam navigation within waters under its jurisdiction.

Within a very few years the profits from steam attracted capital which did not relish being beholden by license to anyone. One of the capitalists was Thomas Gibbons, a native of Georgia who had formed a partnership with former Governor Aaron Ogden of New Jersey to exchange passengers and freight in a ferry service between New York and New Jersey. The monopolists objected, and Ogden yielded to the extent of taking a license from them. Gibbons refused and started running his boats in direct competition with his former associate. Ogden went before Chancellor Kent in New York for an injunction. Gibbons's chief defense was that he held a coasting license from the Federal government which entitled him to enter any port he wanted and navigate any waters within United States jurisdiction.

Kent held that the Federal coasting license could not invalidate all State law on the subject, but he suggested in his opinion that it would be a sound idea to discover whether the Federal courts agreed. The State's highest court, rejoicing in the title of Court for the Trial of Impeachments and the Correction of Errors, upheld the injunction. Whereupon Gibbons took Kent's hint and appealed to the Supreme Court. Everyone who saw profit in State monopolies, everyone who believed in the individual State as the paramount authority in government was on Ogden's side. Those who foresaw greater development under nationwide commercial supremacy, those who opposed monopolies altogether, those who wanted the country developed as rapidly as possible and those who believed in Federal supremacy supported Gibbons. Obviously the Court's decision would be as important as the law for internal improvements, and when the argument opened on February 4, 1824, a good deal of the usual Congressional gallery crowded into the basement room under the Senate to hear the gladiators.

[4]

The monopolists had originally employed Pinkney and Thomas Addis Emmett, eloquent brother of a famous Irish martyr. But Pinkney had died, and they substituted Thomas J. Oakley, New York's Attorney General, believed to be the kind of clear logician judges like. On the other side Webster was associated with Wirt.

Webster, who saw himself as Pinkney's successor in reputation before the Court—"ambitious as Caesar," his colleague in this case described him—had determined to make a big part of that reputation in this one argument.

Webster opened the proceedings with a presentation over which he had worked intermittently for three years and intensively for at least a week. He addressed himself to the Chief Justice, and years later he wrote:

"I think I never experienced more intellectual pleasure than in arguing that novel question to a great man who could appreciate it, and take it in, and he did take it in, as a baby takes in its mother's milk."

Modesty was no part of Webster's equipment, and he was quite sure that he had converted Marshall that day. Actually, the Chief Justice was already committed thoroughly on the main issue in the case, and had been for nearly four years, although no one in the room knew of it. On its face, *Gibbons* vs. *Ogden* centered around the question of whether a Congressional law on the subject of navigation nullified contradictory State legislation. On circuit in the case of the brig *Wilson*, Marshall had avoided Johnson's "democratic snag" by basing his decision on just this point. He had decided the Congressional act was paramount. His opinion had not been published, so it was not among the wealth of precedents cited.

Of course he listened to Webster as if he had never thought about the point before. So did Johnson, whose ruling about Elkison should have left no doubt as to where he stood, and that had been only a few months earlier, attracting wide attention. Webster rehearsed the history of the country to show how just the sort of chaos which would follow a victory for the monopoly had been the chief argument for the Constitution. Oakley followed with a closely reasoned analysis of the position taken by Kent, a figure who commanded respect in any gathering of lawyers. But Oakley realized that he was treading in the footsteps of a great

orator, too. One of the newspaper correspondents who listened
said of his speech:

"He broke ground at a great distance from the immediate question, and commenced a system of mining."

What he had to say amounted to the position taken by the men
who in 1788 had argued for ratification. The survivors, Marshall
at least, were a little weary of being quoted out of the past. The
monopolists, however, had an argument which Webster had not
considered. Oakley mentioned and Emmett further developed the
fact that Fulton had a patent. The patent laws were designed to
confer some protection upon inventors. Therefore, the monopoly
was founded upon the justice which ought to be done to men of
ingenuity. Wirt undertook to defend Gibbons against the operation of the patent laws. He pointed out that a patent might give
Fulton a monopoly of making the kind of steam engines protected
by that instrument, but hardly a monopoly in the use of them
after they were made and sold.

The lawyers argued until late in the afternoon of February 9,
and the Justices took several weeks to prepare their decision. This
was longer than usual, but not because of any basic disagreement.
They knew they were deciding a fundamental issue on which the
development of the country's transportation system would depend. So they took more time than usual, discussing the decision
line by line. Additional delay was due to the fact that Marshall
slipped on a carriage step while coming away from a White House
reception and was confined to his room for two weeks with a
dislocated shoulder. This was the occasion when he wrote his
letter to Polly about their courtship. Although there was a rumor
that Story was drafting the decision because of the Chief's accident, Marshall's letter to his wife showed that he had no trouble
with a pen. The language of the opinion itself is unmistakably his.

On March 2, he was able to resume his place on the bench. The
courtroom was crowded as he was helped into his robe, and as
soon as Court was opened he began to read. His voice was so

feeble that spectators left their seats to crowd around him. They stood for a long time; the Chief Justice was underlining his points by repetition. The main one, of course, was that no State could grant a monopoly in this field because Federal laws took precedence. Lest this seem a little less exciting to later generations than it did at the time, it may be mentioned that Felix Frankfurter, who has lived to see far more sweeping powers justified, considered this decision to be "audacious doctrine." For it was nothing less than a pronouncement that the authority of a State is subject to such limits as the Supreme Court thinks are needed to protect the nation as a whole. Of equal audacity was the broad meaning which Marshall gave to the commerce power of the Federal government.

As usual Marshall went further than the mere decision of the point at issue between Gibbons and Ogden. He also took a leaf out of the book of the strict constructionists and challenged them to prove by the Constitution itself that it was supposed to be construed in narrow terms.

"It has been said," he noted, "that these powers ought to be construed strictly; but why ought they to be so construed? Is there one sentence in the Constitution which gives countenance to this rule? . . . We cannot perceive the propriety of this strict construction, nor adopt it as a rule by which the Constitution is to be expounded."

Marshall expressed the opinion that State rights advocates had resorted to "refined and metaphysical reasoning." The real effect of their argument, if admitted, would be to "explain away the Constitution of our country and leave it a magnificent structure indeed to look at, but totally unfit for use." The fears that a central government would abuse power just because it was a central government were very real. One of the quite seldom cited passages in Marshall's opinion dealt with these fears and showed that the danger they contemplate cannot be allayed by words on paper, even on such a sacred document as the Constitution. In a republican form of government, he pointed out, the forces which prevent abuse of power are "the wisdom and the discretion of Congress, their identity with the people, and the influence which their constituents possess at election." These, he said, "are the restraints on which the people must often rely solely, in all representative governments." In other words, the people themselves must be vigilant to preserve their rights and their liberties; no one will do it for them. Perhaps this is as valuable for posterity as any precedent of broad construction of the commerce clause in the Constitution.

For once, too, Marshall was on the popular side of the question. The *New York Evening Post*, in calling his opinion "one of the most powerful efforts of the human mind that has ever been displayed from the bench of any court," only reflected the general enthusiasm for the blow which crushed monopolies in transportation—at least monopolies conferred by States. The populace was rejoicing because steamboat fares immediately came down. Capitalists who did not happen to have a monopoly rejoiced because they had an opportunity to enter the tremendously lucrative new field. Within a year Niles noted in his *Register* that the number of steam vessels out of New York had increased from six to forty-three. By that time, too, there had been inaugurated a new run from Boston to New York with a fare of $5 for a twenty-four hour trip as against the stage coach's $10 and fifty-six hours.

[5]

As a man who mingled much with his fellows and heard their views on public affairs freely expressed, Marshall was well pleased with the popularity which his steamboat decision brought him. But he could not enjoy it to the full, because the state of the docket gave him concern for the good name of his Court. It had far more work to do than the leisurely tribunal which he had joined in 1801. Cases were piling up, both in Washington and on circuit, and elderly judges were being harried by travel and a backlog of unheard arguments.

Justice Todd, with the whole of the West to visit once a year, was being slowly jolted to death on the road. Brockholst Livingston had died before the steamboat case came up, and Marshall had spent some time worrying about the caliber of his successor. It would have relieved him to know that the politics he feared in the appointment were not to be played quite so shamelessly as he suspected. Actually Attorney General Wirt recommended Chancellor Kent, saying that even so ardent a Federalism as the New York jurist held would not be a handicap on the bench. Rufus King was urging his Senatorial colleague, Martin Van Buren, and that master politician expressed himself as willing to cut himself off from all party matters "like taking the vow and veil in the Catholic Church." But Monroe saw an opportunity to combine political opportunism with a respectable nomination. Almost all his Cabinet hoped for a Presidential succession, and their competition was wearing. So Monroe got rid of one by sending to the Senate for the Supreme Court place the name of his Secretary of the Navy, Smith Thompson.

This New Yorker was an able judge, but he was hardly robust enough for the place. He was physically weary, as were most of his colleagues, when the 1825 term opened with 164 cases on the docket. Marshall estimated that this was four times as many as could be handled comfortably; actually they got through only thirty-eight.

A number of expedients were suggested, but the most obvious one was never mentioned. No one proposed that the practitioners before the bar of the Supreme Court be commanded to curb their eloquence. No one suggested that it would be possible for a lawyer to present his case in something less than three days. At least no one suggested it publicly, although Story, an ardent versifier, scribbled in the notebook which he used on the bench to jot down the best and worst points of counsel:

> You wish the Court to hear, and listen, too?
> Then speak with point, be brief, be close, be true.

Cite well your cases, let them be in point;
Not learned rubbish, dark and out of joint:—
And be your reasoning clear, and closely made,
Free from false taste, and verbiage, and parade.
Stuff not your speech with every sort of law,
Give us the grain and throw away the straw.

Who's a great lawyer? He who aims to say
The least his cause requires, not all he may.

One of the proposals that was made came from Van Buren. He
introduced a measure to create ten circuit judgeships to relieve
Supreme Court Justices of this labor. This had been offered before and ignored. In 1825, Congress was still indifferent to the
sufferings of elderly jurists, and the bill was lost. But by the time
the next term of court came around, even Congress realized that
something must be done. The docket had risen to 190 cases, and
Van Buren joined forces with Representative Webster to push a
new bill. It was plain that Congress was as much afraid of Presidential patronage in new judgeships as it was of the judges themselves,
so the Webster–Van Buren measure would have created only
three more Supreme Court places and three more circuits to ease
the burden. Webster, for one, thought it was a good thing for
members of the highest court to travel.

"I think it useful," he said, "that Judges should see in practice
the operation and effect of their own decisions."

Representative John Kerr went even further. In opposing any
relief for the Justices, he declared:

"They would in a few years become indolent and lose their
dignity and influence in the eyes of the nation. They will fall into
a natural indulgence in the ordinary literary pursuits or other
occupations."

Kerr's reasoning prevailed. Instead of the Webster–Van Buren
bill, Congress passed a law to lengthen the Supreme Court session

in Washington so the Justices could do more work without interfering with their circuit duties. They had to adjourn by March
20 in order to keep their circuits, so the beginning of the term was
set for the second Monday in January instead of February. By
cutting down on their social engagements, the Court managed to
get through forty-nine cases in the 1826 term before they went
home and on circuit to get what rest they could before their next
and longer ordeal.

Marshall, a green and vigorous seventy, stood it better than
most, but he did not see how he and his aging colleagues were
going to get through their work. Actually, in their first lengthened
session, they made a good deal of headway, although when they
adjourned there were still 109 cases unheard. They had given all
their days to hearings, all their evenings and early mornings to
consultation and the writing of opinions.

Todd had died, killed, his colleagues believed, by the hardships
of travel. Robert Trimble of Kentucky took his place, and although he was twenty-two years younger than Marshall, he survived the rigors of his post only two years. However, he was a
member of the Court which reversed the Chief Justice on his
corporation case and then went on to overrule him on a Constitutional issue for the first and last time. Even Bushrod Washington "revolted" and actually wrote the majority opinion.

Appropriately enough, it was Marshall's pet clause on the obligation of contracts which was at stake. On this point he was as
strict a constructionist as Jefferson, if not stricter. The Constitution said that no State could impair obligations of this kind. After
the Dartmouth College case, it was generally supposed that if a
State government wanted to protect itself, it could write saving
clauses into a charter. It was also argued that contracts entered
into after a State law was passed could be assumed to include the
operation of that statute.

Now, in this case of 1827, *Ogden* vs. *Saunders*, Marshall wanted
the Court to hold that a State could not pass laws which would
impair the obligations in contracts to be entered into after the law

was passed. The Constitution, he argued, made no exceptions. So States could not make any either. This was too much for the majority. They very sensibly said that no contract could really be impaired when both parties to it knew the provisions of the law governing their agreement before they signed.

It was at this term, too, that Marshall first became impressed with a new luminary of the bar. He commented with approval on Maryland's new Attorney General, Roger B. Taney, a man almost as tall as the Chief Justice and no more careful of his dress. Both his features and his mind were sharp, and he had as great a faculty as Marshall for going straight to the heart of a constitutional issue. He lost his chief case in Court that year, but he won the regard of the man he was to succeed.

XXII

Last of the Federalists

JUDGES DO NOT spend all their lives on the bench nor devote all their thoughts to law. Especially if they are judges like John Marshall, they are an active part of the life around them. To an increasing degree in the later years of his career, the subject of human slavery and the problems which it brought were complicating the existence of all men, but particularly Southerners. It cropped up in all sorts of political debates, as when John Randolph remarked of Congressmen who contended for authority to use Federal funds for internal improvements:

"They may emancipate every slave in the United States—and with stronger color of reason than they can exercise the power now contended for."

Marshall occupied a ground which was becoming increasingly untenable for men engaged in political activity, and he could maintain it only because he was outside political strife. It was the ground of Jefferson and most of his generation. To Marshall and the rest, slavery was an evil to be eliminated gradually.

The Chief Justice himself was an exponent of a slow process
of emancipation and the removal of the freed slaves to Africa.
When Virginia organized a Colonization Society—there were a
number of them devoted to this resettlement project—Marshall
was elected President. It was a mark of his popularity after the
steamboat decision as well as of his interest in the aims of the
Society. The Governor, James Pleasants, took second rank as
Vice President, but a few years earlier no elected official in Virginia would have yielded place to the Chief Justice.

Marshall was not pleased to see the slavery issue complicated
by other reform schemes. He watched with some misgivings the
introduction of slavery discussions into talk of the new Bible so-
cieties which were spreading across the land, of organized efforts
to reclaim the frontier from godlessness, drink, and mayhem, of
the novel Utopias where the evils of society were to be purged
and the world instructed in a better mode of life. In 1824, Robert
Owen arrived to establish New Harmony. The same year Fanny
Wright appeared with the aged hero of the Revolution, Lafayette,
in whose honor Marshall joined the rest of polite society for spec-
tacular tributes. Fanny, handsome and talented and protected by
the friendship of the revered Marquis, was soon preaching emancipation for both slaves and women.

While Lafayette was being accorded honors which were unprecedented in America, Fanny sought to get from the national
leaders who were his friends some encouragement for an elaborate project which she had evolved on the basis of little knowledge but much good will and entitled "A Plan for the gradual
Abolition of Slavery in the United States without danger of loss
to the Citizens of the South." She proposed that the Southern
States receive public lands on which they could establish plantations, like the one which Fanny herself had started at Nashoba in
Tennessee, where slaves could earn their freedom in from one
year (on the richest cotton land) to ten. Once they were free
they might remain as tenants or be colonized in other lands. She
submitted this plan to Lafayette, who wrote:

"Chief Justice Marshall has, under seal of secrecy, your pro-
spectus, and will shortly write me his opinion confidentially. You
know he is nominal head of the Colonization Society. They say
their approbation will do more harm than good but I found their
good will sincere and my daily conversations during the Virginia trip indicate a gradual amelioration of public opinion."

Marshall's confidential opinion has not survived, but there is
evidence that he was sympathetic to Fanny's aims. A couple of
years after Lafayette's visit he wrote to Pickering that he feared
"that nothing portends more calamity & mischief to the Southern
States than their slave population." When Rufus King proposed
to devote funds derived from the sale of public lands to help the
colonization projects for removing free Negroes to other shores,
Marshall agreed heartily, calling the plan "the most effective that
can be devised." Marshall wrote a few years later:

"The removal of our colored population is, I think, a common
object, by no means confined to the slave States, although they
are more immediately interested in it. The whole Union would be
strengthened by it, and relieved from a danger whose extent can
scarcely be estimated."

Another benefit which Marshall anticipated was that there
would be a use for surplus government funds—he lived in a queer
time when the Administration was puzzled as to how it could
spend all its revenues—without creating an unseemly State
scramble for what came to be known as the pork barrel. Of course
the Colonization Society was no solution to the slavery problem.
It was in many respects nothing more than an attempt to get rid
of free men of color. It was not intended as a step toward general
emancipation.

Although a slaveowner himself and confining his public efforts
to colonization schemes to which no one took exception, Marshall could not avoid running afoul of the criticism which ardent
pro-slavery spirits directed against any move which seemed to

reflect upon their peculiar institution. A few years after Miss Wright sought his advice, he presided at the hearing of a case in which the slavery issue could not be dodged, as he had avoided it in the matter of the brig *Wilson*. For the Supreme Court was called upon to decide whether a slave was a human being or a piece of merchandise.

The point arose because a slaveowner named Robert Boyce sued the owner of a steamboat, one Anderson, for the value of a Negro drowned in an accident on the Mississippi. Boyce and most other slaveholders were grievously and loudly offended when Marshall, with all the rest of the Justices concurring, said of the slave:

"In the nature of things, and in his character, he resembles a passenger, not a package of goods. It would seem reasonable, therefore, that the responsibility of the carrier should be measured by the law which is applicable to passengers, rather than that which is applicable to the carriage of common goods."

Men jealous of the favors which courts have shown to transportation companies might read into that decision a preoccupation with mercantile property rather than all property. The slave-owners did not so regard it. They denounced the decision as a reflection on the institution of slavery itself and therefore as a blow at all property rights.

[2]

Marshall's aloofness from the slavery debate was part of his general abstention from politics. Since 1804, when he had voted against Jefferson rather than for Pinckney, he had not cast a ballot because in the absence of secrecy the mere exercise of the suffrage amounted to taking a partisan position. Even in 1824, when the son of the man who had appointed him Chief Justice was a leading candidate, Marshall remained away from the polls.

He watched with interest as the electoral vote was distributed among Jackson, Adams, Crawford, and Clay in that order. None had a majority, so the House of Representatives had to choose among the first three. That eliminated Clay, and Crawford had suffered a paralytic stroke, so that only his die-hard supporters were voting for him in the House. The contest, therefore, narrowed to Jackson or Adams, and Clay's influence among Representatives was decisive.

"I cannot believe that killing two thousand five hundred Englishmen at New Orleans qualifies for the various, difficult, and complicated duties of the Chief Magistracy," remarked the accomplished and sarcastic Speaker, and threw the election to Adams.

The inauguration ceremony which followed shortly was a greater pleasure than usual for the man who had to administer the oath to the new President. He derived genuine satisfaction in sharing the joy of the old man sitting at home in Quincy trying to conceal his pride in his son. But there was more satisfaction to Marshall in the new President's inaugural promise that the central government would govern, and in his support of Federal power to improve the lot of people through aid to roads and waterways, scientific expeditions, even the free distribution of seeds. Although Adams trembled so that he could hardly hold the paper on which his speech was written, Marshall thought he came through the ordeal well.

His administration, however, was one of those unsuccessful efforts which are sometimes produced by men who seem to have everything for success. Adams had more training for the Presidency, probably, than anyone who ever occupied the White House. He had more ability than most, and complete integrity. He even did a creditable job, but in the eyes of the country he was a failure, for he had all the qualifications which the post requires except the temperament. He was generally sour, suspicious, ungracious, wholly lacking in persuasive powers or the ability to see an opponent's point of view.

His Presidency was marked by the formation of two new political parties. Adams and all three of his rivals had campaigned as Republicans. But now two brands of Republicans began to appear.

The more conservative spoke of themselves as National Republicans. The radicals, rallying under the banner of Jackson, actually adopted a former term of reproach and were called Democratic-Republicans.

The aging John Randolph was just the man to make the party divisions more bitter. He still clung to his erratic insurgency, and when Adams appointed Clay Secretary of State, Randolph was not slow to pick up the charge that there had been a corrupt bargain for the Presidency with the Kentuckian exchanging votes for first place in the Cabinet. Washington drawing rooms rocked with laughter at gibes about "our Clay President," but Randolph was not the man to stop at jokes. One day in the House he denounced what he called "the coalition of Blifil and Black George —the combination, unheard of till then, of the puritan with the black-leg." Clay promptly challenged, and the two statesmen took the road to Bladensburg. At the first fire, Clay discharged his pistol quickly and put the ball through Randolph's long white coat. Randolph paused while his rival waited stoically and then discharged his weapon into the air. The nearest he came to a reconciliation was the peevish remark:

"Mr. Clay, you owe me a new coat."

The bitterness of party was only temporarily modified by the fiftieth anniversary of the Declaration of Independence. Celebrating appropriately but privately, Marshall heard only many days later that John Adams had died on the Glorious Fourth.

"Thomas Jefferson still lives," the old man had whispered just before the end, not knowing that the death of his friend had taken place on the same day four hours earlier.

An age had died with them, and it was the age which Marshall understood. Their passing emphasized for him the changes which most disturbed him. At this time, Marshall was contemplating with somewhat premature alarm the end of free land in America. When that happened, he said, the country would face a fearful future, although he thought more general education might alleviate or postpone the disaster.

"As the supply exceeds the demand, the price of labour will cheapen until it affords a bare subsistence to the labourer," he wrote. "The superadded demands of a family can scarcely be satisfied and a slight indisposition, one which suspends labour and compensation for a few days, produces famine and pauperism. How is this to be prevented? . . . as our country fills up, how shall we escape the evils which have followed a dense population?"

Marshall was not one of the progressive spirits who anticipated a labor movement which would give the worker some equality in bargaining power with the employer. The Chief Justice was not so far ahead of his time as to envisage measures of social security. Certainly he did not think that the radicals who actually were wearing the badge of "Democrat" as an insignia of honor could possibly provide any part of a solution to the problem of the landless worker. Marshall so profoundly distrusted men who could call themselves Democrats that, for the first time in nearly a quarter of a century, he was preparing to vote.

The campaign of 1828, beginning early—in fact, some historians think it began on inauguration day, 1825—was not one which Marshall could admire. It was almost as bitter as that of 1800, and on a far lower level of propriety. Adams was accused of attending church barefoot, of filling the White House with gambling paraphernalia (he had bought a billiard table and a set of chess men), of a corrupt bargain with Clay. Jackson was accused of illiteracy, of murder, of having married a loose woman. The General always believed that the nasty stories told about his Rachel had killed her, and Mrs. Adams was sincerely distressed by the gossip she heard about her husband.

Knowing very little of Jackson (and that not much to his credit), profoundly distrustful of the State rights men and petty politicians who supported the Westerner, Marshall was strong for Adams. He talked about it so much that one day in March, a Baltimore paper quoted him as saying he would regard Jackson's election as the signal for destruction of the government. This forced the Chief Justice into a public statement in which he said he would support Adams "from the strong sense I felt of the injustice of the charge of corruption against the President & Secretary of State."

But more than judicial reasoning was needed to save Adams. The voters were persuaded that in General Jackson they had a champion, that he understood their needs, that he would not be swayed from the path of rectitude by the blandishments, threats or tricks of the masters of money. Jackson, carefully stage-managed by Van Buren, won a comfortable majority in the popular vote and a landslide in the electoral college.

Marshall completely failed to understand the new forces which had swept Jackson into office. He believed that the new Administration would be a cruder, a more violent reflection of Jefferson's two terms, catering even more to the petty interests of State and section, ignoring the strength of the Federal government as it had been carefully built up and explained by the Supreme Court. Like most of the old Federalists, he expected Jackson to be the dupe and tool of scheming, not to say wicked, men. Some were worried about the new President's age, but Marshall could not be of their number, for he was nearly twelve years older himself, and he did not feel decrepit.

But old Jeffersonians and old Hamiltonians alike distrusted the new regime. This was not the triumph of the people as the heroes of 1800 had foretold it. John Randolph thought the country "ruined past redemption." Story envisaged "the reign of King Mob." Surely Jefferson himself had never wanted a backwoods farmer like Jackson and the son of a Kinderhook tavernkeeper like Van Buren to govern the country. The Jeffersonians had expected the people to elect men of dignity and talent and learning. Marshall, of course, had not expected anything of the kind, and he was grimly on the defensive. The Supreme Court had upheld the central government against what he considered the onslaughts of Jefferson. At seventy-three he felt he might still have time to lead the judicial battle against this new apostle of the democracy.

He was thoroughly displeased with the nature of the opposition which he saw embodied in the crowds of hopeful, curious, and vociferous Jacksonians entering Washington with him when he came back for the term of 1829. These people were agreeing with old conservatives in supposing that there had been a revolution. The newcomers rejoiced, however, for the revolution they contemplated was a redistribution of government favors with themselves as recipients. Day by day they poured into the city in hundreds, crowded the grog shops and the gambling rooms, churned the mud of Pennsylvania Avenue as they rushed busily about, laying the groundwork for preferment and astonishing the "old residents"—the species of capital society which would one day be called "cliff dwellers" was already scornful of the provinces.

"The whole world is said to be here," Marshall wrote home, and wished he could follow his letter away from what he called "the pomp and parade of the inauguration."

Jackson himself arrived on February 11, and from that moment was almost continuously besieged by office seekers. The old soldier was known to be grateful for support; he was notoriously loyal to his friends without discrimination; he was reputed to be implacably hostile to anyone who had opposed him. So in thousands, the office-hungry swarmed around him. Other thousands were only curious, and some of them had ridden, walked or poled their way along rivers for as much as 500 miles to see their hero inaugurated.

Small wonder that Webster never in his life had seen such a crowd—hunters from Kentucky, old Indian fighters from Tennessee, woodsmen from the wilds of Michigan. In front of the Capitol, Marshall estimated—and he had the unrivalled view of proceedings which Chief Justices get at these ceremonies—there were twelve to fifteen thousand people, "a great number of them ladies."

Before this animated gathering, under a warming March sun, two tall, erect old men faced each other as the President repeated the oath of office after the Chief Justice. Jackson, with his crown of thick white hair and his face seamed by the pain of illness and his Rachel's recent death, looked the elder. Marshall had only a little gray in his head, and all his life he had enjoyed remarkably good health.

He was able to escape the ordeal which the President and a good deal of official Washington went through immediately after the ceremony. He retired to his quarters, but most of the crowd pursued the President to the White House, stormed through the rooms, forced Jackson finally to flee through a window in Old Hickory's only recorded retreat. Men who had come 500 miles to see him were not to be balked by rules of etiquette which they had never heard anyway, and the elite of the capital were shocked beyond measure to observe visitors to the "President's Palace" standing on the upholstered chairs in their muddy boots and tearing the draperies in their anxiety to get a little closer to Jackson.

The inaugural ball that night was also a terrific crush. Marshall told Polly about it in a letter next day, but in a very few words, explaining that "of course I did not attend it." His daughter-in-law had died a few weeks before, so he had a good excuse, but he assured his wife that he felt no desire to attend under any circumstances.

[3]

Leaving Jackson to struggle with the difficult job of reconciling all the different varieties of "people's men" who had contributed to his victory, Marshall set out for home and a battle nearer to his taste than the contemplation of democracy in action. In those first days of the Administration, he saw only the feuds and the follies; he missed the fresh ideas which were being brought into Washington, and he never appreciated the better political health which accompanied the shouting and the bluster. Nor did he understand the consummate skill with which Jackson drove his strangely assorted team of Northern plunderers and idealists, Western expansionists and dreamers, Southern planters, and small farmers. This wide variety of type and interest is a characteristic of any democ-

racy, and it needs the instincts and firmness of a Jackson to maintain any kind of harmony among them. That is why the great
people's leaders of this country have always been men of great
charm in public as well as ability in conference, capable of leading
as well as reconciling divergent views.

Marshall never realized that the new President had this unique
capacity. He would not have appreciated it, because he was not
interested in how democracy could be made to work. For him it
was still the term of reproach which had embittered the politics
of thirty years before.

He was to make his views clear in the battle at home. This was
to be fought in a convention which Virginia had called to revise
her constitution of 1776, and her most distinguished sons were to
take part in it. Marshall had not wanted to be one of them at first.
While he was still in Washington, he had written to Polly asking
her to authorize their son-in-law to decline for him. Three months
later he wrote Story:

"I am almost ashamed of my weakness and irresolution when I
tell you that I am a member of our convention . . . I have acted
like a girl addressed by a gentleman she does not positively dislike,
but is unwilling to marry. She is sure to yield to the advice and
persuasion of her friends."

Marshall had yielded, but he wrote that the convention would
be full of "a great deal of eloquence as well as talent, and yet will
do, I fear, much harm with some good." He would meet old
friends as well as old rivals at the convention. Madison would be
there and Monroe, the much sobered Giles, who was now Governor; John Randolph, still crusading, unpredictable and dangerous;
Abel Upshur, a future Secretary of State; Philip P. Barbour, a
future Supreme Court Justice; Littleton Tazewell, a popular
pleader before the Supreme Court. It was a highly distinguished
gathering, but it wrought a less wondrous constitution than the
men with whom Madison had worked in Philadelphia forty-two
years before.

The convention opened its sessions on October 5, 1829, in Richmond, and Marshall was released from his duties there just in time to get to Washington for the 1830 term of court. The two former Presidents, seventy-eight and seventy-one, and the Chief Justice, seventy-four, were the most interesting figures in the Hall. Monroe, nominated by the frail Madison, was presiding officer, and was escorted to his chair by Marshall.

At no time in his life did Marshall display so surely the crusted but polished conservatism of his philosophy. As a guardian of property, he was more alert than younger men, and the prestige of his age and his office—for it was beginning to have prestige, now—helped the old men of Virginia defeat the younger reformers. He had come a long way since he had listened to his father describe the victories of the backwoods delegates led by Patrick Henry. He had thrilled then to the defiance expressed by spokesmen of the West. He was allied now to the men of the East in defense of property.

The issue was the measure to be used for calculating representation in the legislature. The stake was control of the State government, which had been in the hands of the owners of many slaves, mostly Easterners. The smaller farmers of the West, including that part of the State which is now West Virginia, proposed to shift this control to themselves by apportioning representatives on the basis of the free white population, and by giving the franchise to all adult males in that population. Marshall was a leader of the forces who contended that property qualifications were essential to intelligent voting and that representation ought to be on the basis of what was called "Federal numbers," that is, the whole white population and three-fifths of "other persons." This, as Marshall pointed out, was equivalent to representation on a basis of property, since the "other persons" were chattels. "I think the soundest principles of republicanism do sanction some relation between representation and taxation," he said.

In the end, the conservative property holders of the East achieved a compromise which was really a victory. Property

qualifications were retained. The apportionment of members of
the two houses of the legislature was fixed without mentioning
"Federal numbers" but on a basis not much different, and which
left the East in control of the legislature.

The convention also gave Marshall an opportunity to express
himself on the role of judges in a republic more freely than he
ever was able to do from the bench. He took part several times in
a debate on the reform of the State judiciary, and although it was
manned largely by his opponents, he was strong against change,
and carried the day, with the invaluable help of Madison and
Monroe.

The convention reformers proposed to make higher judges re-
callable by the legislature. Against this proposition Marshall rose
repeatedly, and reached one of his rare heights of eloquence, crying:

"I have always thought, from my earliest youth until now, that
the greatest scourge an angry Heaven ever inflicted upon an ungrateful and sinning people was an ignorant, a corrupt, or a de-
pendent judiciary. Our ancestors thought so; we thought so till
very lately; and I trust the vote of this day will show that we
think so still. . . . You do not allow a man to perform the duties
of a juryman or a Judge, if he has one dollar of interest in the
matter to be decided; and will you allow a Judge to give a decision when his office may depend upon it?"

Memories of the bitter debates of Jefferson's first administration stirred in some of the hearers as a prominent figure in the
bitterest of them, Giles, rose to reply. But he made a conciliatory
little speech in which he said that he had learned to doubt his own
opinion when he differed from the Chief Justice. However, he
continued to differ, although in the end Marshall won his point by
a small majority.

He had reason to be pleased with his work in the convention.
The political power of the wealthy had been preserved, and the
privileges of the judiciary maintained on the best possible basis, a

general belief that those privileges were essential to good government.

[4]

Any sense of triumph lingering from this gathering in Virginia disappeared when Marshall got to Washington for the second Monday in January, 1830. The Court, that grave and learned body which for the most part had wheeled and manoeuvred as he led, was slipping from his grasp. He had seen the handwriting on the wall late in 1828 when he had heard of Trimble's death and Jackson's triumph at almost the same time. For the first time since he became Chief Justice, he tried to intervene directly in the choice of an associate. He had Story tell Adams that he recommended Senator John J. Crittenden of Kentucky, an able lawyer who was drifting toward the right wing of the Jeffersonian party and was to serve two Whig Presidents as Attorney General.

"The objection I have to direct communication of this opinion to the President," Marshall explained, "arises from the delicacy of the case. I cannot venture, unasked, to recommend an Associate Justice to the President, especially a gentleman who is not personally known to me. It has the appearance of assuming more than I am willing to assume."

Adams took his advice after two favorites of his own had declined, but the Senate refused to confirm Crittenden. The majority would not let the President follow in his father's footsteps by appointing a Justice after his defeat at the polls. They determined to hold the post vacant for a Jackson man, and it did not matter much to them that the Court was thus to be a man short through the 1829 term. This in itself was a serious matter for these aging and, for the most part, increasingly feeble gentlemen. Duval was nearly seventy-seven, three years older than the Chief, and so deaf that it was said he had not heard a Court argument for years. He was ill at home when this term opened. So was Thompson, and Washington was frequently indisposed these days. The youngsters, Story and Johnson, both on the sunny side of sixty, were expected to carry on for years, but Johnson had been injured when his stagecoach upset while crossing North Carolina. When Court was supposed to open, therefore, Marshall, Story, and Washington were alone. Congress was obliged to pass a special law to permit the Court to wait twenty days before calling off the whole term, and in that time the absent members arrived. Under the circumstances, they all resented the extra work which delay in naming Trimble's successor was imposing upon them. Marshall was worried for fear the progress made in clearing the docket would be checked.

On March 6, he got a glimpse of the new spoils system as introduced by Jackson and Van Buren into national politics. It was by no means the worst example, but it came closest to him, and so he disapproved of it. State leaders like "little Van" were determined to reward their followers as they had been accustomed to do with State jobs after a victory. Jackson himself supposed that what he was achieving was a recognition of the principle of rotation in office. He thought government was "so plain and simple that men of intelligence may readily qualify themselves." He thought more harm was done by laziness and apathy on the part of those who had security than could be gained by their experience. Neither he nor Van Buren were prepared to replace as many officials as became customary in later administrations, but far more than ever before were turned out.

The biggest and richest trough for the patronage-hungry then, as for many administrations to come, was the post office. But the Postmaster General, John McLean, a holdover from Monroe's administration, had old-fashioned views about dismissing civil servants for party reasons. He had been a Jackson supporter himself, so it was inadvisable to banish him summarily, yet he blocked the party program. Fortunately he was a lawyer of some talent and hailed from Ohio, part of the Western circuit. It was for just such an emergency that the Senate had left Justice Trimble's place vacant. So on the second day of Jackson's administration, McLean was nominated to it.

The choice was quite respectable; Marshall, Story, and Washington had expected far worse. But they were not gratified by the nomination of an Associate Justice for no better reason than because the President wanted him out of the way of what they regarded as a more shameful distribution of loaves and fishes than it really was. McLean was welcomed with some stiffness, but the fraternity of the Court soon drew him into the close companionship of the boardinghouse, although with Thompson he proved to be almost immune to Marshall's logic and persuasive powers.

That was the situation when Marshall was at the Virginia Convention. A more serious blow to Court solidarity fell during the meeting of the Convention. Bushrod Washington had died in December. The little man with the snuff-stained clothing, the eye patch and the marble countenance would no longer lend his patience, his industry and his inflexible Federalism to the decision of difficult cases. He had not been outstanding among the judges of the nation, but there was something about him that made it one of Henry Clay's greatest claims to an iron nerve that he had once helped himself uninvited to a pinch from the Justice's snuffbox.

Marshall missed him as a friend. He missed him even more as a colleague. For now the Chief Justice was the last of the Federalists on the Court. True, he had won Story and Duval, even Johnson most of the time, but the South Carolinian was independent. There were a few dissents in which he had joined Thompson and McLean, unregenerate Republicans (or Democrats as some called them), and now the Court would get another Jacksonian. Marshall was gloomily certain that the precedents he had set were to be upset, "or," as he told Story, "to use a more fashionable phrase, to be nullified by the Supreme Court of the United States."

There had been no delay in appointing Washington's successor. As soon as news of the Justice's death arrived, Jackson sent the name of Henry Baldwin of Pennsylvania to the Senate, and he was promptly confirmed. Just Story's age, he looked much younger, with a smooth, handsome face, and hair cropped quite close for the fashion of the day. Perhaps nothing indicated so much the change in the character of the Court since Marshall joined it than the fact that a man of fifty could appear so youthful among his associates. But Marshall knew that this was the least of the changes; Baldwin was far from being a Federalist.

"The crisis of our Constitution is now upon us," the Chief Justice wrote in a private letter.

What he really meant was that Johnson, with his old leanings toward Jeffersonian doctrine, held the balance of the Court. Furthermore, it was a time when the principles of the old Federalist party, not the degenerate breed who had toyed with disunion, were in Marshall's mind a good deal. The old fights of '98, divorced from their foreign complications, were raging again, and above his head as he sat in his basement courtrooms this January a tremendous storm was sweeping through the Senate.

Daniel Webster was there, promoted from the House by the masters of Massachusetts, who were grateful for favors received and recognized an accomplished advocate. An almost equally eloquent Senator was Robert Hayne of South Carolina, and he was setting forth a doctrine which reminded Marshall of the one Jefferson and Madison had made famous in their Virginia and Kentucky Resolutions of 1798, but which more than thirty years later had been expanded by extremists into nullification. Hayne was its strongest exponent in the Senate, and was directing his fire against the tariff. Politicians from South Carolina were vehement in their talk on this subject, for they spoke with the fervor of converts. In the first phase of protection a dozen years before, their State had been eager for these duties, and Calhoun had been one of the chief sponsors of protection. There had always been a strong tinge of Federalism in South Carolina, and in the beginning of Monroe's administration this had been reinforced by local hopes of new manufacturing industries. Those hopes had been disappointed, and when duties were raised again, South Carolina was one of the first to use the expression "Tariff of Abominations."

So now, under the cold but approving eye of Calhoun, presiding as Vice President, Senator Hayne was explaining that his State was prepared to resist Federal usurpation. He recalled the glorious days of '76 and he declared that South Carolina would be found now as she had been found then, "acting on a principle she has always held sacred—resistance to unauthorized taxation."

Next day Webster replied. The reply has kept the name of Hayne alive. The peroration has been recited by more school children than any other piece of American oratory except the Gettysburg Address. If it was admired by posterity, it was almost venerated by contemporaries, for no generation thrilled to the godlike Daniel's eloquence as much as his own. His words went echoing through the hearts of his countrymen as well as down the corridors of time when he thundered: "Liberty *and* Union, now and forever, one and inseparable!"

There was some reassurance to words like these, but in the minds of men like Marshall there was great doubt as to what the old Indian fighter in the White House would do to maintain the country intact. Since the Chief Justice had little contact with Jacksonian circles on either side, he was among the most pleasantly surprised of Americans when, not long after the end of the court term of 1830, he read about Jackson's attendance at a celebration of Jefferson's birthday in April. Calhoun, with whom the President had not yet definitely split, had arranged the dinner, and toasts were drafted in carefully calculated order so that they would build up to a fine demonstration of State rights. They were going splendidly, too, until the white-haired old warrior placed himself decisively on record with a choice sentiment of his own. With the voice which knew both how to command, to browbeat and to cajole, he proposed:

"Our Federal Union—it must be preserved!"

This compensated in part for the feeling that the Court was getting out of hand, a feeling which had been intensified by the vigorous dissent of three Justices on a major Constitutional point. Actually this was one issue on which Marshall was reversed completely and rapidly after his death. He had handed down a ruling that the State of Missouri, in issuing loan certificates in amounts of ten dollars and less to citizens short of hard money during the depression, had violated the constitutional clause which forbids states to "emit bills of credit." The Missouri certificates were designed to provide a medium of exchange at a time when banks were closed and little cash was in evidence.

Justices Thompson, Johnson, and McLean thought the case involved no more than the right of the State to float loans. However, if the opinion Marshall wrote had been carried through logically, State bank notes would have been outlawed too, and the course of United States economic history been very different—and perhaps happier.

[5]

His disagreements with Jacksonian philosophy did not carry with them the unpopularity which had repaid his disputes with Jefferson. For one thing, they were not so immediately embodied in judicial opinions. For another, it is difficult for Americans to dislike a good-natured old man, and Marshall at seventy-five still retained the simple, pleasing habits of his youth. He was one of the landed gentry, but it was impossible to suspect that if one saw him walking down the street or exchanging jests and philosophy with the frequenters of modest taverns.

He was too old, he thought, to take much part in the dining out, the fashionable crushes or the gambling along Pennsylvania Avenue. When he did venture forth, it was more or less in line of duty. He reported on a dull party at the French Minister's, at least it was dull for him because the envoy and his wife spoke no English and he no French. He also dined with Van Buren—"a grand dinner and the secretary was very polite, but I was rather dull through the evening." Almost wistfully he wrote to Polly:

"A person as old as I am feels that his home is his place of most comfort, and his old wife the companion in the world in whose society he is most happy. I dined yesterday with Mr. Randolph.

He is absorbed in the party politics of the day & seems as much engaged in them as he was twenty-five years past. It is very different with me. I long to leave this busy bustling scene & to return to the tranquility of my family & farm."

When he did go back, he relished entertainments which the fashionable of Washington would have scorned, and which even some of his peers in Richmond thought undignified. His passion for quoits remained undimmed, and a stranger who attended a popular barbecue in the country was surprised to see an old man emerge from the bushes along a stream, staggering under an armload of flat stones.

"Here," he exclaimed, as he dumped his burden beside the fire, "are enough quoits for everybody."

Of course it was the Chief Justice. Not content with getting a game himself, he wanted others to enjoy his favorite sport.

In Washington he walked a great deal, sometimes with Adams, discussing literature and law. The Chief Justice walked in the funeral of Pinkney, the first lawyer to whose death the Supreme Court paid the tribute of an adjournment. He walked once across the path of that indefatigable gossip writer, Mrs. Royall, and hastily bought a copy of her book, "to avoid a worse castigation," said Story, who also purchased a copy. But then there was a story going around that Mrs. Royall was a dangerous woman, that she had trapped Adams during his Presidency while at his favorite sport of swimming in the Potomac and refused to go away from his clothes so he could come out of the water and get dressed until he had submitted to an interview on topics of the day. Marshall had to be caught on one of his walks, because he was usually at work.

Most of the time, he told Polly, he rose early, pored over law cases, went to court and passed the evening in consultation with his associates. Few visitors called, and those visits were returned only by card. This regimen did not seem to agree with him. Early in February, Wirt and Adams had a long talk about the Chief Justice, for both were concerned about the state of his health

which seemed to them to be breaking down. That night, Adams
wrote some rare words of praise in his diary, noting:

"He . . . has done more to establish the Constitution of the
United States on sound construction than any other man living."

Adams was sincerely worried about what would happen after
the old Chief Justice was forced by death or disability to step
down from the bench. If it happened while Jackson was in office,
"some shallow-pated wild-cat like Philip P. Barbour, fit for noth-
thing but to tear the Union to rags and tatters, would be appointed
in his place." Actually, Barbour made a very good Associate Justice when he was placed on the bench in 1836.

Without using quite the same fierce language as Adams, Marshall felt much the same way. He would have liked to retire, but
he was not prepared to leave the field to Jackson. Retreating from
the rigors of the Washington winter in March, 1831, he was ob-
sessed with the idea of getting out of harness. He was so eager that
he forgot what year it was, and began making plans in the belief
that there would be a Presidential election in the fall. If Jackson
should be defeated for re-election, an eventuality which all his
opponents confidently predicted, Marshall decided he himself
would step down gracefully from the Supreme Court.

His miscalculation was part of the result of sudden and intense
physical pain which the Chief Justice suffered that spring. His
malady was stones in the bladder, but the medical profession of
Richmond was baffled, and the tall frame was wracked with
agony. Having enjoyed unfailing good health all his seventy-five
years, Marshall was ill prepared for the torture, but he bore up
under it and solaced himself with thoughts of retirement, writing
confidentially to Story:

"You know how much importance I attach to the character of
the person who is to succeed me, and calculate the influence which
probabilities on that subject would have on my continuance in

office. This, however, is a matter of great delicacy on which I cannot and do not speak . . . but recent events produce such real uncertainty respecting the future as to create doubts whether I ought not to await the same chances in the fall of 32 which I had intended to await in the fall of 31."

Story protested such thoughts, but the old man was not to be diverted from them. As the pain grew worse and more incomprehensible to his physicians, he determined to go to Philadelphia to consult the miracle man of contemporary medicine, Dr. Philip Syng Physick. Sometimes called "the father of American surgery," he had improved both the teaching and the techniques of his profession.

Dr. Physick discovered the real cause of Marshall's pain, but warned that there was only about an even chance that he would survive an operation. Marshall gladly accepted the gamble, and in October went through the exquisite tortures of the "cutting for the stone" which modern man can scarcely appreciate. In the absence of anaesthetics, the technique had scarcely improved since young Sam Pepys went through the experience, which remained in his mind the great day of his life. The old jurist's stoicism amazed Dr. Physick's assistant, young Dr. Jacob Randolph, who chronicled the fact that their patient hardly murmured once as they cut through and removed at least a thousand of the tiny stones which had been torturing him.

Good spirits and the habit of forgetting himself played a big part in his rather speedy recovery. Dr. Randolph had been surprised on the morning of the operation to find his patient eating a hearty breakfast without any trace of fear. Marshall had explained cheerfully that if it was to be his last meal on earth, he wanted it to be a good one. After the operation, Randolph was sure that "the calm and philosophical views which he took of his case" pulled him through. Just before the operation, Marshall himself had written in his usual vein to Polly:

"I anticipate with a pleasure which I know you will share the time when I may sit by your side by our tranquil fire side & enjoy the happiness of your society without inflicting on you the pain of witnessing my suffering."

But while his strength was returning, hers was ebbing. Marshall got back to the house in Richmond only to find that Polly was physically, as well as nervously ill. She herself seemed to realize that this illness was different from her usual afflictions. On Christmas eve she told him she had something for him, and hung around his neck a little locket containing a curl of her hair. The next day she died, and some time later, probably two or three years at least, he wrote:

"This day of joy and festivity to the whole Christian world is, to my sad heart, the anniversary of the keenest affliction which humanity can sustain. While all around is gladness, my mind dwells on the silent tomb, and cherishes the remembrance of the beloved object which it contains.

"On the 25th of December, 1831, it was the will of Heaven to take to itself the companion who had sweetened the choicest part of my life, had rendered toil a pleasure, had partaken of all my feelings, and was enthroned in the inmost recess of my heart. Never can I cease to feel the loss and to deplore it. Grief for her is too sacred ever to be profaned on this day, which shall be, during my existence, marked by a recollection of her virtues."

They had been married for nearly forty-nine years. During most of that time, she had been regarded by others as a burden and a trial, difficult and capricious, but to her husband she had "the sweetest temper which can accompany a just and modest sense of what was due to herself." To the children, she was the reason why they had to be quiet; to Marshall she was a collection "of as amiable and estimable qualities as ever adorned the female bosom." To their friends, she was a cause of apprehension; to him simply "the woman I adored." He was writing for himself, not for others nor for publication; the paper was found only after his death. Little Mary Ambler had placed her brand upon his heart that day in Yorktown more than a half century before, and it had never faded.

XXIII

Justice and the Indians

THE FACT THAT he had to leave Richmond immediately after Polly's funeral for the Supreme Court session in Washington was almost a welcome relief to Marshall. With returning health, he was able to lose himself to some extent in work and in observation of the extraordinarily interesting politics of that election year.

"I strengthen considerably," he wrote to his son, "and am able, without fatigue, to walk to court, a distance of two miles, and return to dinner. [He also went calling, usually in Story's company, and one day the two judges kept Adams from his dinner while they discussed gradual emancipation of the slaves.] At first this exercise was attended with some difficulty, but I feel no inconvenience from it now. . . .

"This session of Congress is indeed peculiarly interesting. The discussion on the tariff and on the Bank, especially, will, I believe call forth an unusual display of talents. I have no hope that any accommodation can take place on the first question. The bitterness of party spirit on that subject threatens to continue unabated. There seems to be no prospect of allaying it."

Marshall was intensely interested in both the issues. In his opinion on *McCulloch* vs. *Maryland* he had saved the Bank of the United States, and as a Hamiltonian he was a firm believer in the necessity of such an institution. But Jackson was an even more bitter foe of the Bank than Jefferson had been of its predecessor, and was determined to smash it. The Chief Justice watched the alignment of power, and believed with most of Jackson's enemies that the Bank was stronger than the President. Nicholas Biddle, aesthete turned financier, who had been president of the Bank for nearly ten years, was arrogantly confident of defeating the rude warrior who occupied the White House. He controlled what he considered the best minds in Congress. Webster and Clay were retained at high prices as counsel. They, as well as Calhoun and George McDuffie, chairman of the House Ways and Means Committee, had unsecured loans from what its enemies were calling "the Bribery Bank." A great many other Congressmen and assorted politicians had also been accommodated with credit on easy terms.

To Marshall, the tariff issue seemed more dangerous to his principles. For the South, despite Webster's great speech, was not professing itself willing to obey any protective tariff law. This seemed to Marshall harking back to the dangerous days of his own Congressional career. As he saw it, the Kentucky and Virginia Resolutions of that time meant that a State could obey or disobey a Federal law, Presidential order, or Supreme Court decision as it saw fit—or else those resolutions meant nothing at all. The Chief Justice thought the new men who talked of nullification drew their inspiration from this source.

Therefore he had been delighted when Madison wrote that the practice which Marshall supposed him to have advocated in '98 would break up the Union and that the Union was worth preserving. In a letter to Edward Everett, which was published in the *North American Review*, the father of the Constitution even supported the Marshall principle that there was no other body in the country except the Federal judiciary which could interpret the Constitution in the last analysis. Said Madison:

"It would seem that, with but few exceptions, the course of the judiciary has been hitherto sustained by the predominant sense of the nation."

This was generous, since the "course of the judiciary" included some policies of which a more active Madison had publicly disapproved.

"He avows the opinions of his best days," Marshall exulted, recalling their collaboration in the ratification fight so long ago, "and must be pardoned for his oblique insinuations that some of the opinions of our Court are not approved. Contrast this delicate hint with the language Mr Jefferson has applied to us."

The contrast had given the Chief Justice a great deal of pleasure, and he hoped that it would be useful in influencing Southern opinion against nullification. There were no signs of it, however, in the torrid Congressional debates. Marshall heard few of them because during these early months of 1832 his own Court could offer a rival attraction.

[2]

The case, which was to be only second to the tariff at this time in testing the support which Madison's views would receive from the country, was another chapter in the sorry story of United States relations with the Indians. It was also in part a holdover from the Yazoo fight.

When the Federal government took over these lands from Georgia, it was provided that all the rights of the Indians whether in ceded lands or in lands remaining within the State would be respected. However, the Federal authorities undertook to do their best to acquire title from the Indians to the land in Georgia as well as to that ceded. In other parts of the country it had been easy to persuade or swindle the aboriginals to sign away tribal lands.

The Cherokees of Georgia could not be handled in this way. They had adopted a good many of the white man's ways (including the institution of slavery) and many of them had acquired the white man's education. They had a constitution of their own, courts, schools, and much of the machinery of civilization. They were not inclined to sell their lands and move to some remote part of the country about which they knew nothing. They did not fall easy victims to the usual swindles. So negotiations to buy them out had been fruitless.

Then gold was discovered in their territory. That is a lure for which white men have seldom failed to rise, and at once Georgia grew clamorous for possession of the Cherokee lands. The Georgia legislature adopted resolutions declaring that the whole territory belonged to the State. Soon laws were passed regulating the search for gold and the tenure of land. White men were permitted to enter only with a permit from the State, and all Indian institutions of government were abolished. Meanwhile, the Federal government had been trying to persuade the Cherokees to move to what is now Oklahoma. The Indians sent a delegation to explore the offered land. They came back with a vigorously adverse report—no one then knew that there was oil under those barren plains, and no one would have cared anyway—but in May, 1830, Congress passed a bill to remove the Cherokees to the wilderness whether they liked it or not.

"The bullies of Georgia have succeeded in the project of extirpating the Indians by the sacrifice of the public faith of the Union and of all our treaties," John Quincy Adams wrote in his diary.

Marshall was equally disturbed. The Cherokees had retained former Attorney General Wirt to represent them, and he persuaded Judge Dabney Carr, an old friend of himself and of the Chief Justice, to sound out Marshall on the advisability of appealing to the Supreme Court. Marshall, of course, was noncommittal, but he did write:

"I have followed the debate in both houses of Congress with profound attention and with deep interest, and have wished most sincerely, that both the executive and legislative departments had thought differently on the subject. Humanity must bewail the course which is pursued, whatever may be the decision of policy."

Wirt thought he saw encouragement in this letter, and proceeded to file his suit. Before anything could come of it, Marshall was involved in the Cherokee case through a murder. Georgia, having abolished the Indian courts in an act of usurpation which the Indians did not recognize, had tried and convicted a Cherokee named Corn Tassel for killing another man. The Indian contended that Georgia was without jurisdiction and demanded to be tried by the courts of his own people. His attorneys applied for a writ to Marshall, who granted it along with a stay of execution until the case could be argued in the Supreme Court. In what Story later called an "intemperate and indecorous" defiance of the Chief Justice and the Federal authority, Georgia executed Corn Tassel on December 24, only a few days after the Marshall writ had been received.

Here was nullification in action. The rival parties growing up around this issue were violently aroused, although Jackson was not interested, probably because he had almost as little regard for the Supreme Court as for an Indian. The press was full of comments on both sides. Niles's *Register* published the eloquent defiance of the Georgia legislature which authorized the Governor to use force to repel any interference from anywhere with their laws against the Indians. The *Washington Globe* held up Marshall as a strong man, saying in doubtful praise of his career:

"He has achieved for them [Federalists] infinitely more in the Court than all the rest of them have been able to effect elsewhere."

Kind words in the press did not bring Corn Tassel back to life, nor did they make the task of the Supreme Court any easier when, a little more than two months after the execution, the

Cherokees formally brought their case to the bar. For two days in March, 1831, Wirt and John Sergeant of Philadelphia, chief counsel for the Bank of the United States, argued for an injunction to restrain Georgia from carrying out its laws against the Cherokees. The Indians were a foreign nation whose affairs were regulated by treaty with the United States, they contended, and therefore no State had any jurisdiction over them. Nor could a State take away their lands, since all the land originally belonged to the Indians and could be acquired only by treaty. Wirt drew tears from the eyes of stoical red men in the audience and crowds of spectators gazed curiously at weeping Indians.

Georgia did not appear by counsel to contest his argument. But if she had been represented, her attorney might have produced an eight-year-old decision by the Supreme Court which brushed aside Indian titles almost as brusquely as did Georgia. For in a land case involving some fifty million acres between the Wabash and Illinois Rivers, the Court had ruled that title to land in this country originated in Great Britain's possession by right of discovery and passed to the United States by the act of independence. All the Indians had had, said the Court, was a right of occupancy, apparently acquired by the mere accident of having been born on the lands, and having used them for generations.

After five days of deliberation, the Court this time avoided a direct clash with Georgia. There were some protracted sessions of argument and searching of the laws of nations in the Justices' boardinghouse, because unanimity was impossible. Story was one of the minority and tried desperately to convert his Chief to his point of view. He failed, and in the end he and Thompson filed a dissenting opinion.

Marshall dismissed the case on the grounds that the Cherokees were not a foreign nation. He pointed out that the Constitution made a distinction between foreign nations and Indian tribes in the commerce clause and the treaty power. A case which involved the title to land might be heard, but not a request by a tribe posing as a foreign nation.

"If it be true that the Cherokee Nation have rights, this is not the tribunal in which those rights are to be asserted," he concluded. "If it be true that wrongs have been inflicted, and that still greater are to be apprehended, this is not the tribunal which can redress the past or prevent the future."

It was not an encouraging decision for the Indians. There was no other tribunal to which they could turn. Georgia courts were hopeless. Jackson had refused to intervene. Congress had passed a law exiling the Cherokees to the remote West. If the Supreme Court would not rule on their case, they had in practice no right to justice. This was recognized in the dissenting opinion, drafted by Thompson. He and Story held that while the Constitution made a distinction between foreign nations and Indian tribes, that distinction did not apply when a controversy between one of them and a State arose. The Federal government was the protector of the Indians, and the Federal courts as the arm of that government must have jurisdiction. Wirt and Sergeant decided that there might be some way of applying part of the majority opinion to the dispute, and they immediately began to prepare a case on grounds which would come within the scope which Marshall had outlined.

[3]

They had found it by the time Polly died, and the results of their labors were waiting for the Chief Justice when he came back to Washington in 1832, looking for work to distract his mind. To the layman, the point on which the Cherokees now rested their plea for justice was less important than the one they had lost. The whole validity of a State's right to make laws for the Cherokees had been challenged in the earlier case. Now it was narrowed down to the right of Georgia to imprison a white man for refusing to obey those laws.

The white man was a missionary, Samuel A. Worcester, a Vermonter with something of the Granite State's stubbornness. When Georgia ordered all those without State permits to quit Cherokee territory, he and a few others refused. They were pardoned on condition that they leave Georgia for good, and most of them did so. Worcester declined the offer, and appealed to the Supreme Court against his conviction.

The personalities of the lawyers who had charge of the missionary's interests gave the case a close connection with the engrossing politics of an election year. Wirt was a candidate against Jackson, having accepted in September at the first of the country's party conventions the nomination of the National Anti-Masonic Party. This group was one of the periodic examples of intolerance which have cropped up in American history from time to time, but saw no inconsistency in the fact that Wirt himself was a Mason. His colleague, Sergeant, added to the political flavor of the hearing because he was, as counsel for "the Bribery Bank," an object of Jackson's complete aversion.

Georgia again was not represented, but had taken the trouble to issue a formal protest against the whole proceedings. When the arguments began on February 20, interest was so great that fifty or sixty members of the House promptly left their seats and hurried down to the basement. By two o'clock other members were offering motions to adjourn so that all could attend. Shortly before three, one of the motions carried, but the late comers heard very little. Wirt, who had been speaking, was so exhausted that shortly after three he asked for an adjournment until next day, at which time he was in his best vein.

"Judge Marshall was affected to tears by the eloquent peroration of Wirt," Story used to tell his law students many years later.

Only the fact that the Court had dismissed the previous case against Georgia could have given any reason to doubt the decision. Some thought the majority might find another loop-hole, but this time Marshall and Story were in complete accord. On March 3, the Chief Justice came with their opinion neatly written in his own hand—the *New York Daily Advertiser* wanted it preserved to become an object of veneration for posterity—and spectators crowded up as close as they could get to hear him. In his recently

enfeebled voice, he read for an hour and a quarter. The laws and
Constitution of the United States, he said, obviously governed the
Indians, and at least in some respects these people retained the
characteristics of a foreign nation. Story had been converting his
Chief, for he said:

"A weaker power does not surrender its independence, its rights
to self-government, by associating with a stronger, and taking its
protection. A weak state, in order to provide for its safety, may
place itself under the protection of one more powerful without
stripping itself of the right to self-government, and ceasing to be
a state."

It is true that a weak state may have these rights, but history
records sparingly instances where they have been respected under
the circumstances in which the Cherokees found themselves. It is
a little difficult to reconcile this passage with the decision of the
previous year denying that the Cherokees could as a nation protest the laws of Georgia. Marshall, however, had no scruples now
about reversing the decision of the Georgia court which had convicted Worcester. He had decided that Georgia law could not
interfere with Cherokees.

"The whole intercourse between the United States and this
nation is by our Constitution and laws vested in the government
of the United States," he said.

Washington buzzed with speculation as to what would happen
next. The morning after the decision was read, Story went into
Marshall's room and found the Chief Justice in tears, but it was
over Polly and not the Cherokees. A few days before he had asked
Story for a bit of verse which the younger man had written on
friendship, and now in return he was copying out for his associate
some lines which Gentleman Johnny Burgoyne had written on
the death of his wife. (Later Marshall wrote them out for himself,
only substituting "Mary" for the British General's "Anna.")

"He has said to me several times during the term, that the moment he relaxes from business he feels exceedingly depressed, and

rarely goes through a night without weeping over his departed wife," his friend wrote a few hours later to Mrs. Story.

The business of the term was nearly over, but the reaction to the Cherokee decision had just begun. Georgians sizzled with rage, and professed themselves ready to die rather than bow down to the "alien" court. Northern enemies of Jackson hoped to deprive him of votes by suggesting that he was in league with the nullifiers of Supreme Court decisions. The *New York Daily Advertiser* even demanded his impeachment if he failed to act. Probably at this time began the legend, first embalmed in print by Horace Greeley many years later on the authority of George Briggs, a Representative from Massachusetts at the time, that Jackson had said:

"Well, John Marshall has made his decision; now let him enforce it!"

Incredible as it may seem, there was no machinery for enforcing it. Story, writing to a friend five days after the decision, spoke of the "very strong sensation" which *Worcester* vs. *Georgia* had created, and expressed the opinion that Georgia would resist "the execution of our judgment." He added:

"The Court has done its duty. Let the nation do theirs. If we have a government let its commands be obeyed; if we have not it is well to know it at once, & to look to consequences."

Story predicted that the President would not interfere, but in fact he was not asked to take any action. The Supreme Court adjourned on March 17 without issuing any order in the case at all, for the simple reason that there was no provision in law for it to issue writs of habeas corpus for anyone except prisoners in Federal custody.

[4]

The Cherokees were soon forgotten as an issue in themselves. Injustice to them became of interest in politics only as it could be used to prejudice a political opponent in the eyes of the voters, and Indians had no votes. The Bank and the tariff were still the issues around which new parties were forming—one soon to avow itself frankly as Democratic, the other to seek a nostalgic return to the past as Whigs.

The standard bearers for these two groups were to be Jackson and Clay, still calling himself a National Republican. Clay forced through Congress a bill to recharter the Bank, which Jackson promptly vetoed, and then the Speaker won passage of a tariff which, while still protective, reduced duties somewhat. He thought he would sweep to victory on the heels of those two measures. The tariff was a challenge to those Southerners who were saying the only way to keep them in the Union was to permit them to decide themselves which laws they would obey. Hardly anyone supposed that Jackson would disagree with them as vigorously as he did, certainly not a Virginian who wanted to resign from the Supreme Court if only Old Hickory were defeated.

"If the prospects of our country inspire you with gloom," he wrote to Story toward the end of September, "how do you think a man must be affected who partakes of all your opinions and whose geographical position enables him to see a great deal that is concealed from you? I yield slowly and reluctantly to the conviction that our Constitution cannot last. I had supposed that North of the Potomack a firm and solid government competent to the security of rational liberty might be preserved. Even that now seems doubtful. The case of the South seems to me to be desperate. Our opinions are incompatible with a united government even among ourselves. The Union has been prolonged thus far by miracles. I fear they cannot continue."

Jackson had warned South Carolina, the center of nullification sentiment, that he would tolerate no defiance of proper Federal authority. But the State was ready to push to the brink of civil war if not actually to go over it. Popular opinion had been whipped to that pitch when on November 24, a convention specially summoned to consider the tariff adopted a resolution that the Act

of Congress was "null, void and no law" in South Carolina, that
the State would resist force, that any attempt to impose force
would be the signal for South Carolina to secede from the Union.

By the time news of South Carolina's action reached Washington, Jackson knew that he had acquired a mandate such as
few Presidents have received from the voters. If there was a little
confusion as to just what the voters had authorized him to do,
that did not bother him. He took it as a vote of confidence to do
what he thought was right. The main point, as he and his supporters saw it, was that he had 219 electoral votes to 49 for Clay.

Marshall was afraid that the government would leave nullification to the customs officers and the courts, who would be powerless to enforce their decisions. Jackson was just as firm for Union,
however, as the Chief Justice and if anything more forceful and
direct. On December 10, he issued a Nullification Proclamation
which asserted his inflexible belief that no State had a right to
nullify an Act of Congress, withdraw from the Union or resist
enforcement. He backed it up with what was called a Force Bill
in Congress, authorizing the President to use the army and navy
to collect customs. At the same time, he left a way open for South
Carolina to save face by urging lower duties. Clay jumped on this
bandwagon and prepared a compromise tariff, which was signed
on the same day as the Force Act. South Carolina could gracefully suspend its own nullification ordinance, protest against the
Force Act and escape for the time being from the position of
being obliged to back down or fight.

Before that happened, Marshall was gloomily confident that
force would be required to bring the South Carolinians and some
of their supporters elsewhere in the South to their senses. He spent
the first anniversary of Polly's death writing Story an immensely
long letter on the state of the nation.

The occasion was his receipt of proofs of his associate's *Commentaries on the Constitution of the United States,* dedicated to
himself. He was touched. He well knew the labor that went into
these productions—this year he had finished revising his own

biography of Washington for the centennial of his hero's birth, and brought it out in four volumes, using the first as a separate "History of the Colonies." But he was principally concerned with the effects of the Nullification Proclamation and the events of the day which were perhaps an even better commentary on the Constitution than Story's.

Marshall was a little amused that the Virginia legislature, then in session in Richmond, was bestowing on the President "the only epithet which could possibly weigh in the scales against the name of 'Andrew Jackson,' and countervail its popularity." He added:

"Imitating the Quaker who said the dog he wished to destroy was mad, they said Andrew Jackson had become a Federalist, even an ultra-Federalist. To have said he was ready to break down and trample on every other department of the government would not have injured him, but to say that he was a Federalist—a convert to the opinions of Washington, was a mortal blow under which he is yet staggering."

Recapitulating the division of parties in Virginia, he told Story that if South Carolina actually managed to get a "southern league," his State would not be unanimous. Anticipating what actually took place thirty years later in an even greater crisis, he wrote:

"The northern and western section of our State, should a union be maintained north of the Potomack, will not readily connect itself with the South."

Then abruptly he turned to the long dead past. The minds of old men and the minds of historians are inclined to wander backwards, and Marshall was both.

"We are now gathering the bitter fruits of the tree even before that time planted by Mr Jefferson, and so industriously and perseveringly cultivated by Virginia," he wrote.

At seventy-seven, Marshall still cherished bitterness against the kinsman whose policies he had so deeply resented. Few men were old enough or implacable enough to join him in attributing the modern secession theories of Calhoun and his South Carolina school to the influence of the more philosophical and more basically democratic beliefs of Jefferson. But to Marshall all these measures to weaken the Federal government were cut from the same piece of cloth, and he was willing to give sincerely meant tribute to the uncompromising Jackson who had preserved that government. He was sufficiently outspoken that Story could write of the President:

"Since his last proclamation and message, the Chief Justice and myself have become his warmest supporters, and shall continue so just as long as he maintains the principles contained in them. Who would have dreamed of such an occurrence?"

XXIV

☆ ☆ ☆

The Final Decision

PLEASED AS HE was with Jackson's strong stand in the nullification crisis, Marshall was not tempted to trust him with the nomination of a new Chief Justice if it could be helped. For one thing, he did not believe in what he regarded as the President's conversion. For another, he saw that the incipient battle over secession was postponed, not ended. Like so many of the men who could remember keener struggles, he believed that the political eruptions of this age were the death agony of the republic rather than the birth pangs of a broader democracy. In fact, Marshall probably would have said those two were the same thing. It had become necessary to appeal directly to the mass of the people, explaining political issues to them rather than convincing mere groups of leaders, and Marshall agreed with Adams's sneer at candidates who were campaigning for popular support:

"This fashion of peddling for popularity by travelling round the country gathering crowds together, hawking for public dinners and spouting empty speeches, is growing into high fashion."

370

Adams himself was so popular now in his home district that he did not need to seek favor. He had found a vocation for ex-Presidents which his successors unfortunately failed to imitate. He accepted election to the House, and for seventeen years gave the benefit of his experience and his integrity to the service of those causes in which he believed. Adams was constitutionally a pessimist. Marshall had acquired that habit of thought by contemplating political developments which he did not altogether understand. He saw only the influences which were dividing the country. The cement composed of the belief that the people had a stake in the country was still liquid. He could not see that it would harden into a form which would prevent the secessionists from tearing themselves away. He looked upon the party strife as just so much froth, losing sight of the permanent gains because the ignoble struggle for office, loot, and privilege was so blatant. He did not think that even great works like Story's *Commentaries* would be very effective, and upon receipt of the printed version, he wrote to the author:

"I greatly fear that south of the Potomack, where it is most wanted, it will be least used. It is a Mohammedan rule, I understand, 'never dispute with the ignorant,' and we of the true faith in the South abjure the contamination of infidel political works. It would give our orthodox nullifyer a fever to read the heresies of your Commentaries."

Shaking his head over the state of the world, convinced that there was small chance of happiness for his country, Marshall still clung to one hope as far as his own department was concerned. He would try to hold on until Jackson's term expired. Perhaps it would be possible; he came of long-lived stock, and he was in splendid health, far better than the President, when on March 4, 1833, he administered the oath to a Chief Executive for the last time.

At the opening of the 1833 term, Story thought that Marshall looked more vigorous than ever and "seemed to revive and enjoy anew his green old age." He presented each of his associates with a copy of his revised biography of Washington, and was pleased with their words of praise for a work which he knew in his heart was defective. In the growing bitterness of the political struggle for the succession to Jackson, which began as soon as Old Hickory had been re-elected, the Supreme Court seemed to enjoy a fleeting moment of popularity. Washingtonians, who had never known a time when Marshall was not an important figure in the city, were especially fond of the old Chief Justice these days. They cheered him when he went to the theatre to see Fanny Kemble. Story, who was with him in the box, wrote home:

"He behaved as he always does, with extreme modesty, and seemed not to know that the compliment was designed for him."

The incomparable Fanny, as Mrs. Haller in *The Stranger*, drew tears from virtually everyone in the house, and "the Chief Justice shed them in common with younger eyes." Between terms he sometimes visited his children, but he still preferred the brick house in Richmond where he had been happy with Polly for so many years despite her moods and crotchets. There, as in Washington, he was an institution, and if few admired his politics, everyone admired his person.

He kept well up to his work, and Harriet Martineau on her visit to the capital was struck by the business of the Supreme Court where the arguments spun their interminable length, "watched by the groups of idlers and listeners around them; the newspaper corps, the dark Cherokee chiefs, the stragglers from the far West, the gay ladies in their waving plumes, and the members of either House that have stopped in to listen; all these I have seen at one moment constitute one silent assemblage, while the mild voice of the aged Chief Justice sounded through the Court."

There were new men coming up all the time. Webster and Clay, of course, were veterans by now. Taney was a powerful pleader of a different sort. But younger men were crowding the capital—James Buchanan and Charles Sumner, George Bancroft and William Cullen Bryant, the Blairs and an odd character named Sam Houston who had been tried before the House for indulging in a street brawl with a member. Bancroft, who saw the Chief Justice when he called on his friend Story, was struck by the old man's "venerable coolness of manner" and by the absence of any marks of genius.

The deference of the young was pleasant. There were advantages in age, when it brought so much kindness and respect. It was pleasant, too, to feel that differences with old friends no longer mattered, and to send off a copy of the colonial history inscribed to James Monroe "as a mark of the affectionate resolutions excited in the bosom of the author as he looks back to times long since gone by." There was less joy in dining out, for as he neared eighty, it upset his digestion even to contemplate what a Washington hostess thought it necessary to set before her guests.

Mrs. Samuel Smith, giving a little dinner for twelve in honor of Miss Martineau—none of the guests knew for what the British visitor was distinguished, but they were falling all over each other to pay tribute to her genius—had to struggle hard to cut down Henry Orr's elaborate ideas as to what she should serve. Henry was the most fashionable waiter in the city, and informed Mrs. Smith rather haughtily that when Mrs. Levi Woodbury, wife of the Secretary of the Treasury, entertained, she had thirty meat dishes. Mrs. Smith was firm, and Henry was reduced to this menu:

Soup, fish, canvasback ducks, a small ham, a small turkey, partridges, mutton chops, a macaroni pie, an oyster pie, four vegetables, ice cream in forms, a pyramid of fruit, jellies, custards, blanc mange, cakes, sweetmeats and sugar plums. (Miss Martineau, her hostess noticed, ate nothing but a mite of turkey and a little ham.)

Marshall himself gave Story minute directions about the best route for Miss Martineau to take on her journey through Virginia. He wrote out a letter of introduction, which Story delivered, urging her to keep it as "the memorial of a man of eighty, still in the possession of his glorious mind, whose death, whenever it may happen, will cause a sensation in America, unequalled except by that of Washington." Story did not exaggerate more than friendship permits. Chancellor Kent had told him that Hamilton had been "the greatest and wisest man of this country" because he saw events fifty years before they happened, but he had added:

"Next to him in wisdom and sense, intuitive rectitude and truth and judgment is Ch. J. Marshall."

[2]

Affairs of the Court ran less smoothly than the affairs of Marshall's private life. He was not the only one whose health gave his associates concern. When the 1834 term opened, Johnson was too ill to attend, and Duval was so feeble that he expressed his intention of resigning before the next one.

For a time, however, the Chief Justice was able to supply with his own ingenuity the place of his failing associates. At this term two cases were argued which he thought might upset two of his cherished principles—the constitutional bar against States issuing any kind of bills of credit and the exclusive right of Congress to legislate on navigation, or anything connected with it. Kentucky had authorized a State bank to issue notes which were in effect legal tender for most purposes. New York had given the city administration authority to exclude undesirable passengers arriving in port from other States or foreign countries. Story and Duval stood by the Chief Justice in considering both these measures unconstitutional. Thompson, McLean and Baldwin wished to uphold them. It had always been supposed that in case of an even division, the judgment of the lower court would be affirmed, and both these cases had been decided in favor of the State legislation. Marshall, fighting a losing rear-guard action, at this point read a new rule. It was something of a judicial discovery, never known before, but the Chief Justice gave it an air of antiquity, saying:

"The practice of this court is not, except in cases of absolute necessity, to deliver any judgment in cases where constitutional questions are involved, unless four judges concur in opinion, thus making the decision that of a majority of the whole court."

He therefore directed that the two cases be argued over again at the next term. By that time, he hoped, Johnson would be well enough to attend, and he knew that this associate agreed with him. But time was against him. Before the next term began, Johnson had died and Duval had carried out his intention of resigning. When Marshall opened his last term on January 12, 1835, Johnson's successor had already been appointed, and the Chief Justice could appraise James M. Wayne of Georgia. He saw a sturdy man of forty-five with a strong face, well-shaped head crowned with a thick head of hair swept back from the broad forehead and an inflexible expression. A little conversation proved that he was no blind upholder of Jackson, but neither was he devoted to Marshall's theory of national supremacy. Wayne would go along with the old majority of the Court only to the extent of recognizing the Union as something more than a loose federation.

Duval's successor had not been appointed when Court opened, but Jackson gave Marshall a rather pleasant surprise by sending to the Senate the name of Roger Brooke Taney of Maryland, his former Attorney General and Secretary of the Treasury. The Chief Justice had been much impressed with Taney on his appearances before the Court. He was confident that so able a lawyer as the ungainly, untidy Marylander would make a sound Federal judge, if not a sound Federalist. But Jackson was feuding with the Senate, and Taney was a stout Jacksonian. Senators, therefore, were spitefully blocking the President—they had already virtually assured the election of Van Buren as next President by rejecting his nomination to be Minister to England and thereby making him the darling of Jackson and the people. Marshall thought he was old enough and near enough to the end of his time to attempt a bit of lobbying for the nominee. Senator Leigh of Virginia was a fellow member of the Barbecue Club, and to him the Chief Justice wrote:

"If you have not made up your mind on the nomination of Mr. Taney, I have received some information in his favor which I would wish to communicate."

Marshall's intervention was without avail. The Senate was not interested especially in Taney's qualifications. Members merely wished to spite Jackson, and on March 3 the nomination was rejected. In the Supreme Court itself, the absence of a full membership gave Marshall the opportunity to postpone the unpalatable Kentucky and New York cases for another term. He predicted what actually happened, of course, that when the cases were finally decided, it would be in favor of the States.

As if to show the world that, although seventy-nine, he retained as much vigor as ever, Marshall never missed a moment of a single sitting that term, and he delivered most of the opinions as usual. In his whole time of service on the bench, the Court considered 1,215 cases, and in 109 no opinion was rendered. Of the remaining 1,106 which required written decisions, Marshall had composed 519, and in his thirty-five terms of court he had filed exactly nine dissents. In his last term, there were no suits of special importance, but Story complained that these seemed to need long and intricate arguments which he thought could have been compressed into one-third the time.

"But this is the very region of words," he declared; "and Americans, I fear, have a natural propensity to substitute them for things."

The Chief Justice listened with his usual patience. But the apprehensive Story was worried all through the term, and on the day before the Senate rejected Taney, he wrote:

"Chief Justice Marshall still possesses his intellectual powers in very high vigor, but his physical strength is manifestly on the decline."

A few days later, the Court closed its work with a decision in a Florida land case. There had been a motion to continue it on the ground that it might be possible to reach a settlement out of court, and Marshall indulged in a bit of judicial irony, saying:

"Though the hope of deciding causes to the mutual satisfaction of parties would be chimerical, that of convincing them that the case has been fully and fairly considered may be sometimes indulged. Even this is not always attainable. In the excitement produced by ardent controversy, gentlemen view the same object through such different media that minds not infrequently receive therefrom precisely opposite impressions."

But judges would see more clearly than anyone else. It was an axiom with Marshall, and by and large he believed that his experience on the bench confirmed it, that a judiciary set above the political strife of the nation wore spectacles less definitely tinted than anyone else.

"The Court," he said in this case, ". . . must see with its own eyes, and exercise its own judgment, guided by its own reason."

This was Marshall's last pronouncement from the bench over which he had presided for so long that many men could not realize that there had ever been other Chief Justices. For the last time, he handed the manuscript of his decision to the clerk. For the last time he bowed to the bar and the spectators. For the last time he allowed himself to be helped out of his black robes and walked slowly from the basement room between the pillars which supported the floor of the Senate. For the last time he parted with his associates at their boardinghouse and climbed into the coach for Richmond. How many times he had made that journey, always until the last few years with high anticipation! But this time there was nothing to return to except an empty house.

[3]

Old men, even when they are surrounded by affectionate children and are enjoying the veneration of their neighbors, allow their minds to wander in the past. Marshall was no exception. He spoke of his wife and his parents, telling stories of his youth. If he men-

tioned his judicial career, no one was sufficiently interested to set
down his words. There was an added serenity to his tone, which
came from satisfaction with his work, and with the place which
that work had won in the minds of men. It had won a place, too,
in the hearts of some, and in a little time more, Story would be
telling Miss Martineau:

"I am in love with his character, positively in love . . . I never
hope to look upon his like again."

Story was a good friend, but the verdict which he passed upon
his revered Chief was accepted by posterity. The Supreme Court
has settled a great number of knotty problems since Marshall died
—problems which in other republics have been soluble only by
civil strife, loss of liberty or political chicanery. Marshall made
the traditions of that Court more than any other man, and he
made them so sanely that after a century Justice Frankfurter could
write:

"But he had too much of an instinct for the practical to attempt
rigidities which could not possibly bind the future. He wished to
promote the national power, but he left open the choice of doctrine for the attainment of his purpose."

On the centenary of Marshall's accession to the bench, there
was an extremely elaborate legal jubilee. The most interesting
analysis of his influence was made by Oliver Wendell Holmes, the
greatest of liberal Justices as Marshall was the greatest of the conservatives.

"There fell to Marshall perhaps the greatest place that was ever
filled by a judge," said Holmes, and then he explained how the
place had been filled. With no great reverence for the actual decisions as men wanted them applied to these later days, Holmes
added: "I should feel a . . . doubt whether, after Hamilton and
the Constitution itself, Marshall's work proved more than a strong
intellect, a good style, personal ascendancy in his court, courage,
justice, and the convictions of his party."

Men have risen to greatness on less; few would ask greater praise from posterity. Marshall himself would have been more than content, although he would have relished even more Adams's private reflection that the Chief Justice had "settled many great constitutional questions favorably to the continuance of the Union."

In the course of his work he had made the judiciary really an equal and co-ordinate branch of government and had laid the foundation for a judicial strength which from time to time has caused critics of the Supreme Court to complain that it is all-powerful. In the early days of the republic, foreign students of our customs and institutions had wasted little time on the Supreme Court, but toward the end of Marshall's career, Alexis de Tocqueville wrote:

"The peace, the prosperity, and the very existence of the Union are vested in the hands of the seven Federal judges. Without them the Constitution would be a dead letter: The Executive appeals to them for assistance against the encroachments of the legislative power; the Legislature demands their protection against the assaults of the Executive; they defend the Union from the disobedience of the States, the States from the exaggerated claims of the Union, the public interest against private interests and the conservative spirit of stability against the fickleness of the democracy."

This is exaggeration, but it indicates the importance to which the Court had risen. Marshall's share in the process was so widely appreciated that the bar spoke of him with unusual respect. Even the bumptious Webster wrote somewhat apologetically of "having spoken somewhat more freely than usually befits the mouth of an humble attorney at law, like myself, of the 'manifest errors' of the Great Chief."

All this was achievement. So was the long list of precedent-making decisions, although most of these were to be modified or reversed by the ingenuity of later judges and the necessities of later generations. But the crowning achievement was Marshall's contribution to that special feature of the American system which gives to the country, in its Supreme Court, a real court of last resort. In all other governments which are based on the will of the people, the courts take second place to the legislature. It would be rash to say that without Marshall, the judicial power inherent in the Constitution could not have been realized. Nevertheless, Marshall was the man who laid the foundation for that power and built a good deal of the superstructure. He found the Court a subordinate branch of government, used by the Executive and not definitely independent of Congress. He left it a force which neither President nor Congress could flout with impunity, a force which gained in power after his death until more than a century later so sober and respected a journal as *The Christian Science Monitor* could declare:

"When an American proposes disobedience to a decision of the U.S. Supreme Court he is proposing revolution."

It is this reputation, which Marshall took the lead in establishing, which has made the Supreme Court at one and the same time a handmaiden of property and a guardian of liberty. As Mr. Dooley so well put it, the Justices follow the election returns, but they have been the great apostles by and large of "middle of the road" progress. Their influence has been so strong because in the years of Marshall's service on the bench, their authority was put beyond partisanship. This, far more than the actual decisions he handed down, have been the Richmond lawyer's great contribution to the growth of the American Republic.

[4]

The tributes and the future alike were hidden from the old man resting, in the hope of outlasting Jackson's second term, at his brick house in Richmond. There, in May, 1835, that staunch New York Federalist, Chancellor Kent, found him "very emaciated, feeble & dangerously low." He had hurt his back when a coach in which he was riding was upset, but he was optimistic about his recovery. He insisted that Kent should come to see him in Washington the next winter.

Reports of his condition were circulating through the country. There was some talk of a deal by which, if he would resign, Jackson would appoint Webster to the place. The godlike Daniel's shifts from one set of principles to another in the past made it easy to believe that he would welcome such an arrangement, and it was said that he was making overtures to the President, his only condition being a softening of the Administration attitude toward the Bank. There was also a strong rumor that Benton of Missouri was slated for the post. That outspoken gentleman was saying that Marshall ought to resign because:

"The elevation of the station requires that a man should descend from it with grace and dignity, instead of hanging on until he tumbles off."

But the Senator had no desire to mount the bench himself. His first choice was Taney, his second Barbour. He was of one mind with Jackson, for it was to Taney that the President gave the first place in the Court, which a chastened Senate meekly confirmed, while Barbour took Duval's seat.

However, Marshall was not ready to give up yet. While Benton was expressing himself without reserve, the Chief Justice had set out for Philadelphia to see if Dr. Physick could perform another miracle. But after a careful examination through several June days, the eminent surgeon diagnosed a liver disease which not even his skill could check. He told the Chief Justice quite frankly that his case was hopeless, and the old man sent for his children while he composed himself to die. Story, almost beside himself with grief, talked of coming down to cheer his "loneliness" and wrote his friends long letters about Marshall's virtues.

For two weeks, the patient slipped slowly out of life. Although the liver was so greatly enlarged that it pressed against the stomach in such a way that the patient could not retain food, he was relatively free from pain, cheerful and composed. Three of his sons reached his side. He never knew that the eldest, Thomas, had been killed by a falling chimney in Baltimore on the way to join his father. Independence Day found the old man just barely able to hold a pen, and he traced the words he wanted for his epitaph. They were:

JOHN MARSHALL

The son of Thomas and Mary Marshall
Was born on the 24th of
September, 1755; intermarried
with Mary Willis Ambler
the 3d of January, 1783;
departed this life the —th day
of ———, 1835.

They filled in the blanks just two days later.

☆ ☆ ☆

Bibliography

Adams, Abigail, *Letters*
Adams, Henry, *History of the United States*
———— *The Life of Albert Gallatin*
Adams, John, *Works*
Adams, John Quincy, *Diary*
———— *Memoirs*
Adams, Samuel Hopkins, *The Godlike Daniel*
Alexander, Holmes, *Aaron Burr, the Proud Pretender*
American Historical Association, *Annual Reports*
American Historical Review
Ames, Fisher, *Works*
Anderson, D. R., *William Branch Giles*
Atlantic Monthly (Vol. 84)

Bates, Ernest Sutherland, *The Story of the Supreme Court*
Beard, Charles A., *An Economic History of the Constitution of the
    United States*
———— *Economic Origins of Jeffersonian Democracy*
———— *The Supreme Court and the Constitution*
Beard, Charles A. and Mary R., *The Rise of American Civilization*
Benton, Thomas Hart, *Thirty Years' View*

Beveridge, Albert J., *The Life of John Marshall*
Biddle, Nicholas, *Correspondence*
Binney, Charles Chauncey, *The Life of Horace Binney*
Boudin, Louis B., *Government by Judiciary*
Boudinot, J. J., *The Life, Public Services, Addresses and Letters of Elias Boudinot*
Bowers, Claude G., *Jefferson and Hamilton*
———————— *Jefferson in Power*
———————— *The Young Jefferson*
Bradford, Gamaliel, *As God Made Them*
———————— *Damaged Souls*
Bruce, William C., *John Randolph of Roanoke*
Bryan, George, *The Imperialism of John Marshall*
Bryan, W. B., *A History of the National Capital*
Buchanan, James, *Works*

Carrington, E. F., *Battles of the American Revolutionary War*
Carson, Hampton Lawrence, *The History of the Supreme Court of the United States*
Clay, Henry, *Private Correspondence*
———————— *Works*
Cleves, Freeman, *Old Tippecanoe*
Columbian Centinel
Corwin, Edward S., *The Constitution and What It Means Today*
———————— *John Marshall and the Constitution*
———————— *The Twilight of the Supreme Court*
Craigmyle, Baron, *John Marshall in Diplomacy and Law*

Davis, Matthew L., *Memoirs of Aaron Burr*
Dictionary of American Biography
Dillon, John F., *John Marshall*
Documents Illustrative of the Formation of the Union of the American States
Dodd, William E., *Statesmen of the Old South*
Dunbar, Seymour, *History of Travel in America*

Ernst, Morris L., *The Ultimate Power*

Ferrand, Max, *The Records of the Federal Convention*
Fisher, Sydney George, *The True Daniel Webster*

Flanders, Henry, *The Lives and Times of the Chief Justices of the Supreme Court of the United States*

Foote, William Henry, *Sketches of Virginia, Historical and Biographical*

Frankfurter, Felix, *The Commerce Clause under Marshall, Taney and Waite*

Gallatin, Albert, *Writings*

Gay, Sidney Howard, *James Madison*

Gazette of the United States

Gilmer, Francis Walker, *Sketches of American Orators*

Goodrich, Samuel G., *Recollections of a Lifetime*

Green Bag, The (vol. 13)

Hamilton, Alexander, *Works*

———, James Madison and John Jay, *The Federalist*

Haskins, Charles H., *The Yazoo Land Companies*

Horton, J. T., *James Kent, a Study in Conservatism*

Hudson, Frederic, *Journalism in the United States*

Hughes, Charles Evans, *The Supreme Court of the United States*

Independent Chronicle

Irving, Washington, *Letters of Washington Irving to Henry Brevoort*

James, Marquis, *Andrew Jackson*

Jay, John, *Correspondence and Public Papers*

Jefferson, Thomas, *Writings*

Kennedy, John P., *Memoirs of the Life of William Wirt*

Kent, William, *Memoirs and Letters of James Kent*

King, Charles R., *Life and Correspondence of Rufus King*

Levy, Beryl Harold, *Our Constitution: Tool or Testament?*

Lewis, William Draper, *Great American Lawyers*

Liancourt, Duc de la Rochefaucauld, *Travels Through the United States of North America*

Lodge, Henry Cabot, *Life and Letters of George Cabot*

Loth, David, *Alexander Hamilton, Portrait of a Prodigy*

——— *Public Plunder, a History of Graft in America*

Madison, James, *Writings*
Magruder, Allan B., *John Marshall*
Marshall, John, *An Autobiographical Sketch*
———— *The Life of George Washington* (1st and 2d eds.)
Massachusetts Historical Society, *Collections*
———— *Proceedings*
Mayo, Bernard, *Henry Clay, Spokesman of the New West*
McCaleb, Walter F., *Aaron Burr Conspiracy*
Meade, (Bishop) William, *Old Churches, Ministers and Families of Virginia*
Monaghan, Frank, *John Jay*
Monroe, James, *Writings*
Morison, Samuel Eliot, *The Life and Letters of Harrison Gray Otis, Federalist*
———— and Henry Steele Commager, *The Growth of the American Republic*
Morris, Gouverneur, *Diary and Letters*

National Gazette
National Intelligencer
Nelson, Sally, *Love Stories of Famous Virginians*
New York Daily Advertiser
New York Evening Post
Niles's Register

Oster, John Edward, *The Political and Economic Doctrines of John Marshall*

Palmer, Ben W., *Marshall and Taney*
Parton, James, *The Life and Times of Aaron Burr*
———— *Life of Thomas Jefferson*
Partridge, Bellamy, *Sir Billy Howe*
Pellew, George, *John Jay*
Perkins, A. J. G. and Theresa Wolfson, *Frances Wright, Free Enquirer*
Pickering Papers (Massachusetts Historical Society)
Pickering, Octavius and C. W. Upham, *Life of Timothy Pickering*
Plumer Papers (Massachusetts Historical Society)
Plumer, William, Jr., *Life of William Plumer*
Poore, Ben: Perley, *Reminiscences of Sixty Years in the National Metropolis*

Porcupine's Gazette
Powell, F. H., *Richard Rush*
Proceedings and Debates of the Virginia State Convention of 1829–1830

Quincy, Edmund, *Life of Josiah Quincy*

Randolph, Jacob, *A Memoir on the Life and Character of Philip Syng Physick, M.D.*
Rives, W. C., *History of the Life and Times of James Madison*

Safford, William Harrison, *The Blennerhassett Papers*
Schachner, Nathan, *Aaron Burr*
Schoepf, Johann David, *Travels in the Confederation*
Scott, Winfield, *Memoirs of Lt. Gen. Scott Written by Himself*
Semmes, J. E., *John H. B. Latrobe and His Times*
Smith, C. W., Jr., *Roger B. Taney, Jacksonian Jurist*
Smith, Margaret Bayard, *The First Forty Years of Washington Society*
Smyth, Clifford, *John Marshall, Father of the Supreme Court*
Stanard, Mary Newton, *Richmond, Its People and Its Story*
Stevens, William Oliver, *Washington the Cinderella City*
Story Papers (Massachusetts Historical Society)
Story, William Wetmore, *Life and Letters of Joseph Story*
Styron, Arthur, *The Last of the Cocked Hats; James Monroe and the Virginia Dynasty*
Sumner, Charles, *Works*

Taylor, John, *Construction Construed and Constitutions Vindicated*
Thayer, James Bradley, *John Marshall*
Ticknor, George, *Life, Letters and Journals*
Tocqueville, Alexis de, *Democracy in America*

Umbreit, Kenneth Bernard, *Our Eleven Chief Justices*
United States Courts, *Condensed Reports of Cases in the Supreme Court of the United States*
——————— *Reports of Cases Argued and Adjudged in the Supreme Court*
——————— *Reports of the Trials of Colonel Aaron Burr, etc.*
United States Department of State, *Authentic Copies of the Corre-*

spondence of Charles Cotesworth Pinckney, John Marshall and Elbridge Gerry, etc. (XYZ Papers)
United States Senate, *Trial of Samuel Chase*

Van Buren, Martin—*Autobiography*
Van Santvoord, George, *Sketches of the Lives and Judicial Services of the Chief Justices of the Supreme Court of the United States*
Virginia Historical Society, *Collections* (The History of the Virginia Federal Convention of 1788)
Virginia Magazine of History and Biography

Warren, Charles, *The Supreme Court in American History*
Warville, J. P. Brissot de, *New Travels in the United States of America*
Washington Federalist
Washington, George, *Writings*
Webster, Daniel, *Letters*
———— *Private Correspondence*
———— *Writings and Speeches*
Wharton, Francis, *State Trials of the United States During the Administrations of Washington and Adams*
Wharton, Henry, *Some Account of the Life, Writings and Speeches of William Pinkney*
Wildes, Harry Emerson, *Valley Forge*
Wilkinson, James, *Memoirs of My Own Times*
William and Mary College Quarterly
Wilstach, Paul, *Patriots Off Their Pedestals*

☆ ☆ ☆

Index

Adair, John, 219, 223
Adams, Abigail, 156
Adams, John, 25, 65, 122, 125-7, 133, 138, 143, 144, 146-7, 148-9, 151, 152, 153, 154, 155, 156-8, 161, 165, 175, 241, 255, 337
Adams, John Quincy, 202, 203, 206, 207, 250, 262, 264, 273, 288, 335-6, 337, 338, 339, 345, 351-2, 356, 359, 370-1, 378
Alexander, Czar, 237
Alexander, William, 40
Allan, John, 187
Allen, Ethan, 29
Alston, Joseph, 237-8
Ambler family, 54, 57, 78, 116, 185
Ambler, Eliza, 52, 54, 55, 57, 58, 76, 78, 115
Ambler, Jacquelin, 54, 63
Ambler, John, 63, 78
Ambler, Mary (Mrs. John Marshall), 52; courtship, 53 ff.; marries, 63; references to, 67, 76-8, 102, 110, 126, 128-9, 130, 142, 143, 153, 183, 185-7, 242, 276, 325, 341, 350, 351, 364, 372, 382; illness and death, 354-5
Ambler, Nancy, 54
Ames, Fisher, 123, 148, 151, 199

Anderson, Richard, 53, 55
Anderson, Robert, 55
Arnold, Benedict, 32, 33, 58-9
Aurora, The, 194, 195

Bache, Benjamin Franklin, 119
Baker, John, 75, 233
Baldwin, Henry, 347-8, 374
Bancroft, George, 372, 373
Barbecue Club, 121, 375
Barbour, James, 314
Barbour, Philip P., 342, 352, 381
Barlow, Joel, 181
Barras, Paul, 126, 130
Barron, James, 236
Beard, Charles A., 201
Beaumarchais, Pierre Augustin Caron de, 135
Bellamy (XYZ affair), 133, 134, 135, 139
Benton, Thomas H., 381
Beveridge, Albert J., 193, 208, 231
Biddle, Nicholas, 357
Blackwood's Magazine, 241
Blennerhassett, Harman, 219, 221, 223, 230, 236, 243-6, 248, 249
Blennerhassett, Mrs. Harman, 243, 245

Bollman, Erich, 221, 223-6, 228, 230, 231
Bonaparte, Jerome, 199, 226
Bonaparte, Mrs. Jerome, 199, 226, 268
Bonaparte, Napoleon, 121, 130, 133, 135, 156, 189, 195, 216, 237, 255, 269, 279, 280, 283
Boston Gazette, 257
Botts, Benjamin, 233, 246
Boudinot, Elias, 140
Bowers, Claude G., 194, 208, 231
Boyce vs. *Anderson*, 335
Boyce, Robert, 335
Braddock, Edward, 18
Brandywine Creek, Battle of, 37-8
Breckinridge, John, 178-9
Brevoort, Henry, 269
Brig Wilson vs. *U.S.*, 309-10, 324, 335
Briggs, George, 365
Bright, Michael, 259
Briscoe vs. *Commonwealth's Bank of the State of Kentucky*, 374, 376
Brown, John, 219
Bryant, William Cullen, 373
Buchanan, J., 121
Buchanan, James, 319, 372
Burgoyne, John, 39, 364
Burr, Aaron, 45, 155, 158-60, 172, 199, 205, 208, 250, 272; "conspiracy" and trial, 218 ff.; acquittal, 249
Burr, Theodosia, 159, 219, 232, 243, 249
Burwell, Rebecca, 54

Cabot, George, 123, 151, 199
Calhoun, John C., 268, 282, 286, 309, 327, 348-9, 357, 369
Call, Daniel, 116
Callender, James T., 154, 166, 209, 210-12
Campbell, Alexander, 122
Campbell, Archibald, 23, 33
Campbell, George W., 208, 252
Canning, George, 263
Carr, Dabney, 359
Carrington, Edward, 79, 116, 248
Carrington, Paul, 99
Chase, Samuel, impeachment, 198, 200, 202, 203, 207 ff.; death, 273; references to, 151, 154, 166, 168, 181, 196-7, 216, 226, 248, 270, 277
Cherokee Nation vs. *Georgia*, 360-2
Chisholm vs. *Georgia*, 164
Christian Science Monitor, The, 380
Claiborne, William C. C., 230

Clay, Henry, 111, 257-8, 268, 269-70, 282, 286, 288, 291, 311, 319, 335-6, 337, 338, 347, 357, 366, 367, 372
Clinton, De Witt, 281, 282
Clinton, George, 199, 281
Clinton, Sir Henry, 44, 46
Cobbett, William, 139
Cohen, M. J., 313-5
Cohen, P. J., 313-5
Cohens vs. *Virginia*, 313-5
Colston, Raleigh, 142
Commager, Henry S., 214
Cooper, Thomas, 144
Corn Tassell, 360
Cornwallis, Earl, 35, 36, 59, 60
Corwin, Edward S., 232
Craig vs. *Missouri*, 349-50
Craigmyle, Baron, 136
Crawford, William H., 335-6
Crittenden, John J., 345
Cushing, William, 163, 167, 181, 253, 270, 272, 277

Dartmouth College vs. *Woodward*, 292-7, 301, 330
Daviess, Alexander H., 116, 220, 221
Dayton, Jonathan, 219
Decatur, Stephen, 227, 236, 288
Denny, Richard, 110
Dexter, Samuel, 123
Dunmore, Lord, 30, 31
Du Pont de Nemours, E. I., 237, 238
Du Pont de Nemours, Victor, 144
Duval, Gabriel, 273-4, 294, 295, 345, 347, 374, 375, 381
Dwight, Timothy, 257

Early, Peter, 208
Eaton, William, 226-7, 232, 235, 242-3
Edinburgh Review, 241
Elkison, Henry, 321, 324
Ellsworth, Oliver, 49, 151, 157, 162-3, 166
Ellsworth, William W., 319
Emmett, Thomas A., 323, 325
Everett, Edward, 357

Fairfax estate, 20-1, 74-6, 115-6, 122-4, 133, 142, 205, 261, 284
Fairfax, Baron, 17, 20, 75, 101, 103, 284
Fairfax, Denny M., 124, 284
Federalist, The, 86, 90, 94
Fenno, John, 112

Fisher, George, 116
Fletcher vs. *Peck*, 261-2, 264-7, 293
Fletcher, Robert, 261
Fordyce, Captain, 31
Foushee, William, 91, 233
Frankfurter, Felix, 326, 378
Franklin, Benjamin, 13, 26, 65, 83
Freneau, Philip, 112
Fries, John, 151, 209, 250
Fulton, Robert, 281, 322, 325

Gallatin, Albert, 72, 144, 151, 153, 204, 257, 272
Gazette of the United States, 112
General Advertiser, 306
Genêt, Edmond C., 114-5, 267
Germantown, Battle of, 38
Gerry, Elbridge, 126, 131 ff.
Gibbons vs. *Ogden*, 322-7
Gibbons, Thomas, 322-3, 325, 326
Giles, William B., 188, 202, 224, 233, 342, 344
Gilmer, Francis, 73
Gladstone, William E., 85
Granger, Gideon, 206-7, 272
Greeley, Horace, 365
Greene, Nathaniel, 33
Grenville, George, 24-5
Griffin, Cyrus, 229, 245, 271-2

Hamilton, Alexander, 13, 14, 33, 35, 44, 45, 79, 85, 86, 90, 106, 109, 111, 112, 116, 118, 119, 123, 127, 128, 138, 141, 143, 153, 155, 159, 164, 168, 199, 204, 205, 215, 219, 220, 221, 229, 239-40, 287, 302, 305, 374, 378
Hand, Learned, 11
Harper, Robert G., 208, 213
Harper, William, 176-7
Harrison, Benjamin, 61, 94
Hauteval (XYZ affair), 134, 135, 139
Hay, Eliza, 291
Hay, George, 230, 233, 234, 237-8, 248, 249
Hayne, Robert, 348-9
Henry, Patrick, 22, 27, 30, 50, 56, 61, 67, 72, 73, 87, 88, 93-4, 95-6, 97, 98, 99, 100, 102, 104-5, 109, 110, 120, 122, 149-50, 343
Hite et al vs. *Fairfax et al*, 74-6
Hite, Joist, 75
Holmes, John, 293
Holmes, Oliver Wendell, 11, 378
Hooe, Robert, 176-7

Hopkinson, Joseph, 139, 208, 219, 293, 302
Hottenguer (XYZ affair), 133, 134, 135, 139
Houston, Sam, 373
Howe, Sir William, 32, 36, 37, 38, 39, 44
Hughes, Charles E., 11
Hunter, David, 284
Hylton vs. *U.S.*, 164, 193

Innes, James, 93, 99, 122
Iredell, James, 163
Irving, Washington, 232, 269

Jackson, Andrew, 12, 219, 222, 232, 235, 238, 283, 335-6, 337, 338, 339, 340-2, 345, 346, 347, 349, 352, 357, 360, 362, 363, 365, 366-9, 370, 371, 372, 375, 376, 380, 381
Jackson, Francis J., 263, 267
Jay, John, 65, 90, 106, 118, 119, 157-8, 163-5
Jefferson, Thomas, as Governor, 49-51, 58, 59; licenses M. as lawyer, 57-8; suggests M. for judgeship, 111; opinion of M., 115, 241, 249, 272, 311, 317; first administration, 175 ff.; re-elected, 202; second administration, 210 ff.; death, 337; other references to, 12, 13, 14, 17, 22, 27, 32, 54, 55, 56, 61, 70, 73, 80, 81, 93, 106, 108, 109, 112, 114, 119, 122, 127, 129, 130, 139, 140, 141, 146, 148, 149, 156, 158-60, 166, 167, 172-3, 239-40, 266, 270-3, 277, 286, 308, 309, 317, 318, 330, 335, 339, 344, 348, 358, 368-9
Jeffreys, George, 166
Johnson, Richard M., 268, 318
Johnson, Samuel, 154
Johnson, William, 200-1, 205, 224, 226, 256, 270, 274, 277, 285, 294, 299, 317, 319, 320-1, 324, 345-6, 347, 348, 350, 374, 375
Jones, Joseph, 63
Jones, Walter, 302

Keith, James, 17
Keith, Mary, 17-18 (*see also* Marshall)
Kemble, Fanny, 372
Kent, James, 294, 296, 323, 324, 328, 374, 380-1
Kerr, John, 329
Key, Philip B., 209

King, Rufus, 112, 123, 136, 199, 281, 284, 287, 311-2, 334
Knox, Henry, 73, 111

Lafayette, Marquis de, 45, 59, 222, 256, 333-4
Lee, Gen. Charles, 44-5
Lee, Charles, 120, 190, 192, 209
Lee, Henry, 47, 93, 117, 150, 318
Lee, Richard Henry, 61
Leigh, Benjamin W., 375-6
Lincoln, Abraham, 12
Lincoln, Levi, 173, 204, 272, 273
Livingston, Brockholst, 224, 270, 273, 294, 296, 328
Livingston, Edward, 271-3
Livingston, Robert, 322

McCulloch vs. *Maryland*, 302-6, 307, 308, 315, 319, 357
McCulloch, James, 302
McDuffie, George, 357
McHenry, James, 153
McLean, John, 346-7, 350, 374
MacRae, Alexander, 233

Madison, Dolly, 262, 277, 288
Madison, James, in Virginia Constitutional Convention, 90 ff.; Court appointments, 270-3; other references to, 79, 80, 83, 85, 106, 109, 111, 112, 148, 176-7, 192, 204, 256, 260, 263, 267, 268, 279, 280, 282, 283, 308, 318, 342-3, 348, 357-8
Marbury vs. *Madison*, 176-7, 189-94, 238, 309
Marbury, William, 176-7, 190-2, 194
Marchant, Henry, 163
Marie Antoinette, 108
Marshall family, 17, 19, 21, 22, 24, 59, 78, 88, 185
Marshall, Charles, 23
Marshall, Edward C., 218
Marshall, Humphrey, 116, 221, 257-8
Marshall, Jacquelin A., 88
Marshall, James (brother of M.), 78, 88, 115-6, 124, 185, 190, 284
Marshall, James (son of M.), 153
Marshall, Jane, 185-6
Marshall, John (grandfather of M.), 17, 18
Marshal, John (son of M.), 142, 143
Marshall, John:
    Early Life—Birth, 18; ancestry, 16,

17; boyhood, 16, 19 ff.; education, 21-4; early homes, 18, 20, 24; exposure to revolutionary doctrine, 22-4, 27, 30; early experience as soldier, 27, 28-9; first battle, 31; joins Washington's army, 32; promotions, 33, 45; at Brandywine, 37-8; at Germantown, 38; at Valley Forge, 40-4; at Monmouth, 44-5; at Stony Point, 46-7; raid on Paulus Hook, 47; leaves army, 48; meets Mary Ambler, 52; courtship, 53-61; studies law, 55-7; admitted to bar, 58; joins attack on Arnold, 58-9; inoculated, 36, 60; elected to legislature, 61, 71, 84, 107; named councillor of state, 62; marries, 63; appearance, 29, 42, 52, 54, 62, 74, 102, 115, 131, 184
    Professional Life—Prospects at marriage, 65; fees and expenses, 66, 84, 88, 102, 120; service in legislature, 67-8, 70, 71, 87-8, 120; growth of political philosophy, 69, 80, 84-5; practice of law, 69, 71, 76, 83, 88-9, 107; resigns from Executive Council, 71; retires from legislature, 71, 110; anecdotes concerning, 74, 184, 275, 351; in *Hite et al* vs. *Fairfax et al*, 74-6; domestic life, 66, 71, 72, 76-9, 84, 88, 110-11, 116, 121, 142-3, 185-7, 218, 239, 350; views on Shays's Rebellion, 80; drafts ratification compromise, 87-8; in Virginia Constitutional Convention, 90 ff.; defends judiciary, 99-104; refuses Attorney Generalship, 107, 120; partner in Fairfax purchase, 115-6; last army service, 117-8; refuses French embassy, 121; in campaign of 1796, 122; in *Ware* vs. *Hylton*, 122-3, 164; XYZ negotiations, 125 ff.; return and reception, 139 ff.; refuses Supreme Court post, 143, 146-7; visits Washington, 146; campaign for Congress, 147-50; leadership in House, 151 ff.; as Secretary of State, 153 ff.; on Burr-Jefferson tie, 159-60; views on politics, 107-8, 113, 117, 118, 255, 267, 278, 337-8, 339, 356-7, 359-60, 366, 367-8, 370, 371
    Chief Justice—appointed, 158; administers oath to Jefferson, 161, 172-3; constitutional rulings and opinions, 191-4, 207, 212-3, 217, 246-8, 259-60, 264-5, 296-7, 299-300, 304-5,

310, 314-5, 325-7, 361-2, 364, 374; biographer of Washington, 168-70, 176, 181-2, 196, 198, 201-2, 207, 217-8, 229, 235-42, 367-8, 372; opinion of Jefferson, 159-60, 172-3, 174, 317, 318, 368-9; first case, 175; in *Marbury* vs. *Madison*, 176-7, 189-94; in Chase impeachment, 207 ff.; in *U.S.* vs. *Fisher*, 212-3; on responsibility of government officials, 217; on meaning of treason, 228, 246-8; in Burr trial, 229 ff.; in *U.S.* vs. *Peters*, 259-60; in *Fletcher* vs. *Peck*, 264-6; on obligation of contract, 264-6, 300, 330-1; gives verdict for Jefferson, 273; on judicial distinction, 275; life in Washington, 274-6, 350-1, 372, 373; manner on bench, 191-2, 231, 274-5, 277; on war of 1812, 278, 279-80, 283; on immunity of foreign warships, 278-9; mentioned for presidency, 280-1; heads exploring expedition, 281; on rights of neutrals, 286; in Dartmouth case, 294-7; defines corporation, 296; in *Sturges* vs. *Crowninshield*, 297-300; in *McCulloch* vs. *Maryland*, 302-6; replies to Roane, 306; in *Brig Wilson* vs. *U.S.*, 309-10; on slavery, 310, 332-3, 334, 335; in *Cohens* vs. *Virginia*, 313-7; in *Bank of U.S.* vs. *Dandridge*, 321; in *Gibbons* vs. *Ogden*, 322-7; overruled on Constitutional issue, 330; heads Colonization Society, 333; in *Boyce* vs. *Anderson*, 335; abstention from politics, 335-6; on population, 337-8; supports Adams for President, 338-9; in Virginia Constitutional Convention, 342-5; on representation of property, 343-4; on judiciary, 344; on appointment of Justices, 345; in *Craig* vs. *Missouri*, 349-50; plans to retire, 352-3; illness, 352-3; mourns his wife, 354, 365; Georgia defies his writ, 360; in *Cherokee Nation* vs. *Georgia*, 362; on rights of Indians, 360-65; in *Worcester* vs. *Georgia*, 362-5; fights rearguard action in Court, 374 ff.; summary of Court cases in his time, 376; hears last case, 376-7; illness and death, 381-2; appraisal of his work, 12-14, 378 ff.

Marshall, Judith, 23
Marshall, Lucy, 23, 78

Marshall, Mary (daughter of M.), 187
Marshall, Mary Ambler (wife of M.), *see* Ambler, Mary
Marshall, Mary Keith, 18, 21, 60, 382
Marshall, Nancy, 60
Marshall, Thomas (brother of M.), 45
Marshall, Thomas (father of M.), 17, 18, 19, 20, 21, 22, 23, 24, 26-7, 28, 30, 32, 34, 38, 52, 58, 60, 61, 63, 66, 88, 116, 382
Marshall, Thomas (son of M.), 24, 71, 382
Marshall, William, 23, 154, 166, 210
Martin vs. *Hunter's Lessee*, 284-5
Martin, Luther, 208, 233, 234, 236, 237, 249, 253, 262, 264, 302-3
Martineau, Harriet, 372, 373, 378
Mason, George, 50, 83, 85, 94, 96, 98, 100, 101-2, 103, 110, 179
Mason, Jonathan, 138
Mayor, Aldermen and Commonalty of the City of New York vs. *Miln*, 374, 376
Mead, Cowles, 223
Merry, Anthony, 218
Mitchel et al vs. *U.S.*, 376-7
Monmouth, Battle of, 44-5
Monroe, James, 23, 24, 33, 34, 40, 61, 63, 67, 71, 96, 106, 114, 118, 121, 125-6, 233, 238, 256, 279-80, 282, 284, 291, 311-2, 315, 319, 328, 342-3, 346, 373
Montgomery, Richard, 32
Moore, Alfred, 168, 181, 200
Moore, Thomas, 199-200
Morgan, George, 244
Morison, Samuel E., 214
Morris, Gouverneur, 85, 108, 118, 179
Morris, Hester, 115-6
Morris, Robert, 34, 90, 108, 115-6, 123-4, 126, 133, 142, 152, 212

Nash, Thomas, 152-3
National Gazette, 112
National Intelligencer, 194, 294
New York Daily Advertiser, 363, 365
New York Evening Post, 179, 327
Nicholas, George, 93
Nicholas, W. C., 233
Nicholson, Joseph, 208
Niles, Hezekiah, 298, 306, 327, 360
Noailles, Vicomte de, 114
North American Review, 357

Oakley, Thomas J., 323, 324-5

Ogden vs. *Saunders*, 330-1
Ogden, Aaron, 323, 326
Ogden, David B., 313-4
Olmstead, Gideon, 259-60
Orr, Henry, 373
Otis, Harrison Gray, 288
Owen, Robert, 333

Paine, Thomas, 33
Paterson, William, 158, 167, 181, 195, 224, 277
Patterson, Betsy (*see* Bonaparte, Mrs. Jerome)
Peck, John, 261, 265
Pendleton, Edmund, 63, 71, 93, 94, 99, 100
Pepys, Samuel, 353
Peters, Richard, 166, 259-60
Physick, Philip S., 353, 381
Pickering, John, 189-90, 198
Pickering, Timothy, 143, 147, 153, 199, 213, 255, 263, 278, 283, 334
Pinckney, Charles C., in XYZ mission, 125 ff.; other references to, 122, 141, 172-3, 199, 201, 202, 256, 308, 335
Pinckney, Thomas, 122
Pinkney, William, 276-7, 295, 297, 304, 313-4, 323, 357
Pleasants, James, 333
Plumer, William, 203, 208, 212
Poe, Edgar Allan, 187
Porcupine's Gazette, 139, 140
Priestley, James, 144

Quincy, Josiah, 267, 278
Quincy, Mrs. Josiah, 226

Rall, Johann, 35, 39
Ramsey, Dennis, 176-7
Randolph, Edmund, 75-6, 85, 90, 91-2, 93, 96, 98, 99, 106, 111, 233
Randolph, Jacob, 353
Randolph, John, in Chase impeachment, 208 ff.; other references to, 28, 188, 205-7, 220, 223, 233, 235, 254, 256, 262, 266, 269, 332, 337, 339, 342, 350-1
Randolph, Mary Isham, 17
Rittenhouse, David, 259
Roane, Spencer, 200, 306, 307, 316
Robins, Jonathan, 153
Rodney, Caesar, 208, 256
Ross, General, 283
Royall, Mrs. Anne, 351

Rutledge, John, 165

Schoepf, Johann D., 62
Scott, Dred, 193
Scott, Sir Walter, 269
Scott, Winfield, 233
Sedgwick, Theodore, 123, 142, 148, 151
Sergeant, John, 361-2, 363
Shays, Daniel, 80
Slaughter, Philip, 42
Smith & Buchanan, 298
Smith, John, 219, 250
Smith, Robert, 279-80
Smith, Mrs. Samuel, 373
Spectator, The, 194
Steuben, Baron F. W. von, 43
Stevens, Colonel, 31
Stirling, Earl of, 40
Stoddert, Benjamin, 280-1
Story, Joseph, appointment to Court, 273; character, 274-5; other references to, 77, 252-4, 264-5, 267, 284, 285, 294, 296, 299, 301, 304, 305, 308, 310, 316, 317, 320, 321, 325, 328-9, 339, 342, 345, 346, 347, 352-3, 356, 361-2, 363-4, 365, 366, 367-9, 371, 372, 373-4, 376, 378, 381
Sturges vs. *Crowninshield*, 297-300
Sumner, Charles, 372
Swartwout, Samuel, 221, 223-6, 228, 230, 231, 232

Talbot vs. *Seeman*, 175-6
Talbot, Silas, 175-6
Talleyrand-Perigord, C. M. de, 128, 131-2, 133, 134, 135, 136, 137
Taney, Roger B., 331, 372, 375-6, 381
Taylor, George K., 185-6
Taylor, John, 75, 179, 211, 310-1, 314, 317
Tazewell, Littleton, 342
Thompson, James, 22-3
Thompson, Smith, 328, 345, 347, 350, 361-2, 374
Tocqueville, Alexis de, 379
Todd, Thomas, 252, 270, 285, 294, 295, 328, 330
Trimble, Robert, 330, 345, 346
Truxtun, Thomas, 149, 227, 236, 243
Tupper, General, 244
Tyler, Comfort, 230
Tyler, John, 271-3

U.S. vs. *Dandridge*, 321

U.S. vs. *Fisher*, 212-3
U.S. vs. *Peters*, 258-60
Upshur, Abel, 342

Valley Forge, 39-44, 48, 54
Van Buren, Martin, 328, 329, 339, 346, 350, 375
Villette, Mme. de, 135

Wadsworth, Jeremiah, 123
Ware vs. *Hylton*, 122-3, 164
Washington Federalist, The, 180
Washington Globe, The, 360
Washington, Bushrod, 146, 147, 150, 167-70, 176, 181, 182, 202, 270, 273, 277, 280-1, 294, 299, 302, 306, 330, 346, 347
Washington, George, offers M. Attorney Generalship, 120, 121; offers M. French mission, 121; urges M. to run for Congress, 145-6; rejoices in M.'s election, 150; M.'s biography of, 167-70, 176, 181-2, 196, 198, 201-2, 207, 217-8, 229, 239-42, 367-8, 372; other references to, 12, 17, 19-51, 59, 60, 80, 83, 85, 90, 92, 93, 95, 107, 108, 110-2, 117-8, 126, 128, 130, 135, 165, 168, 175, 267, 301
Washington, Lawrence, 20
Wayne, Anthony, 44, 45, 46, 47, 52, 59

Wayne, C. P., 169-70, 176, 182, 198, 202, 217, 229, 239
Wayne, James M., 375
Webster, Daniel, 276, 277, 286, 291, 293, 294, 297, 300, 301, 302, 305, 318, 323-4, 329, 340, 348-9, 351, 372, 379, 381
Weekly Register, 298, 306, 327, 360
Weems, Mason L., 182
Western World, The, 221
White, Edward D., 319
Whitney, Eli, 204
Wickham, John, 231-2, 245
Wilkinson, James, 219, 221-3, 225, 227-8, 231, 232, 234-5, 238
Wilson, Woodrow, 174, 177
Wirt, William, 233, 245-6, 248, 293, 302-3, 323-4, 325, 328, 351, 359-63
Wolcott, Alexander, 273
Wolcott, Oliver, 153
Woodbury, Mrs. Levi, 373
Worcester vs. *Georgia*, 362-5
Worcester, Samuel A., 362-4
Wright, Frances, 333-4
Wythe, George, 50, 56, 57, 85, 93, 94, 99, 100

XYZ Papers, 139

Yazoo Frauds, 203-7, 261-2, 264, 266-7